For Barbara Tayt

ᔆᦙ THE DIARY ᦙᔆ
OF A SHROPSHIRE
FARMER

A YOUNG YEOMAN'S LIFE AND TRAVELS
1835–37

PETER DAVIS
EDITED BY MARTIN DAVIS

Martin Davis
²⁷/₈/₁₂

AMBERLEY

First published 2011

Amberley Publishing
The Hill, Stroud
Gloucestershire GL5 4EP

www.amberleybooks.com

British Library Cataloguing in Publication Data.
A catalogue record for this book is available from the British Library.

ISBN 978-1-4456-0013-0

Typesetting and Origination by Amberley Publishing.
Printed in Great Britain.

Contents

List of Maps and Illustrations

Maps

Illustrations

(All photographs by Martin Davis)
Cover: *Haymaking*, by Claude Hayes

1 The county boundary runs down the middle of the River Teme, between Burford and Tenbury.
2 Lower Nash, the home of the Davis family until 1822.
3 Bickmarsh Hall, Warwickshire, where Peter Davis and his family lived from 1860.
4 *The Bull* bred by Peter Davis – '1st prize 15£ & silver medal to the breeder, Birmingham 1865'.
5 Page 1 of the transcription of the travel diary by Edith Howard Freer.
6 Page 1 of Peter Davis' original travel diary, rediscovered in 2009.
7 Nelson Monument, Exchange Flags, Liverpool, designed by Matthew Cotes Wyatt and sculpted by Richard Westmacott: 'This monument, which is executed in bronze, consists of a marble basement and a circular pedestal, supporting figures emblematical of Nelson's principal victories. The statue of the dying admiral rests one foot on a prostrate enemy, and the other on a cannon; and he is receiving upon his sword a naval crown from Victory.' (From an account of Liverpool in 1839, published in *The Penny Magazine*).
8 A steam locomotive of the Planet class, one of which would have pulled Peter Davis' train from Liverpool to Manchester.
9 Lancaster Priory.
10 Bowness-on-Windermere.
11 The rowing boats for hire at Bowness today are perhaps little different from that which Peter Davis rowed up the lake in 1835.
12 Looking north up Lake Windermere towards the Langdale Pikes.
13 Carlisle Castle.
14 The National Monument, Calton Hill, Edinburgh, with Salisbury Crags in the background; the Monument was designed (by W. H. Playfair) as a memorial to those who had died in the Napoleonic Wars, and it remained uncompleted after funds ran out.
15 St Stephen's church, New Town, Edinburgh, built in 1827–1828.
16 'In St Andrews Square is the house which was the birth place of Lord Brougham,' on 19 September 1778. The Revd George Hall, vicar of Tenbury, had been Lord Brougham's domestic chaplain when he was Lord Chancellor: they were both from Westmorland.
17 Drill grubber, pulled by one or two horses.
18 The west front of Durham Cathedral, with the River Wear in the foreground.

43 Oath of the executors of the will of Samuel Davis senior, administered by the Revd David Jones of Burford.

44 The Lodge (or Dean Lodge), Nash, was the former home of Peter Davis' aunt, Eleanor, and her husband, William Partridge.

45 The front of the former Poor Law Union Workhouse, Teme Street, Tenbury (more recently the local Council offices); designed by George Wilkinson, it cost £1,365 to build in 1837.

46 The nearest we have to a portrait of the diarist.

Introduction

This is no great literary discovery. It is in fact only remarkable for its ordinariness, a couple of mostly commonplace daily accounts set down on the threshold of the Victorian era by a countryman, full of youthful enthusiasm. Peter Davis' record none the less presents us with a microcosm of life at a time of immense change.

Born in Burford, Shropshire, in 1812, Peter Davis still lived there at the time he wrote the two diaries published here. They cover a fortnight's travels north in June 1835, and daily life in Shropshire during most of the two years that follow. No other writings by him are known to have survived.

The family background

Peter was the third son of Samuel Davis of Burford and his wife Elizabeth, née Reynolds. They lived in what is still today – in Simon Jenkins' words – 'a lovely corner of old Shropshire'. In 1831, Burford, at the southern extremity of the county, comprised eight separate 'townships' with 1,086 inhabitants. Just across the River Teme lay the market town of Tenbury, Worcestershire (later known as Tenbury Wells): its population in 1831 was 1,768.

Little is known about the background of the diarist's father. Samuel Davis – 'a more upright and honest man never was in existence' – seems to have been a successful yeoman farmer. In his lifetime, while he managed to buy property, he continued to pay rent for his house and farmland. His income derived from cattle, sheep, pigs, arable products, hops and cider, and horticulture.

Samuel and his wife Elizabeth were thirty-five and twenty-two respectively when they married on 26 June 1804, in the chapel at Burford's Nash Township: one of the witnesses was William Reynolds,

1. The county boundary runs down the middle of the River Teme, between Burford and Tenbury.

Elizabeth's eldest brother. He and two other brothers, Peter of Kemberton and Joseph of New House, feature in the diary, along with their sisters Eleanor Partridge and Maria Reynolds. The Reynolds family were also farmers: Elizabeth, baptised at Kinlet, 12 miles north-east of Burford, was a daughter of Peter and Mary Reynolds, who seem to have moved to Burford sometime shortly after Elizabeth's birth.

Elizabeth and Samuel Davis themselves had five children: William, Caroline, who died aged seven, Samuel junior, Peter himself, and finally Eliza, her mother dying in childbirth aged thirty-one. Samuel and Eliza were thus named for their parents, whilst William and Peter were named for their mother's brothers and father. So, Peter Davis grew up with two older brothers and a younger sister, their father having lost not only his wife, but also his elder daughter.

In 1822, the family, which may already have included Aunt Maria Reynolds, moved from Lower Nash to nearby Dean Park, a farm of some 480 acres situated in Boraston Township, just to the north-east of Burford itself. Next to the farmhouse are extensive agricultural buildings, some now converted to housing. All have the appearance of predating the diary.

2. Lower Nash, the home of the Davis family until 1822.

The Park has been said to be so named because its early owners were the Dean and Chapter of Worcester Cathedral. Another theory, possibly more likely in view of its position (at the top of a steep drive), is that 'Dean' is a form of 'Dinas', in Old and Middle Welsh meaning 'fort' or 'citadel'. On early maps of Worcestershire, Dean Park is shown – even though just over the county border – looking very much like a citadel.

Tunstall Evans, in his 1840 *History of Tenbury*, refers to Dean Park in florid terms:

> Of this tenderly remembered villa, wherein we wore away the happiest
> of our days, we perhaps might say too much; therefore shall say nothing
> – only that it is a distant bowshot from Tenbury Bridge.

It is odd – in the light of this rather tantalising fragment – not to find Mr Evans mentioned in the diary. Possibly he wrote his history under a pseudonym.

Where were the Davis children educated? Peter's next brother, Samuel junior, is the only one of the family about whom we know something certain: he was admitted as a Pensioner of St John's College, Cambridge, on 23 October 1830. He did not take up residence then for whatever reason, but eventually did so at Christ's College, three years after Charles Darwin, who was then about to depart on the *Beagle*. Samuel progressed

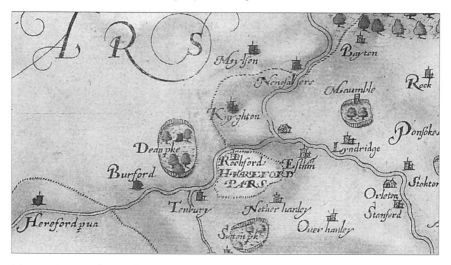

Map 1. Extract from Christopher Saxton's 1577 map of Worcestershire, showing Dean Park, just over the county border in Shropshire.

well, reading mathematics under the tutorship of the Revd Edward John Ash; he was described as a Scholar as of 1 November 1832, and obtained his BA as 33rd Wrangler in 1835[1]. From Cambridge, he moved to Devon and entered the Church.

In Tenbury, since 1816, there had been a National School, supported by voluntary contributions. In addition, there was a combined boarding and day school in Teme Street, Tenbury: on 2 March 1837, Peter Davis describes in his diary visiting Mr Home (the schoolmaster) 'for the new books'. Possibly a more promising clue is given on 1 May 1837, when Peter reports that he dines with Mr Tinson, a Ludlow schoolmaster.

Considering that he most likely left school a good decade before the period in hand – for an outdoor life involving much manual labour – Peter Davis reveals himself as tolerably well-educated. The diaries' style is natural, sometimes pithy, the handwriting even and mostly intelligible. As is the case with many (if not most) diaries, grammar and spelling show signs of eccentricity: Peter Davis' are published warts and all, the warts being part of the self-portrait they afford.

He was not afraid of tackling a serious book: 'Begin reading the second volume of Southey's life of Cowper' (3 March 1836). 'Finish reading the first volume of Hume's History of England' (18 March 1836). Later,

… This the most beautiful and striking appearance of the Aurora I ever beheld. By 11 clock this awful meteorous phenomenon had disappeared. M. Libos attributes the aurora to the decomposition of the two airs which compose the atmosphere, oxygen and nitrogen, in the polar regions by an accumulation of the electric fluid there. [18 February 1837]

Further evidence of Peter Davis' intellectual curiosity, from the travel diary, is given below.

The travel diary

The twenty-three-year-old Peter embarked on a fortnight's journey northwards on 8 June 1835. In this, 'the first tour of any distance from home I ever made', 800 miles were covered, more than 100 of them on foot. From Shropshire he proceeded to Liverpool, on to Edinburgh and then back via more eastern counties, coming as far south as Northamptonshire. His experiences are recorded in a discrete notebook, clearly not part of any general diary; the later diary, by contrast, begins on 26 January 1836 and finishes on 26 November 1837, filling a complete book; this marks it out as one of a series.

Written by a young farmer at a time of change in so many areas of British life, the travel diary naturally notes the different soils, crops, animals and farming methods he observed, but also much more of general interest about the landscape, people and buildings. Besides coach travel and a good deal of walking, he writes of the novelty of a journey by train, one of half a dozen different modes of transport he used while away.

The diary's style is mostly telegraphic, but its author waxes lyrical once in a while. Of Bowness-on-Windermere, for instance:

> Here is a village at the margin of the largest and most beautiful lake in the whole country, with boats &c in great number on it: with islands here and there studded as if placed by art to give sublimity to the scene:– and mountains round which far surpass anything I ever witnessed before. Talk of visiting large Towns and such like places, indeed here is a sight worth all the towns in the Kingdom put together. [11 June]

Peter Davis may have written as he went along: more likely, he made notes. The diary would then have been filled in at home – as from 21 June it certainly was, the entry beginning:

> Rather over-lie myself, not rising until half after five. Been dreaming of witnessing the wedding of Mr. H. Davis, the surgeon of Tenbury, to Miss Henderson. N.B. Find, when I reach home, that this wedding actually took place on the very day previously.

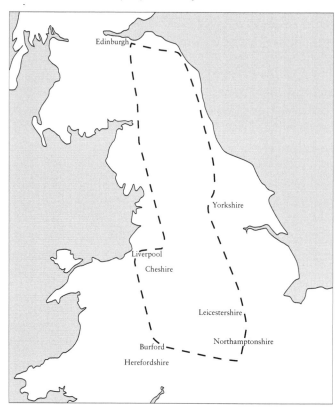

Map 2. Peter Davis' route during his fortnight's travels in June 1835: he journeyed 800 miles, progressing clockwise from Burford, Shropshire.

By the time of his travels, Peter had learnt not just how to look after himself, but to know his own mind. Besides farming, he had a variety of other interests. He writes, for instance, of a visit to Edinburgh University:

> Hear Dr. Jameson deliver a lecture on natural history at this place to a rather large audience of young men. Do not think very highly of the Dr. as a lecturer although he may be an able man and good scholar. His illustrations consisting of specimens of the different animals fishes insects skeletons &c &c were good and formed the chief attraction. There was a full length skeleton of a human being. [15 June]

The travel diary is hardly a unique work. At a time when the Industrial Revolution was proceeding apace, anyone who wanted to learn about new developments would set out to see for themselves, and many naturally wrote up their experiences.

Peter followed a punishing schedule (see Appendix 1). On his fourth day, for example, he walked 30 miles to reach Bowness-on-Windermere. On day 11, he arrived in Tadcaster on foot at 11 p.m., only to be off by 4.30 the next morning to walk towards Doncaster. (From the later diary, however, it is clear that early morning starts were as much the rule as the exception.)

The forms of agriculture Peter observed as he went through the different counties are noted carefully: you might conclude this was the true purpose of his journey. He shows awareness of the agricultural pioneers of his day, for instance in the entry for 13 June:

> Pass Netherby Park one of the most extensive, beautiful and best cultivated in England. This belongs to Sir J. Graham: it was the more interesting to me having read the report from the farm, published in the Farmers Series.

In Scotland there are visits to plant nurseries and a Mr Hope's farm, which using the latest steam threshing machine:

> Find it a very complete thing of the kind & quite recently erected – made by Douglass of Edinburg. Find that the machine when in full motion thrashes 10 Boles or 40 imperial Bushels pr. hour – which is an amazing quantity – only 6 horse-power.

Unlike in his other diary, Peter Davis does not come across as a particularly sociable man on his travels. Only a single passing encounter is described, and that briefly:

> Meet with one young man upon the road a farm servant, whom I had a good deal of talk with. Find him deficient in the detail of his own business even. [11 June]

And when, in Newcastle, he called upon a Worcestershire connection, he writes:

> I was induced to stay the night with them although with some reluctance.

On the other hand, he went to a coffee room in Edinburgh, 'to see my traveling companion there', and perhaps implies some disappointment when he failed to appear.

Nor does Peter Davis reveal any great sense of humour, certainly not when – on his first night in Liverpool – he was disturbed 'by a lot of beasts … in a workhouse close under the chamber window'.

He only reveals a scintilla of imagination when noting the dream about his namesake's wedding.

We learn little about what Peter Davis ate or drank, nothing of how much he carried with him or the appearance of the people he came across: what fascinates him are the logistics of his journey; agricultural methods; the scenery, in particular the great landed estates; and the scale of the recently-erected civic buildings in Liverpool and Edinburgh.

That Peter Davis' tour made an impression on him is shown by his subsequent recording of efforts to set up a reading room in his home town: he had seen for himself the benefits of such institutions in the North. Further, from the article on Peter Davis' farm published in the 1867 *Journal of the Royal Agricultural Society of England* (see below, page 24), it is clear that he was a pioneer in the use of agricultural machinery, the early example of which he had seen in action in East Lothian.

The 1836/7 diary

Whilst the motivation for keeping a travel diary is readily understood, we have no clue as to why Peter Davis wrote any other diaries. Was it for his own future reference? Every day he records the weather. New events are noted (the first tooth extracted, the first wedding witnessed, the first brace of birds received as a gift, for instance). Milestones are celebrated: the end of hop-picking, with a dance on the green in the moonlight, and a sheep roast for the return of the squire's son as an MP.

There is only an isolated instance of Pepysian coyness to indicate caution in case the diary reached a wider readership:

Go to Bromyard Fair and come home without doing any business for a certain reason which I will not record here. [3 May 1837]

By 1836, the family home and a major part of Samuel Davis' farming business had been handed over to Peter's eldest brother, William. Their father still held tenancies from Mr Hope (Greete) and Mr Salwey (Court of Hill). Nevertheless he must at least partially have retired, moving to live in one of the rectories adjacent to Burford church, nearly two miles west from Dean Park. In January 1836, we find Peter Davis himself living there too, alongside his father.

With Samuel Davis senior established in a rectory and his second son entering the Church, the place of religion within the family is already clear. Diary entries rarely fail to record when it was a Sunday, and Sundays were kept in accordance with the Fourth Commandment – though not, it seems, obsessively so: as well as visiting friends and family, hopyards were inspected (4 September 1836), 'Parish union business' was discussed (2 October 1836), and rent paid (28 May 1837).

Peter Davis invariably attended church on Sunday, and sometimes went twice ('like a good boy' – 9 April 1837). Holy Communion, administered only on major feast days, warranted prior reflection: 'All partake of the sacrament except myself who had not prepared' (Whitsun, 1836).

It was not always a question of going to St Mary's: besides 'the Mother Church', there were, within Burford parish, three chapels, and Burford was indeed divided into three portions, each with its own rector. Trollope (three years Peter Davis' junior) springs readily to mind. The three rectories were gathered in a group near St Mary's, though by 1836 only two seem to have been lived in. The Old Rectory that survives to this day was almost entirely rebuilt in the second half of the nineteenth century, though some Jacobean features remain.

The rector of Burford's third portion was the Hon. and Revd George Rushout-Bowles MA, JP. Mr Rushout, as he is known in the diary, lord of the manor of Tenbury, was then aged sixty-three, the younger son of the First Baron Northwick of Northwick Park. (Then in the far south-eastern corner of Worcestershire, it is now in Gloucestershire.) His mother was an heiress, Rebecca, née Bowles – hence the addition to his surname.

Mr Rushout was Rector of Burford, both first and third portions, for many years till 1833; he then resigned the first portion, having acquired, in the words of C. R. Dodd, 'conscientious principles respecting pluralities'. Though the holding of two or more benefices by the same person was not prohibited by law until the passing of the Pluralities Act in 1838, Mr Rushout saw which way the wind was blowing.

The Rushout home was Burford House. An extensive property (built 100 years earlier), it lies adjacent to the church and explains why one of the rectories was available for Samuel Davis to rent.

Though Mr Rushout had misgivings about pluralism, he had none about nepotism: having resigned as rector of Burford's first portion, he (as patron of the living) conferred it upon his wife's nephew, the Revd Alexander Stewart MA. Mr Stewart, his wife and young family lived in Church Street, Tenbury, while a new rectory was being built for them at Boraston. On 2 June 1836, Peter Davis reported: 'Eliza and I inspect Mr Stewart's new house.' Alas, he was not to enjoy it for long: by February the following year, he 'lies ill in bed'. On 11 June, Mr Stewart 'still remains in the North of England very ill'. Eventually, on 12 November 1837, the diarist 'went to Nash chapel to hear Mr. Wybrow preach the funeral sermon for the late Rector of Nash & Boraston who died a short time since'. (Henry Wybrow and Alexander Stewart were Oxford contemporaries.) Mr Stewart was just twenty-nine.

Two other clergymen, with whom Peter Davis was on particularly good terms, feature regularly in the diary, the Revd David Jones and the Revd George Hall. Mr Jones and family lived in one of the other rectories at Burford. The rector of Burford's second portion was an absentee, Mr Jones being his curate. His annual salary – at one stage £50 – fed and kept himself, a wife, a son and four daughters.

Mr Hall, vicar of Tenbury, was altogether better off: a contemporary report lists the net value of his livings at £607 p.a., and this was before the partial success of various tithe actions (see entry for 3 July 1836). He was vicar from 1827 until his death in 1845, aged sixty-two. Originally from Shap, Westmorland, George Hall had bought the Tenbury advowson in 1823; when the living became vacant, he petitioned for it on his own behalf. In another Trollopian touch, he used to fish in the River Teme on horseback; when his pony died, the tanyard rejected it, the skin being full of fish hooks. Tunstall Evans' 1840 *History of Tenbury* was dedicated to Mr Hall, 'whose eloquence as a preacher, benignity of heart, splendid talents and enlightened mind justly entitle him to high esteem'. There was, nevertheless, a contrary view:

> Mr. Hall appears to have brought a good deal of north country energy into the Teme Valley neighbourhood … He won a long series of law suits concerning tithes etc. His victory, however, must have been at the considerable cost of popularity with those chiefly concerned. [F. Wayland Joyce]

Indeed, when Mr Hall was taking the service, Mr S. H. Godson and other Tenbury landowners were seen to attend church elsewhere.

The tithe battle continued after 1836: Mr Godson, Mr V. W. Wheeler, Joseph Cooke (the surgeon), Francis Davis and others took their case to the highest court of the land. Not until 1840 was the House of Lords' judgment finally delivered – against them – by Lord Cottenham, the then-Lord Chancellor. The legal costs can hardly have been negligible.

On 14 February 1836, Peter Davis records:

> Mr. Rushout faltered very much in performing the service. His eyesight and the use of his limbs seem to fail him. Write a letter to Samuel acquainting him of it and desiring him to come over as soon as possible to Take the duty.

Peter Davis' brother Samuel – ordained a deacon only a few months previously – complies. Within three weeks he has arrived from Devon, and is officiating at baptisms, marriages and burials, as well as taking Sunday services. Unfortunately, however, he has neglected to tell his bishop (Exeter) what he is up to. Further, he has failed to obtain the prior permission of the local bishop (Hereford) to officiate in Burford. This leads to much frustration:

> A party come from Hill Top to Burford Church thinking to hear Samuel do duty but were of course disappointed on acct. of his misunderstanding with the Bishop. [16 October 1836]

In addition, Samuel's plans for ordination as a priest were put back – to 1837. (The ordination is not mentioned in the diary.)

A strain of unselfishness and public spiritedness runs through Peter Davis' narrative. The reading room project has already been mentioned: 'Call at the Swan … for the purpose of asking Mr. Grove if he had a room in the House he could spare for a reading room, myself and some others proposing to establish such a thing at Tenbury' (10 March 1837). On the farm, Peter Davis behaves with similar altruism: 'Mr. Partridge being shearing his sheep, stay and assist' (8 June 1837). And when his brother comes to help out the ailing Mr Rushout, Peter uncomplainingly moves back up to Dean Park with his 'traps' (3 March 1836).

There is, also, evidence of what we see as a Victorian moral sense: Peter inclines towards the censorious when people drink too much, writing for instance (on 2 January 1837) of the local attorney 'Fuller (who gets beastly drunk before dinner)'. In addition, on 7 March 1836 he records:

> We play at whist, myself being most singularly unfortunate losing more than I ever did in one evening before at the game viz about £4. So much for gaming. However there's one consolation – if one did not sometimes see and feel the evil consequences of vice the practice of virtue would not appear so delightful.

In 1836 generally, much visiting of newly-weds takes place: 'No end to the weddings this year in this neighbourhood' (3 October). Samuel Davis junior was married in June, but more significant for Peter was his sister's marriage two months later. Eliza's husband was a Tenbury attorney, William Trumper. 'The first wedding I ever attended' was a controversial match, possibly because the groom had only been widowed the previous year: the bride's father absented himself, as did her brother Samuel and his new wife. Happily, by 12 October fences have been mended somewhat: 'Mr. & Mrs. Trumper visit the Park together for the first time. Father here and become sociable with them – a step gained!' And by July and August of the following year, during Samuel senior's last illness, the diary records that Eliza and her husband were among the most frequent visitors.

It is this illness, the subsequent death and its aftermath that dominate the entries for the last five months of the diary. Having made his will on 19 June 1837, Samuel Davis became 'very unwell' only three days later. On the following day he was 'taken violently ill in the afternoon. Fell down in a fainting state.' Doctors and surgeons come and go over the next nine weeks. Then, on 26 August, 'My father getting worse very fast – no hopes left.'

For 30 August, the entry reads:

> Warm clear day. This morning about ¼ to 5 o'clock my poor dear Father departed this life without a struggle having bourn a lingering illness of nearly 3 months. In the 69th year of his age. May the Lord have mercy upon the soul of my best friend upon earth. All the family present besides Samuel who arrived at Park by this day's Mail. Aunt Partridge goes home to return tomorrow. Mr. Trumper comes to Tea and takes Eliza home with him.

On the day of the funeral, Peter Davis adds: 'A better Father, a better husband or a more upright and honest man never was in existence.'

Throughout the diary, Peter's search for a farm tenancy is a recurring theme. A total of fourteen farms are mentioned as possibilities, none of them taken at this time. In his will, Samuel Davis states that he has 'lately placed my said sons William and Peter in two Farms formerly occupied by myself'. As mentioned, his eldest son William had taken over the Dean Park tenancy by 1836. The diary does not relate exactly which farm had become Peter Davis' responsibility. That some deal had been done is clear from the entry for 20 April 1837:

> Mr. H. Davis of Orleton comes to take a valuation of the stock, crop, implements &c. upon Burford & Nash between Father & myself including Furniture. Every thing valued to me excepting two lots of wheat the one at Nash the other in Burford Granery, and two Beds, bedsteads &c. viz. the Bed and all belonging to it in White room without a counterpaine, the bed in my room and the steads &c. in Study room.

Nevertheless – from the fact that searching continued – it is evident that arrangements in Burford parish were not satisfactory to Peter in the long term. At an earlier stage, he let his irritation show:

> Father & I go to Broncroft to look over the Lodge Farm but could not agree for it. The farm is 322 acres, the price put 420£ a year. We bid the 400£ and parted. Feel very angry with my Father for not closing upon it, the farm being not only a good one but in a good state and the buildings &c. all very complete or to be made so in a short time. [28 October 1836]

Peter Davis never gave up on Broncroft: by 1841 he was settled there, in Lodge Farm.

Any farming operation at this time was heavily dependent on animals, and Peter was confident in dealing with them. 'The grey nag gets his fore-leg strained at the fetlock. Poultice and bleed him' (13 May 1836). As well as references to horses, we know there are working oxen on the farm, and of course sheep: the entry on 25 May 1836 records: 'Had a right hard day's sheep-shearing. Five of us shore nearly 157 (all large ones).'

Critical though Peter may have been of his father's hard-headedness, he himself knew the value of what he dealt in, and was not inclined to yield on price. On 13 October 1837, for instance, he writes:

> Call on Mr. Baker about the Hay rick at Court of Hill but could not deal, he wanting 100£ for it, much more than the worth (19 Ton).

Six weeks later:

> Go to Nash in afternoon and call on Mr. Baker, he now being in the humour to sell the Hay. But no go for me now thank you.

Earlier, on 22 July 1836, we read:

> Father & I go to the Furlongs to measure a stick of oak Timber which he bot of Mr. Edwards last year, but no go. The right stick was cut off and being fobbed off with another would not do.

The diary records few critical observations. Besides the expression of anger with his father (mentioned above), he voices other gripes during October 1836:

> ... The other estate (Mr. Pheysey's) sold very high, Mr. Trumper the purchaser for him at 8,025£ – 150 acres. This stretch in price was caused by Mr. Wheeler, the opposition bidder, who imagined Trumper was bidding for us! Thus showing his good feeling towards us.

Subsequently, he writes:

> Call on Mr. Rushout to see the Shrewsbury paper to ascertain the day of the revision of the votes for Burford, which happens to be past, being on 24th, William (who is the Burford overseer) having neglected to attend.

Peter Davis is as sparing of accolades as he is with criticism. The tributes to his father, already noted, are all the more affecting for this, as is this earlier comment:

> Mr. & Mrs. H. Davis and Mr. Trumper come here (the Park) to Tea and taste Miss Reynolds Piclets. She being famous for making prime ones as indeed she is for doing everything else in the way of cookery &c. [7 February 1836]

Despite the few compliments handed out in this diary, its tone is generally cheerful. The weather is always the first topic, for which appreciation is often expressed: 'Beautiful day. Fair & sun shiny' (5 February 1836); 'Small frost, very mild fine day' (7 May 1836); 'Most delightful day. Sun shining all day' (3 January 1837).

Peter Davis – being a single man – was often taking meals with friends and relations; he seemed to enjoy hospitality:

> A good dinner prepared by Mrs. Smallman. Uncle Reynolds, B. Sayer, & I leave together and go to spend the evening at Boraston where we meet the Sayers, Mrs. Reynolds &c. and stay playing at cards till between two & 3 o'clock. [2 January 1837]

There is no hint of any romantic attachment during the period covered by the diaries; though Peter Davis only married in 1845, aged 33, he nevertheless appreciated women, and not just for their cooking. Of his sister-in-law, he comments: 'Much pleased with Samuel's choice. She appears a very sensible and well disposed person: rather good looking into the bargain' (25 June 1836). 'Take Tea at Burford along with Saml. and his bride, a truly affectionate and estimable person' (12 August 1836).

Something occurred at the very end of Samuel Davis senior's life to make him change his will so as to reduce young Samuel's share of the estate. The will he made in June 1837 left residue between the sons in three equal shares; by a codicil dated 8 August, however, only William and Peter were to share the residuary estate. Samuel remained entitled to a devise and bequest of 'Dead' or 'Dept' Croft[2], Rye Shutts and the Dingles, Knighton-on-Teme, a total of some 84 acres, together with the cottage called Aston Bank.

Peter Davis does not hint at any falling out. Possibly Samuel senior took the view that his second son was now settled in his choice of profession, with the prospect of taking charge in due course of his father-in-law's parish. (He did so in 1852 – presented by his father-in-law as the patron of the living.) He can hardly have been under the impression that Lucinda Davis would be well-provided for, being one of the eleven children of a clergyman.

Following his father's death, Peter Davis undertook much of the work involved with his estate, including honouring Samuel's bequest.

> William goes to Ludlow market. Sells a load of wheat for me, some for himself. Takes a draft of agreement for Saml. to Mr. Anderson to prepare between Mr. Mytton of Deptcroft and himself for renting that Estate, the draft furnished by me. [4 September 1837]

It appears from the 1836/7 diary that only longer journeys were covered by coach or gig. Long walks seem to have been rare occurrences. The distances between Burford and places mentioned, listed in Appendix 2, show how very much time must have been spent in the saddle. Peter Davis, his father and eldest brother took for granted the need to attend the local markets regularly, and to rise early in order to arrive at distant places in good time, even in the depths of winter. On 28 January 1837, we read:

> Some little snow – very cold wind. Having received a letter from Mr. Blashill dated the 25th stating that Sir J. Cotterill had a farm to offer, William & I start off this morning to see it and get to Garnons (the seat of Sir John) by nine.

Garnons is a good 25 miles south-west of Burford. The letter referred to had taken two days to arrive, Peter's diary predating the introduction of the uniform penny post.

After 1837

As noted, the 1836/7 diary ends with its owner running out of space in his journal. From other sources, however, we can piece together what happens subsequently to the main protagonists.

William Davis continued farming Dean Park, eventually marrying at the age of thirty-eight (in 1844). The faithful Maria remained in the household until at least 1851. In the following year, however, she too was married, at the age of sixty, and living further north in Shropshire, in Kemberton; she died there twenty-five years later.

William and his wife Martha, née Child, had four children; he prospered, acquiring land in Kingsland parish. Eventually, he gave up the farm tenancy in favour of his second son, another Peter Davis, who later lost all his money after investing in South American silver mines.

William's eldest son, Will, married (after a twenty-year engagement) at the age of forty-four. Long before then, he had qualified as a solicitor, practising in Tenbury Wells until his death in 1928. Outliving his wife, who was childless, he lived on at Stanbrook House, Burford, with his spinster cousin Eliza Augusta Davis, a daughter of the diarist, for a companion. Following her eventual death in 1954, a sale took place, where none of the extended family was present to rescue what must have been a considerable bulk of papers and photographs.

The injudicious Peter Davis junior had a daughter and six sons, the youngest of whom, the Revd Ralph Leigh Davis, left behind an invaluable family tree. Married at forty-three, he continued what seems like a tradition of reluctant uxoriousness in that branch of the family.

By contrast, the Revd Samuel Davis married three times, allegedly meeting all his wives on the same day. His second was the sister of R. D. Blackmore, author of *Lorna Doone*. Following ordination, he lived out most of his life in Devon, remaining vicar of Burrington until 1883, shortly before his death. He was said to be of simple, sweet disposition and fine presence, much revered in the neighbourhood. The eldest of his six children followed him to Cambridge and into Holy Orders.

Eliza outlived all three of her brothers. Her husband, William Trumper, died in 1838 after only two years of marriage; they had no children. Four years later, she married John Corser of Byton, near Presteigne, a farmer, eventually moving to Shipton, in Corvedale, not far from Broncroft, where earlier, as a young widow, she had been living with her brother Peter. With John Corser, she had three daughters and a son.

As mentioned, Peter Davis, the diarist, is to be found by 1841 farming Broncroft Lodge near Diddlebury, north of Ludlow, Eliza living in the same household. By 1845 (then aged thirty-three) he has moved some twenty-five miles south to a 600-acre farm at Milton, Herefordshire, and married Jane Jeffries. Fourteen years his junior, she was from a well-established farming family near there. In 1848, Peter won a medal at Smithfield, which is now in the possession of his great-great-grandson Bruce Coates (see below, page 27).

By the time of the 1851 census, Peter (his wife then with three children) was farming King's Head Farm with 480 acres at Bromfield, nearer to Ludlow. Finally, at Michaelmas 1860, he moved some 45 miles south-east, taking on the tenancy of the Bickmarsh Hall estate, Warwickshire. In the 1861 census, he is said to be a farmer of 1,270 acres there, employing twenty-nine men and five boys.

The 1867 *Journal of the Royal Agricultural Society of England* has a full description of farming methods used at Bickmarsh, 'a district of stiff clay, high-backed lands'.

The normal force of horses on this farm would be 38 to 40, certainly not fewer than 36; the introduction of a steam cultivator has enabled

3. Bickmarsh Hall, Warwickshire, where Peter Davis and his family lived from 1860.

Mr. Davis to sell off fully half his teams, and to carry his tillage-work before him with only 18 horses ... His total expenditure on steam culture will be less than half the lowest amount at which we put his saving in horseflesh ... He greatly increases the acreage of root-crops; and his grain-crops yield far better than before, all being attributed by him to steam cultivation and thorough drainage.

A compliment is also paid in the same report to Peter's elder son, John Jeffries Davis (then twenty-one): 'As sound, intelligent and business-like a young farmer as we have had the pleasure to pick up for some time.'

Peter and Jane had a total of eight daughters besides their two sons: all survived them. Full details, along with their grandchildren's, are set out in Appendix 3. Like her father, the eldest daughter, Gertrude Louisa, wrote diaries. Indeed, her collection spans six decades; it has yet to be fully transcribed, but the picture that emerges is of a happy and united family, with God-fearing parents, much respected and well-loved.

Gertrude married Howard Freer of Bidford-on-Avon, after whose death she went to live in Canada with some of her six children. Another daughter, Flora May, left for Australia immediately upon marrying Herbert William Marshall of Birmingham. Her sister Constance Alathea married Trevor Webster of Bewdley; their grandson, also Trevor Webster, likewise emigrated to Australia, driving himself and his wife by car from England, for the most part overland. John Jeffries Davis and his wife Kate Freer had a son who died in New York and seven daughters, three of whom lived and died in Canada. Other descendants are known to be living in New Zealand, Sarawak, the United States, Argentina, Portugal, France, and no doubt other places far flung from south Shropshire.

Unfortunately, no likenesses of Peter Davis or his siblings have survived. There exists, however, an oil painting, known as *The Bull*. By an unknown artist, it has on the front the words 'Ist prize 15L & silver medal to the breeder, Birmingham 1865.' On the back is written 'P. Davis, Bickmarsh'. A cattle show was held annually at Bingley Hall, Birmingham, and the catalogue for the 1865 exhibition confirms that Peter Davis was indeed the winning breeder in the Fat Cattle class for Hereford Oxen or Steers exceeding three years and three months of age. Again, descendant Bruce Coates has the accompanying medal in his possession.

Peter Davis died at Bickmarsh on 3 October 1873, aged sixty-one, and was buried in nearby Dorsington churchyard. His career as an independent farmer had more or less coincided with what became known as the Golden Age of Farming in Great Britain, 1840–1870; and indeed his local newspaper described him as 'one of the leading agriculturalists in this district'. On his imposing gravestone (highly polished red granite) is written: 'This tomb was erected by many friends as a memorial of their esteem and affection.' When his wife Jane eventually died (in 1891), she was buried in the same grave, and a further inscription was added.

My involvement with the diaries

Until 2009, I had no knowledge of my ancestor's 1836/7 diary. Of the travel diary, a transcript had survived, made by Gertrude's daughter, Edith Howard Freer. For Christmas in 1898, Edith (then sixteen) was given an album into which, as was the custom, various friends and relations drew pictures or wrote wise sayings. She had never known her grandfather, but transcribed the travel diary entries into this album, using its blank pages. Some fifteen years ago, I received a photocopy of the album from the trans-continental motorist, Trevor Webster of New South Wales.

It whetted my appetite. What information had been passed down to me about the Davis family was sparse. This is not surprising, as it is grandparents who are the key for handing down stories. My father had never known his grandfather, Arthur Henry Davis, nor had my grandfather known his, Peter Davis. Arthur Henry, in turn, had never known his grandfather, Samuel Davis.

4. *The Bull* bred by Peter Davis – '1st prize 15£ & silver medal to the breeder, Birmingham 1865'.

So, all I knew of Peter Davis were the dry facts: a diary, however, transforms everything. As Judge Jeffreys said at the trial of Lady Ivie in 1684, 'Now, instead of records, the upshot is a little lousy history.'

Publishing the travel diary became a long-term ambition, but not one high on my list of priorities. In November 2009, however, I received a telephone call from Bruce Coates in New Brunswick, Canada, descended from John Jeffries Davis. Bruce's story about the discovery of both original diaries is told briefly in Appendix 4.

Compared to Edith's transcription, which turns out to have been neither complete nor totally accurate, I find the freshness of Peter Davis' original diary provides a valuable insight into both the man and his times. I hope others who read it will agree.

The process of editing the 1836/7 diary has involved some conjecture. Those details I have managed to track down relating to individuals mentioned by Peter Davis are set out in Appendix 5 (this includes brief biographies of the public figures referred to in the travel diary, so as to avoid overloading the endnotes). Initially, my main sources were the International Genealogical Index and UK Census returns. Ages set against

Our Grandfather's Diary.

Peter Davis   Born 1811
at Dene Park

June 8th 1835.

Tenbury Worcestershire

Start from Park at 6. o'clock on horse back to Ludlow – Hay making started near Ludlow Take a place by the "Alert "Coach to Shrewsbury & by "L. Hyrondelle" from thence to Liverpool – Pay at Angel Ludlow 18/- for the whole route – arrive at Shrewsbury about 12 oclock – get on the "L Hyrondelle" & proceed on through Elles. here, Overton, Wrexham Chester to Liverpool where we arrive about 7 at the Birkenhead Hotel – Each person entitled to a Ticket on arriving at the latter place to proceed over the River Mersey on a Steamer which Ticket is procured from the Coachman – Was much pleased with the road & country all the way from Shrewsbury to Ellesmere – the Soil is rich & country level The coach loaded to excess all the way 11. or 12. outside – Being a little behind

5. Page 1 of the transcription of the travel diary by Edith Howard Freer.

adults appearing in our 1841 Census are, however, approximate and some relationships have had to be guessed at.

The Reynolds genealogy is particularly 'ballpark'. The most vexed question concerns Peter Davis' Reynolds grandfather, who is not mentioned in the diary even though his home (New House) was much visited. From other sources, it is clear grandfather Peter was living there: perhaps, aged seventy-nine in 1836, he was senile. Another curiosity is that Peter Davis, while mentioning others as 'cousin' or 'aunt', does not refer to his great-uncles Peter and James and great-aunt Eleanor as such, but only by name.

In compiling the biographical index, I have not included every reference to close family members, only flagging up significant events. For others, however, I have included even quite trivial mentions to indicate the frequency of Peter Davis' contact with them. Appendix 5 and the biographical index may not compensate for the absence of any general index, for which I apologise. As family history is of ongoing interest, I would welcome any information to supplement or correct what is here referred to. I can be contacted via the publishers or my website, www.freerangephotography.co.uk.

Our landscape in times of change: 1835 & 2010 – a personal reflection

In a lecture in May 2009, the Bishop of London expressed his dismay at the state of history teaching in British schools. 'Never have we known so much about now,' he said, 'and never have we been so ignorant of how we came to be here.' Having spent my working life in the law, I sometimes feel I am a thwarted historian. It was my favourite subject at school, where only a conspiracy between the headmaster (a former barrister) and my mother (daughter and granddaughter of solicitors) prevented me reading history at university.

Although as a schoolboy I studied different historical periods, somehow the late eighteenth/early nineteenth century passed me by. The other yawning gap in my education was science. So it was that I never learnt about what has been described as the most significant revolution in man's history, the Industrial Revolution – arguably at its height in 1835.

Reading my ancestor's travel diary caused me to reflect on what was a dramatic period of change for our landscape. In May 2009, therefore, I set out to follow his steps and to reflect in turn on the changes we face today.

In retracing his journey, I planned to cycle through the parts where he walked. Otherwise, I would put my bicycle on the train. All went well until I reached Oxfordshire, and was nearly in the home straight. There, I was freewheeling down an empty road when I failed to spot a large pothole. As my speed would have been approaching 30 mph, my journey naturally ended in hospital (luckily with no long-term ill effects, apart from those suffered by my bicycle and helmet).

Even my camera survived the crash, but being so much in an air-conditioned train had rather limited what I could photograph as I went along. Like my ancestor I kept a diary of my trip. After my return from hospital, however, it sadly vanished. I feel shamefaced that Peter Davis' travel diary should have survived intact for 175 years, while mine went missing after only a few days.

Three factors in particular transformed the landscape during Peter Davis' lifetime: transport, farming and food, and the expansion of the built environment. In all these areas, the early nineteenth century was a period of rapid and intense change.

First, transport. As can be seen from Appendix 1, the greater part of Peter's 800-mile journey was by coach. In those days, coaches travelled at 14 mph maximum between stages or 8 mph on average over a day's journey, allowing for changing the horses. It is hardly surprising that Peter Davis was impressed by his experience of travelling by train.

One of the first steam passenger railways, the Liverpool to Manchester line, had opened just under five years prior to Peter Davis' journey. Having embarked on the train at Liverpool, he recorded an overall speed of 24 mph. He also mentioned crossing the new Leeds to Selby line on his way between Tadcaster and Doncaster, and (north of Towcester) the line of the London to Birmingham railway, which opened eventually in 1838, one of the first inter-city lines, and one of the first to be built into London. Later (25 May 1837), the diary records a visit to the Grand Junction Railway in course of construction.

At the end of 1835, there were 338 miles of track in the UK; by the time of Peter Davis' death, this had risen to some 14,000. The engineering works needed to build these railways transformed the face of Britain.

The second major factor in changing Peter Davis' landscape is farming. On his trip, he inspected (as mentioned) Mr Hope's 6-hp, steam-driven machine, threshing forty bushels an hour, 'an amazing quantity', he wrote. On his father's farm, all the threshing would have been by hand, or with simple, hand-powered machinery. Yet, following Peter's death thirty-eight years later, there were no less than ten lots of steam machinery listed in the particulars of sale of his farming stock.

Though the great period of the Enclosures was the sixty years from 1760 to 1820, when some 3,500 Enclosure Acts were passed by Parliament, it was not till the late 1840s that most of the land in Britain was enclosed. This, together with mechanisation, triggered the Golden Age of Farming referred to earlier, with large areas of wetland being drained and coming under cultivation for the first time. As a result, farmers had the funds to rebuild farmhouses, and also to put up better dwellings for their (fewer) employees.

If it was a time for farm-related construction, it was all the more a time of rapid expansion of towns and cities. Peter Davis marvels at the new buildings in Liverpool and Edinburgh. London's population more than trebled in his lifetime; Manchester's quadrupled. Huge areas of the best agricultural land and market gardens went for building houses and factories, part of the conflict between the black and the green.

Just as Peter Davis lived at a time of change in his nineteenth-century landscape, so do we also stand on the threshold of an equivalent period of dramatic change today. My thoughts dwell in particular on food, fossil fuels and changes in our climate.

We have already entered a period of world food shortages. The British government's Chief Scientific Adviser talked starkly in May 2009 about the growing world population and 50 per cent more food being needed to feed us all by 2030. Twenty-one years before that talk, and the year was 1988: this does not seem so very distant to me. Twenty-one years thence (2030) is likewise not far away, certainly in terms of the need to plan to increase world food output by 50 per cent. Common sense dictates that, as a nation, we need to look to grow more of what we eat. Assuming we take this obvious step, we shall surely see the landscape changing considerably as we move to more intensive farming methods.

Our agriculture and horticulture depend hugely upon fossil fuels. We need them to run our tractors, feed our animals, heat our greenhouses, and refrigerate the lorries that transport our produce; as well as for fungicides, herbicides and insecticides. Water scarcity, but above all fuel scarcity, will dictate major changes in what we grow.

The underlying reason for such rapid change taking place in Peter Davis' lifetime was the availability of cheap energy and raw materials. Today, energy is no longer cheap because neither oil nor gas, two of the major non-renewable resources on which we have come to depend, are any longer plentiful. The experts may not agree on whether we have or have not already passed the point of peak oil production, but that is immaterial: our prosperity over the past 150 years has been based on the availability of oil and gas in ever-increasing quantities. In the foreseeable future this will no longer be the case, dictating major changes for farmers adapting to new systems of food production.

Finally, even if all the energy sources we take for granted were to be cheap and plentiful, the concentration of carbon dioxide in the world's atmosphere is 388 parts per million[3], up by more than one-third on pre-Industrial Revolution levels. If we continue along this path, scientists tell us that our children and grandchildren face a very bleak existence. We need to cut our carbon use. Climate change, caused by increasing greenhouse gas emissions, is the greatest potential threat both to our countryside and to ourselves.

So, we face an unpredictable future, the only certainty being the inevitability of change. Local and small-scale action, by Transition Hereford, Leominster or Presteigne, is not alone going to suffice to prevent our landscape altering. However, without individuals getting together in their local communities to study the problems, and becoming resilient through evolving local strategies, our governments will not be persuaded that the public is willing to play its part in adapting to change.

Peter Davis expresses his joys and sorrows directly in the diaries. Though not in any degree an intellectual, he comments with honesty and intelligence on the events, people and places he encounters. Politically conservative[4], he was not reactionary. In fact, he was nothing if not a man of action, and I like to think he lived in hope: we could do worse than to follow his example.

Martin Davis, great-great-grandson of the diarist
December 2010

Notes

1. In other words, Samuel Davis was ranked 33rd of all those in his year at Cambridge who obtained first-class honours in Mathematics: he was one of only fifteen Wranglers from his college in the years 1833–42. The order of Wranglers was widely publicised in the national newspapers, shaping the public's perception that mathematics was the most intellectually challenging of degree subjects.
2. This property is referred to on local maps, and occasionally by Peter Davis, as 'Deepcroft'.
3. As at October 2010.
4. See the entry for 26 July 1837.

Peter Davis' Travels North: 1835

Burford, Shropshire to Liverpool
Liverpool to Lancaster
Lancaster to Bowness-on-Windermere
Bowness to Carlisle
Carlisle to Edinburgh
Edinburgh to Berwick-upon-Tweed
Berwick to Newcastle-upon-Tyne
Newcastle-upon-Tyne to Tadcaster
Tadcaster to Nottingham
Nottingham to Brackley
Brackley to Pershore
Pershore to Burford

[Monday] June 8th 1835
[Burford, Shropshire to Liverpool]

Start from Park[1] at 6 clock on horseback to Ludlow[2]. Haymaking commenced near Ludlow. Take a place by the Alert Coach[3] to Shrewsbury & by L'Hyrondelle[4] from thence to Liverpool: pay at Angel, Ludlow 18/-[5] for the whole route. Arrive at Shrewsbury[6] about 12 clock. Get on the L'Hyrondelle and proceed on through Ellesmere, Overton, Wrexham, Chester to Liverpool where we arrive about 7 clock at the Birkenhead Hotel. Each passenger entitled to a ticket on arriving at the latter place to proceed over the river Mersey on a Steamer, which ticket is procured from the coachman.

Was much pleased with the road and country all the way: from Shrewsbury to Ellesmere the soil is rich and country level. The coach loaded to excess all the day – 11 or 12 on outside. Being a little behind time at Shrewsbury they were obliged to mend their pace to make up for it – so we went at the

June 8th 1855 —

Start from Park at 6 Clock on
horseback to Ludlow. Haymaking
commences near Ludlow. Take
a place by the Alert Coach to
Shrewsbury, & by L Byron delly from
thence to Liverpool:— pay at
Angel Ludlow 10/6 for the whole
route. Arrive at Shrewsbury
about 12 Clock. Get on the L
Byron dell and proceed on through
Ellesmere, Overton, Wrexham, Chester
to Liverpool where we arrive about
7 Clock at the Birkenhead Hotel.
Each passenger entitled to a ticket
on arriving at the latter place to
proceed over the river Mersey on
a Steamer, which ticket is
procured from the coachman.
Was much pleased with the
road and country all the way:
from Shrewsbury to Ellesmere
the soil is rich and country
level the coach loaded to

6. Page 1 of Peter Davis' original travel diary, rediscovered in 2009.

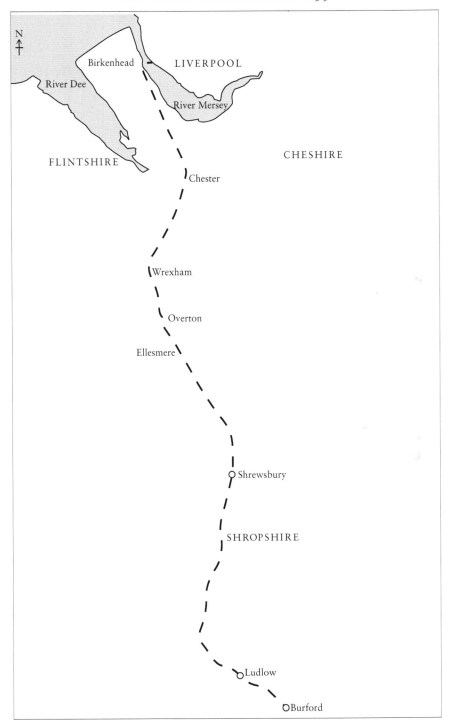

Map 3. 8 June 1835: Burford to Liverpool (99 miles).

rate of 13 or 14 miles the hour perhaps as far as Wrexham. The horses first raters, full of blood. The land changes at Ellesmere from a loose gravelly Turnip and Barley soil to a stiff clay, which last, however does not continue far[7]. Our next stage to Overton, Flintshire. A very level and flat country still but soil improving again. Swede sowing commenced and progressing in most places on the road. Almost invariably planted on the drill system[8]. Potatoes, on account of the flatness of the country, are in this district, viz Flintshire, Denbighshire and Cheshire, all planted on beds about 4 or 5 feet wide with ditches between cut out square at the bottom. This is the general practice, whether in garden or field culture[9].

Get to Wrexham at ¼ past four o'clock[10]. Some delightful views in Denbighshire, the river Dee winding its course round the hills, which being planted with trees together with gentlemen's & noblemen's seats in the distance give the country a most majestic Appearance. Some of the best land (which is nearly all meadow) lies on the borders of Denbighshire & Cheshire: it then falls off and becomes thin and poor in places: all the way very flat and the road almost upon a level from Tenbury to Liverpool, a distance of 89 miles. We get over the river in a packet & arrive at the Docks about ½ past 7 P.M. Proceed into the town; look out for a domicile; fix upon the White Bear in Dale Street[11]. Get some Tea – feel tired and rather fatigued. Go to bed at 11.

[Tuesday June 9th]
[Liverpool]

Rise before four. Get scarcely a wink of sleep from being continuously disturbed by a lot of beasts (or something a little better) in a workhouse close under the chamber window. Start off through Byrom Street & Scotland road. The first circumstance I meet with worth notice is a spirit shop at 4 o'clock full of customers, guzzling away at it, consisting of both men and women. Get an extensive view of the town from a hill neer Shaw Street. Pass the infirmary a splendid building. Come to the Adelphi Hotel, Raneleagh Street[12] a very extensive and even magnificent house – then through Lord Street, St George's Crescent, splendid buildings Shops &c. Come to the new Custom House now being builded near the docks, a truly magnificent erection[13]. Get among the ships in the docks. The first I enter is one kept expressly for performing divine service in: holds a thousand. The next ship I go on board is the Liverpool an American Ship fitted up in the neatest style much more so than the English[14]. Go on board another American and then to breakfast. The stewards and mate's of the American

7. Nelson Monument, Exchange Flags, Liverpool, designed by Matthew Cotes Wyatt and sculpted by Richard Westmacott: 'This monument, which is executed in bronze, consists of a marble basement and a circular pedestal, supporting figures emblematical of Nelson's principal victories. The statue of the dying admiral rests one foot on a prostrate enemy, and the other on a cannon; and he is receiving upon his sword a naval crown from Victory.' (From an account of Liverpool in 1839, published in *The Penny Magazine*)

ships are very civil and even polite men; who will allow you to look over their ships and even show persons over them free of charge. Proceed to the market house, which is the largest I ever saw. Stepped it for upwards of 200 yards long: there are five separate avenues. Enter the Lyceum news room[15], a splendid building of the kind. Visit the Mount Cemetery, one of the most curious and at the same time the best adopted places for the purpose that could well be imagined. Contrived in a kind of valley – with a natural bank on one side planted with shrubs and trees, and a wall and the sloping roads down to it on the other. Been formed about 16 years[16]. The splendidly built houses round give it a still more striking and magnificent appearance.

Exchange 12 o'clock. This is the place which of all others in Liverpool has most attracted my attention. Hundreds, I may almost say thousands, of the most respectable and intelligent inhabitants of the town congregated together. The exchange itself forms a square of large extent with Nelson's most beautiful Monument in the centre, the whole being flagged. The public news room on one side, two or three hundred gentlemen each with a newspaper in his hand or walking to & fro in conversation[17].

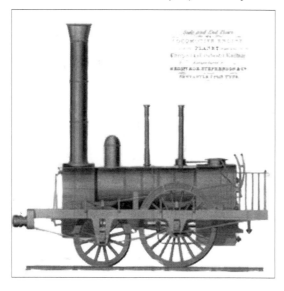

8. A steam locomotive of the Planet class, one of which would have pulled Peter Davis' train from Liverpool to Manchester.

Visit the Clarence Dock Yard[18] where the steam packets put in. They are much larger than I should have expected. Altogether the Docks to a stranger form one of the most attractive, interesting & instructive sights[19]. See the Zoological gardens[20] in the afternoon a very good collection & very tastily laid out. In fact the Liverpool people apper to excel in most things they undertake. This has been an excessively hot day like the two which have preceded it.

Wednesday June 10th
[Liverpool to Lancaster]

Rise at 6 o'clock. Take a place to go by the Railway to Manchester[21]. Get a Ticket which costs 5/6 at the Royal Hotel[22] by the first train. A Ticket for second train costs but 4/-, but that is ½ an hour longer in going on account of carrying luggage, stopping often &c – and the carriages are altogether inferior to the first. Go from the Inn in an omnibus, the charge for which is 6d.

Each passenger's Ticket is numbered and according to that number, he takes his seat in the carriages. Each carriage contains six seats comfortably fitted up, 3 on each side. The whole train is ranged under a covered place till starting-time, when it moves gently first through an excavation cut through the rock. The steamer is then set to and off you go as swift as the wind, the steamer making the most curious oozing noise imaginable. A female who was going by the train wished to take her two

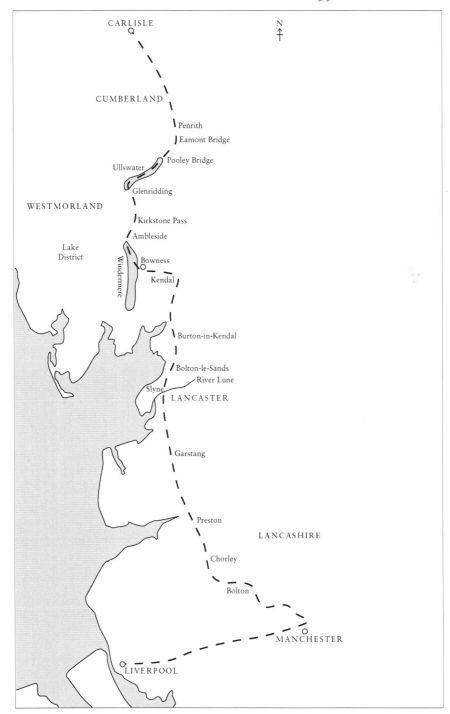

Map 4. 10 June: Liverpool to Lancaster, via Manchester (85 miles); 11 June: Lancaster to Bowness-on-Windermere (30 miles [on foot]); 12 June: Bowness to Carlisle (47 miles).

9. Lancaster Priory.

dogs along in the carriage; but no go – she was soon shown the contrary. We started at 7 minutes past 7 precisely and got to Manchester in one hour and 17 minutes a distance of 31 miles.

Walk into the Town (Manchester). Come to the Mosely Arms[23]. Breakfast there. A first rate Inn. Cost me 1s/8d and bad breakfast into the bargain. Make a vow never to go to one of these Head Inns again if I can avoid it. Soon get tired of Manchester and resolve to leave it by twelve o'clock Coach. Take a place on the "Fair Trader" to Lancaster: fare 10/-. Manchester is a bustling town and some fine public buildings in it, as the Town Hall[24], Infirmary[25] &c. Otherwise a black, narrow-streeted unpleasant Town, at least as far as I have seen it. Get to Bolton 20 minutes past 10 – the Country from Manchester generally uninteresting, the land not good. 11 miles from Manchester to Bolton.

Chorely[26]. 15 minutes to 3. A small Town. A very unpleasant ride from Bolton the road pitched with large stones. Country become more interesting. Some highish hills and tolerable scenery. Preston[27], 5 minutes to 4 clock. Some pretty scenery at the entrance of the town and fairish meadows up the valleys. Garstang. Some fine & extensive scenery at the entrance.

Lancaster[28] – 10 mins. to 7 o'clock P.M. having come from Manchester (54 miles) in 6 hours & 50 mins. Had a most delightful drive from Preston. The heat having abated and the evening been delightful. On entering this town the view is splendid and most extensive. On the hill before descending into the town is seen the river[29], the ocean at a distance and a most extensive range of country including the hills of Westmorland. Here is an ancient and most magnificent old castle[30]. Regret my having arrived too late in the evening to see the interior and view from Top. Get permission however to ascend the steeple of the church[31] which stands close by and is quite as high. From this place the most splendid and extensive view is commanded. The hills in Cumberland, Westmorland, Yorkshire are distinctly seen, as well as the ocean with the vessels upon it to a great distance.

Stay at Noon's Royal Oak Inn[32]. Take Tea here which is the most comfortable Inn I have yet met with. Several other visitors also staying here from Edinburgh, Liverpool &c.

Thursday June 11th
[Lancaster to Bowness-on-Windermere]

Rise at ½ past four and start 10 mins. befor 5 to walk towards Burton[33]. Slayne[34], 3 miles from Lancaster. Here is some of the richest and best cultivated land I have yet met with. Luxuriant crops of grass and grass seeds[35]. Soil appears to be a rich gravelly loam – excellent crops of Barly and Beans are grown. The fences excellent and kept in the best order possible. Some of the land rented at 3 and 4£ per acre. The breed of cattle very much mixed. Some Short Horns – some Scotch amongst them. The sheep long-legged and large – of no particular kind. The drill system of Turnip planting invariably followed.

Burton 5 minutes to 8 clock – walked from Lancaster 10½ miles. Time 2 hours 55 mins. Since leaving Bolton Village[36] the country has not been quite so interesting: the land poorer – stone wall fences by the road side generally. The country round here seems to abound in stone for all purposes. Houses all built with it, gate posts invariably stone. The ploughs all drawn in the 9.o. fashon[37] with two horses – sometimes 1 or 2 in addition if very steep and hard. Land very gravelly about here: the morning unfortunately foggy – so have not had the benefit of the distant views. Get a good breakfast & rest here at the royal Oak[38]. Start off 10 minutes after nine – to walk to Kendal. The first object worthy of notice is Farltom Knot[39] about 2 miles from Burton. This side the town is in Westmorland. The country about here

10. Bowness-on-Windermere.

except for the hills uninteresting. Kendal. Get here on foot by 10 mins. past 12 clock, being 11 miles. Had a very hot fatiguing journey from Burton. The country very barren – hills & stonny cliffs. The district however produces Turnips, Barly, Wheat Oats, seeds, clover & grass between the hills. The two horses & 8.o. plough seen to prevail all through the north of England. The common people about here are not so very active and expert as I was led to believe from Revd. G. Hall. They will salute you with, "Very wa-arm, very wa-arm Sir," quite familiarly. Meet with one young man upon the road a farm servant, whom I had a good deal of talk with. Find him deficient in the detail of his own business even.

Kendal is an extensive town – lies straggling about a widish valley. The houses and buildings have a peculiar appearance. They are all built with the same material (stone) and the slates with which they are covered correspond in colour with the stone erections. There is an obelisk placed on an eminence on one side of the town to the memory of the revolution of 1688[40]. An old castle[41] too appears on a bank or hill on the opposite side of the town.

Crown Inn, Bowness, near Windermere Lake. 7 clock P.M. Just arrived here on foot from Kendal. Feel very much tired[42]. Take tea. Go down into the village and return up to this Inn, which stands on higher ground and commands certainly to speak with moderation one of the most sublime, picturesque and pretty prospects in England. Here is a village at the margin of the largest and most beautiful lake in the whole country, with boats &c in great number on it: with Islands here and there studded as if placed by art to give sublimity to the scene:– and mountains round which far surpass anything I ever witnessed before. Talk of visiting large Towns and such like places, indeed here is a sight worth all the towns in the Kingdom put together. I say this without intending to exaggerate.

The village itself is very beautiful. The houses are all white with Ivy trees creeping along and upon them. As to land the country is certainly very barren all the way from Kendal. Nothing but rocky hills and stone walls. In some places no fields: but all through immense quantities of stone.

Bowness contains two good Inns for visitors viz Allcocks White Lion and Wilsons Crown hotel[43]. There appear few visitors just at present.

June 12
[Bowness to Carlisle]

Start from Bowness in a boat for Ambleside at 1/4 to nine. Belle Isle on the lake near Bowness is the largest on the lake – contains 30 acres – planted

11. The rowing boats for hire at Bowness today are perhaps little different from that which Peter Davis rowed up the lake in 1835.

12. Looking north up Lake Windermere towards the Langdale Pikes.

with trees and a walk round it of 2 miles which strangers are permitted to traverse. Try ones hand at rowing for the first time: rather hard work – soon learn how, which is indeed simple enough. The late Bishop Watson's residence lies to the right of the lake called Colgarth[44]. Mr Curwen's residence opposite to it[45]. The banks of the lake delightful generally planted with trees: very much diversified. Gentlemen's seats seen in different places peeping through the trees. Pass Low Wood public house[46]. Langdale Pikes soon spring into the air to the left; very high[47]. Pass Mr. Browncker's House Tappesgate[48]. Two Ladies rowing a boat alone. Get to the end of the lake, called Water end – 10 clock, being 1 hour & 1/4 from Bowness, about 5 or between that & 6 miles.

Ambleside – Salutation Inn[49]. Hire a poney here to proceed to Ullswater. Arrive there at 1 clock, over one of the most rugged, mountainous & Barren countries I ever came near. This country seems to consist of nothing but mountains rivers and lakes[50]. Hire a boat – to go up the lake[51]. Enter it 25 Mins. past one. At the head of the water stands the house of Wm. Marshall Esq.[52]. The mountains at the head of this lake are not so handsome as Windermere being tipped with stone instead of trees.

Pooley Bridge – Sun Inn[53]. Landed here from the head of the lake in two hours & 25 minutes: had a most interesting & pleasant journey. The country or gentlemen's seats not so numerous as at Windermere. Altogether this is certainly inferior to the other in scenery. Going the contrary way, i.e. up the lake the scenery is much better, or rather seen to better advantage than down the way we came.

Penrith. 6 clock. Have had an exceedingly pleasant walk from Ullswater[54]. The country quite changed from mountains and Lakes to a fine and highly cultivated Agricultural District. The land gradually improves all the way and the farming the same. Pass through the village called Eamont bridge[55] about a mile back which as far as I can remember is the best built and neatest I ever saw. About this place farming seems to be carried on in a scientific manner. The Drill System invariably followed for turnips & potatoes. Penrith is a neat & well built town. The material is stone of a sand or reddish colour with which this district seems to abound, for the half at least of the fences are made with it. Carlisle. Get to this place a little before 10 by coach through one of the best cultivated districts in England, without exception. I have seen a [great] many agreeable sights, but never saw one that has afforded me more pleasure than this drive of 18 miles. Turnips, Barley, Wheat & Seeds grown to the greatest perfection. The people generally more intelligent, active, expert & industrious than in the southern or midland counties. Sup at the Blue Bell[56]. Weather delights me.

13. Carlisle Castle.

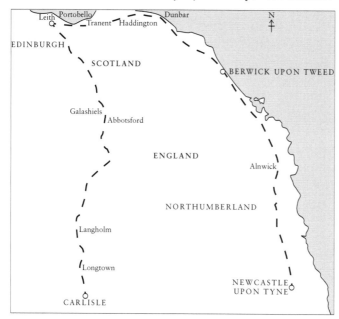

Map 5.
13 June: Carlisle
to Edinburgh (90
miles); 16 June:
Edinburgh to
Berwick-upon-
Tweed (61 miles);
17 June: Berwick
to Newcastle-
upon-Tyne (61
miles).

Saturday June 13
[Carlisle to Edinburgh]

Rise early to look round the town which by the by is well worth the notice
of a stranger. The first object is the county courts built in a very novel and
handsome manner and in separate parts, the street passing betwixt them[57].
They appear very spacious and each court terminates in a round Tower.
There is also a very large Tower[58] & Cathedral.

Longtown. From Carlisle[59] a light, poor soil although well cultivated. Land
improves very much near Longtown. Pass Netherby Park one of the most
extensive, beautiful and best cultivated in England. This belongs to Sir J.
Graham: it was the more interesting to me having read the report from the
farm, published in the Farmers Series[60].

Longholm – ½ past nine. We have come through one of the most romantic
and beautiful countries I ever beheld from Longtown[61] – just entered on
Roxburghshire – all mountain. Cheviot sheep kept – very sound & good
turf for sheep, the surface quite even and no stones.

Edinburgh – ½ past 7 clock. To say that I have been gratified with the
journey from Carlisle[62] here would be to say but little. My impression is
that I never spent so pleasant a day in traveling in my life. Such a diversity

of scenery. The greater part however from Longholm consisting of hill and Dale. In short there is nothing but hills, or rather very high smooth sheep walks with sometimes a little fertile and always well cultivated land along the valleys. Pass within sight of Abbotsford, the Seat of the late Sir Walter Scott a short distance from Gallishiels. Abbotsford is certainly a romantic place, but as it appears to me more novel than splendid.

This mountainous district does not end til we come within 10 or 11 miles of Edinburgh, after which a rich and highly cultivated country steals upon one by degrees[63] until at last your attention is taken with the sight of one of the finest, if not the very finest and most magnificent cities in the whole world. To return however to the country first. All along where the soil is worth cultivation that is done in a very superior manner. There is some lovely scenery up the banks of the Eske River, such as is not often equalled. The richest and most highly cultivated district, however, adjoins Edinburgh, which part is cultivated more like a garden than fields and far exceeds any thing I have met with before[64]. Take up my abode here at Armstrong's Tavern opposite the Black Bull[65] and a very comfortable place.

Sunday 14th June
[Edinburgh]

Rise at six and take a walk into the town. Go to the Castle first but finding that not open today, resolve to visit it again tomorrow. Pass on to Prince's Terrace & Calton Hill – which contains some of the finest buildings in the city. On the Top of the Hill stand Nelson's Monument[66], the observatory[67], the Pantheon, or national Monument of Scotland[68]. Shall visit these places also tomorrow. The inhabitants of this town are exceedingly civil and obliging. If you ask a question of any one, you at once receive a civil and straightforward answer without exception. They not only give you a reply to your question, but some will say, "May there be any thing else or other place I can point out to you" or such like. Having inquired of the Landlady of the house I stay at what time the church service begins at the Kirk Churches, she afterwards brings me in a pair of Bibles[69], and says "Sir, if you are going to Kirk, I have brought you a pair of bibles for your use," for which I of course politely thank her and from this circumstance form a good opinion of her from it. In short, to do them full credit the Scotch are a well-inclined and pious race – much more so than the English. They are also, too, especially the lower orders more intelligent and much better informed. ¼ Past one: am just returned from St Vincent's Church[70] where I have been hearing a very celebrated preacher, Dr. Muir. The Kirk

14. The National Monument, Calton Hill, Edinburgh, with Salisbury Crags in the background; the Monument was designed (by W. H. Playfair) as a memorial to those who had died in the Napoleonic Wars, and it remained uncompleted after funds ran out.

churches in this city all begin morning service at the same time, viz ¼ to 11 clock A.M. It is at once a grand and pleasant sight to witness the different congregations moving toward their respective churches in (I may say) majestic order for there is more decorum and true grandeur in this sight than in any one I perhaps ever witnessed before. St Vincent's is a new Church and very elegantly fitted up: the congregation very large and respectable. The Kirk of Scotch church service is very different to the English – and in my opinion has more effect upon the congregation. The service begins with a Psalm which the minister himself gives out, after which an extemporaneous prayer is delivered. Then a lesson out of the Scriptures – then another Psalm or hymn and after that the Sermon. Dr. Muir preaches extempore. His subject was the preaching of the Gospel: his text taken from St John & that Saint's example, precepts and mode of preaching strongly and eloquently recommended.

4 Clock P.M. Been to St Giles Chapel[71] to hear Dr. Gordon. Service began at 2. The Dr an old man and in my opinion a very inferior preacher to the one I heard before. 6 clock. Just seen about 140 catholic school girls pass by, going to the catholic chapel[72]. The people of this city are all day passing and repassing to the different churches, chapels &c. Go over the way to Black

15. St Stephen's church, New Town,
Edinburgh, built between 1827 and 1828.

Bull coffee room – think to see my traveling companion there but could not.
Being obliged to buy something, call for a glass [of] Gin and water, for which
I pay a shilling[73]! The weather still beautifully warm and pleasant.

Monday June 15th
[Edinburgh]

Arthur's Seat Hill ½ past 5 clock. From this spot, which rises 822 feet above
the level of the Sea (though within a short distance of it) the prospect is most
beautiful. You see the whole city of Edinburgh and portions more or less of
twelve Counties, besides which the Firth of Forth has a most magnificent
appearance – this view is the grandest I ever beheld. Salisbury Crags Walk.
The view from here is most splendid. The town is seen to great advantage.
The three grand divisions are apparent, viz the Southern division, the old
Town with the noble castle at its head as it were and the new Town with
its magnificent and unequalled buildings &c. Holyrood House too at the
foot of the old Town is seen to great advantage here. Ramble back into
the Town. In St Andrews Square is the house which was the birth place of
Lord Brougham and opposite to it in the same square[74] is seen the house in
which the celebrated David Hume died. Visit many other places remarkable
for something or other but too numerous to mention. Nelson's Monument,

16. 'In St Andrews Square is the house which was the birthplace of Lord Brougham', on 19 September 1778. The Revd George Hall, vicar of Tenbury, had been Lord Brougham's domestic chaplain when he was Lord Chancellor; they were both from Westmorland.

Top of Calton Hill. Just ascended the top by 173 steps up the interior. The prospect from the summit is very grand. You see the streets and houses even more distinctly than from Arthurs seat from the situation being parallel with the principal streets. The rain guage at the top is 484 feet above the level of the sea and 130 feet above the base of the monument. Breakfast in the inside on a fine Finnen Haddie[75] fish from Aberdeen a noted place for that kind – costs 1/9d admission into the bargain!

Proceed thence to Holyrood House – go through it and also the Chapel adjoining. To attemp to describe this Royal and ancient edifice here would be out of the question. Suffice it to say that it is a stone fabric forming a square within decorated on all sides with piazzas and a spacious walk. The gallery on the north side is 150 feet long. Strangers are shown the rooms and beds on which Queen Mary[76] and Charles II[77], slept. Also the room where Rizzio was murdered.

Next visit the old Scotch Parliament House which is open to the public and now used for the courts of Law. Near to it in Parliament Square is just erected (only a few days back) a new statue of King Charles II on horseback which has a very elegant appearance[78]. Go next to the Castle. Here is always a regiment of soldiers kept, now amount to 800. Here you are shown into the room in which Queen Mary gave birth to James 1st and by procuring a ticket and paying 1/- for it you are shown into the crown room containing the ancient regalia of Scotland and which has only been exhibited for a few years past having been locked up in a chest in the same room and not opened for a great length of time. Go to the University next which is a most extensive and splendid erection. Hear Dr. Jameson deliver a lecture on natural history at this place to a rather large audience of young men. Do not think very highly of the Dr. as a lecturer although he may be an able man and good scholar. His illustrations consisting of specimens of the different animals fishes insects skeletons &c &c were good and formed the chief attraction. There was a full length skeleton of a human being.

For the sake of novelty and in order to mix with as many different sorts of people company &c as I could, go into a coffee house to take tea called The Temperance coffee house & reading room, which adjoins the college – which of all the others I have been in is at the same time the most comfortable, the cheapest, and most respectable as any. Here are a number of newspapers, Magazines, Reviews and other publications taken in which you may sit down and read with as little interruption as if you were in a private room[79] for the most profound silence prevails except when an order is given or received for anything the company may want. This is a good regulation and the system I have no doubt answers well. Take two large cups of Tea and a sufficient quantity of bread & butter which only costs one 5d: so great is the difference in charges at these places in this city. Walk down to Henderson's nursery on the Leith road – very extensive and kept in the neatest order. All kinds of trees & shrubs appear to be raised here to the greatest perfection. Weather beautiful.

Tuesday June 16th
[Edinburgh to Berwick-upon-Tweed]

Rise at 5 – visit Dickson's nursery and garden[80]. This most extensive and highly, indeed elegantly, cultivated concern occupies about 50 acres of land and comprises a choice collection of all kinds of shrubs vegetables trees &c &c. This as well as the other nurseries is open to the public who are allowed to traverse the different walks in all directions and forms one of the most instructive pleasant and I may say extraordinary sights which have come under my inspection. Its amazing extent and the invariable neatness observed in these nursery's is certainly astonishing and reflects the greatest credit on the owner. 40 men & women are the least number that are constantly employed in this one concern.

Walk thence down to the town of Leith[81] and have been much gratified with seeing it. There are some fine public buildings and the harbour comes direct into the Town. Here are Piers or walks made partly of wood and stone which go a considerable distance into the sea. Reach the end of one – should think it at least 3/4 of a mile long. Girls, boys, men aye and women too, are seen bathing on the Coast close to the town and docks – don't envy them this cold morning – find on enquiring that the practice is general every morning in the summer season. Go back to Edinburgh for breakfast. Proceed towards the Parliament house or law courts as it is now called[82], the advocates Library and the Signet Library[83]. The courts of session I find sitting in the Parliament House. See Lord Jeffry, Lord Cockburn and Lord Corehouse presiding as Judges. This is to a stranger a splendid sight. The advocate's Library adjoins the parliament house and for splendour of appearance quite baffles all description: it is 140 feet long and contains 150000 volumes. The signet library is underneath the above and forms the ground floor, level with the street. This too is very beautiful, but not equal in size or grandeur to the above. Have since visited the Physician's Hall[84], but that is the only place I think in the town, in which I have been disappointed.

At ½ past 11 A.M. leave Edinburgh for Portobello. Trenant[85]. Walked from Edinburgh here 10 miles – came through Portobello where there was a review of a regiment which is there stationed. All the elite of Edinburgh were there assembled. The review takes place on the beach (the town being close to the coast) and is rather a pretty indeed imposing sight.

Call at a Mr. Hope's close to the last named town to inspect a thrashing machine driven by steam which I had been informed was to be seen there. Mr H.[86] not at home – get a very polite reception from Mrs. H. who immediately sends for the Bailiff or Greive as here called to show me to it – find it a very complete thing of the kind & quite recently erected – made by Douglass of Edinburg. Find that the machine when in full motion thrashes 10 Boles or 40 imperial Bushels pr. hour – which is an amazing quantity – only 6 horse-power[87]. This is a very complete place altogether. The buildings are new and well arranged – the farm exceedingly well cultivated. Pass through Musselborough, an ancient & interesting town. Berwick 10 clock at night. Met with a coach at Trenant in the county of Haddington and come by it here 47 miles for 9/-. Have come through I may safely say the best cultivated district in Scotland. The county of Haddington is most

17. Drill grubber, pulled by one or two horses.

delightful all through it without exception. Some of the largest fields I ever saw in Tillage culture and farmed in the very best manner possible. Drill system invariably followed. Beans 2 or 2½ feet apart which freely admit the horse hoe[88]. Noblemens & Gentlemens seats abound in the district – in the neighbourhood where these are the plantations of trees bordering the immensely long and wide Tillage fields give the country a most majestic and delightful appearance, particularly at this season of the year.

Dunbar is a pretty town and most delightfully situated on the coast. We have been within sight of the ocean the greater part of the way. Altogether the journey has been a very agreeable one. Weather still warm and fine. Put in at the red lion[89] the inn the coach goes to at Berwick. This town, as far as situation goes is a delightful place. Cannot say more of it. The town has sometime been of great importance, is enclosed & bounded by double stone walls and which is a curious fact belongs neither to Scotland or England[90].

[Wednesday 17th June]
[Berwick to Newcastle]

Being in want of a Barber to shave and after looking through the whole town I was naturally surprized to find that the town did not contain one – not a person of that calling could I find. A famous place for salmon, one of which or part of one I enjoy for Breakfast. Take a place to Newcastle and start at 8 A.M. Arrive at the latter place at ½ after 4 P.M. after a rather unpleasant ride, it having rained and been rather cold[91]. The country we came through not very interesting although we have come by some picturesque places and beautiful Mansions Castles &c. Amongst the rest Alnwick castle the seat of the Duke of Northumberland which is certainly

18. The west front of Durham Cathedral, with the River Wear in the foreground.

a most curious and ancient edifice. Stands close to the Town (Alnwick) and has a very odd appearance from its varied form and the number of devices, figures &c upon the turrets. The castle was erected in the time of the Romans and even now forms the country seat of the noble owner, who whilst there invariably gives a public Dinner to the most respectable inhabitants of the town and neighbourhood once a fortnight.

Newcastle very gay this week on account of the races taking place. This town is far better than I expected to find it. There are some good public buildings and well built streets in it. The land of the country through which we came is generally poor, or however not by any means good but well cultivated upon the Scotch system, the roads and hedges most excellent.

Thursday morning [18th June]
[Newcastle to Tadcaster]

At Mr Harvey's Newcastle. Called last night, and meeting with a very polite recept from Mr. and Mrs. H. (the late Miss M. Partridge) I was induced to stay the night with them although with some reluctance

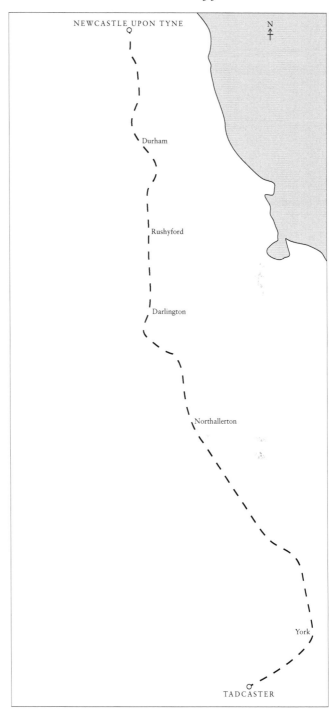

Map 6. 18 June:
Newcastle to
Tadcaster
(93 miles).

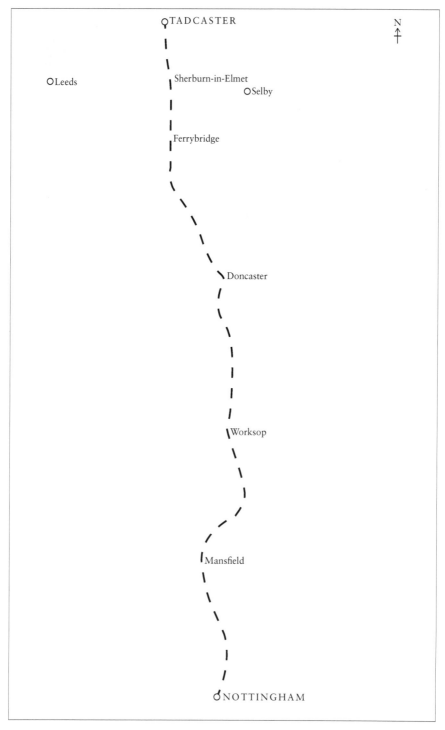

Map 7. 19 June: Tadcaster to Nottingham (73 miles).

19. A coach and four, as drawn and engraved for Dugdale's *England & Wales* (1846).

it not having been mine intention to do so. This place (their Country House) is called Elsureth[92] Villa, and is pleasantly situated at the west end of the town. Miss Partridge has I think been lucky in meeting with a (as he appears to be) very agreeable and well informed little man for a husband. They have not many weeks entered the wedded state and are but just returned from London. The house newly built and elegantly furnished.

Start from Newcastle for York at ½ after 9. Distance 82 miles. Pass by Lambton Hall[93] and Lumley Castle[94], the latter a noble edifice the seat of Earl Scarborough. The country high, but flat – land not very good – cultivation fair but nothing striking so far as to Durham – which town we reach by 11 clock. It has a rather noble appearance on entering. The castle & cathedral are great ornaments to the place and are indeed noble edifices. Busheyford Inn between Durham & Darlington[95]. The country high & bleake – the land stony and not good. York ½ past 7 P.M. From Northallerton (where we Dined) we have passed through a rich and beautiful country, generally very well cultivated. The soil generally appears to be a rich loam, sometimes rather stiff or tenacious: well wooded and some fine Parks &c.

Tadcaster – 11 clock at night[96]. Having started from York this evening to walk a mile or two on the road here, and thinking to sleep at one of the country public houses, I have been not a little disconcerted at finding the houses on the road one after another full and without any accommodation and some indeed of them shut up and people gone to rest! This house that I am in and one other the only ones not shut.

Friday 19 June
[Tadcaster to Nottingham]

Rise at ½ after 4 and proceed on for Doncaster on foot, 3 1 or 2 miles from
Tadcaster. Here the land and whole country is most beautiful. Fine fields of
Barley Wheat & clover not perhaps to be excelled – immense plantations
of Timber are seen in the distance: the soil a light loam and well adapted
for turnips. Here too is a small apple orchard; such a thing as I have not
met with before in any part of the North of England or Scotland; excepting
a few Trees in a garden or so.

The farmers here buy rape cake mostly from Leeds at 5£ per ton which
it appears is the only manure procurable here. The land rented at 1£ to
25/- per acre but the necessity of manure makes the ground cheaper than it
otherwise would be, which remark is peculiarly applicable to this district.
They apply half a Ton per acre for Wheat & Barley and the system of
fallowing for Wheat is here adopted in some instances.

Meet with a crop of <u>Tassels & Wold</u>[97], the former used for the purpose of
com[b]ing cloth at the manufactories: the latter for dyeing. Pass through the

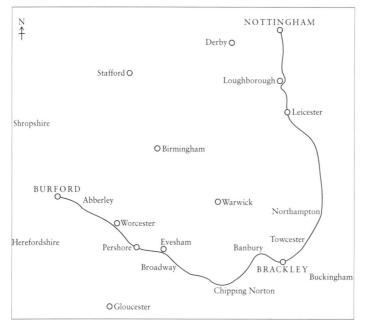

Map 8. 20 June: Nottingham to Brackley (77 miles); 21 June: Brackley
to Pershore (51 miles); 22 June: Pershore to Burford (33 miles).

small Town of Sherbourne[98] – more fields of Tassels and Wold, sometimes the Tassels grown alone or without the wold. Some fine Lucern[99] cut the first time and fast coming to a second crop. Flax also grown here[100]. Go through the village of South Milford. Here the new rail road from Selby to Leeds crosses the road[101].

Doncaster 11 clock. Have come here from Ferrybridge by Mails and had a most delightful drive[102]. The morning exceedingly fine and not too warm. I had no idea of finding in Yorkshire such a district as we have passed through. Taking into account the extent (which is very great) it is the richest and (except East Lothian) the best cultivated district, I may say perhaps in the Kingdom. Generally level and well wooded – the scenery delightful, now too at its best. The soil generally improves all the way, till at Doncaster it is such as is seldom equalled either in richness or cultivation. It consists of a sandy loam, incumbent on limestone – and then rock underneath. Hay-making is just commenced. Seen some beautiful crops of St. Foin cut & uncut[103]. The grass very strong and [a] good crop particularly near the town.

At ferry bridge there are some very extensive lime works: they burn it in Mounds and not kilns as in most places. Sold at 8/- the chaldron of 32 Bushels being 3d per bushel[104].

20. The London to Birmingham railway line, where it crosses high above the Northampton–Towcester road. In the course of construction at the time of Peter Davis' journey, it was one of the first inter-city railway lines in the world, and the first to be built into London.

Nottingham, 8 clock P.M. Just arrived here by coach from Tickhill, having walked to the latter place from Doncaster[105]. Worksop, the first town we come to, itself a clean and beautiful little place. When taken with the suburbs and surrounding country abounding in Mansions & Parks [it] is certainly altogether one of the most delightful rural objects imaginable. The Duke of Portland's seat, Welbeck Abbey and Worksop Manor belonging to Duke Newcastle[106] stand foremost the rest. At the former place there is an old oak, called the Green Dale Oak[107] through which a carriage road has been cut. Clumber Park[108] and Thorsby Park[109] the former the Duke of Newcastle's, the latter the seat of Earl Manners[110] also lie in the immediate vicinity. These four Mansions were at one time the residences of four Dukes and from that the town of Worksop got the name of the Dukery[111]. From the latter town to Mansfield the scenery is most beautiful – the land being rather of an inferior quality has been planted by the different proprietors, chiefly with Fir intermixed with Beech Oak, and other trees and forms for miles one continued series of plantations with openings of square fields here and there and the road winding its way through them.

We also passed through Sherbourne Forest a most extensive plain of wood and common land[112]. Robin Hoods Nest as it is called is a small public house about the middle of the Forest. Newstead Abbey, Lord Byron's property, lies a mile to the right of the road, but not visible therefrom.

Am now at the Kings head, Nottingham[113]. This appears a lively and spirited county town. Many very good shops and the town of considerable extent. Have progressed about 70 miles today and walked 18 of them.

[Saturday] June 20th
[Nottingham to Brackley]

Rise early and take a walk through the town. Take a place by coach for Leicester, the distance being 26 miles for only 3/6! Nottingham is a pleasant and comparatively well built town. Here is the best market place for Butchers meat in proportion to the size I ever saw. The land about this place is very inferior. The soil appears to be a light sand upon a rock underneath.

Leicester 10 clock A.M. Have come here by coach through Loughborough. The country all through delightful. The land through Leicestershire a rich Turnip & Barly soil.

Northampton – come here by coach from Leicester: had a most delightful drive – never enjoyed one more[114]. The country is really beautiful; chiefly

21. The Bell Inn, Brackley, 'the very neatest of a small Inn I ever was in'.

consists of grazing land. Numbers of oxen fatted here for the London Market a great proportion of which are Herefords and Scotch. Leicester sheep appear to prevail generally. Northampton a rather pretty town. Hapend to be market day, Saturday.

Towcester, a small town eight miles distant from Northampton – have walked it. Some pretty good land on the road, but not observed so many beasts feeding as on the other side [of] Northampton. Agriculture is not carried on to nearly so great perfection as farther North. Turnips sowed – and grain generally not drilled[115]. Lord Pomfret has a Park and seat near to this place, well-planted with trees, which have a noble appearance. The new line of rail road from London to Birmingham[116] [is] marked out to cross this road between the two towns above named.

Brackley, a small town, distant from Towcester 12 miles. For want of a better conveyance and being tired of walking, have come this stage in a covered cart. Have met with land here just as barren as some which I passed this morning is rich.

Sunday June 21st
[Brackley to Pershore]

Rather over-lie myself, not rising until half after five. Been dreaming of witnessing the wedding of Mr. H. Davis, the surgeon of Tenbury, to Miss Henderson. N.B. Find, when I reach home, that this wedding actually took place on the very day previously[117].

Brackley is a neat little place with excellent accommodation in the way of Inns for travelers. The one I stayed at [is] the very neatest of a small Inn I ever was in (The Bell[118]). The people too in it as neat as the house. Pass through the village of Furthenhoe[119]. The land about this place is excellent – chiefly in meadow.

Banbury. Have had a pleasant walk here from Brackley. The country is beautiful all the way. Soil good. Great many Vetches grown and fed off with store sheep – cut and put in craches for them[120]. Breakfast, and go to Banbury Church. Hire a poney to ride to Chipping Norton[121]. Get there just in time to meet the Sovereign Coach[122]: proceed on by that to Pershore 28 Miles.

Between Banbury & Chipping Norton wh[ich] is in Oxfordshire the greater part of the land is very high and barren. Likewise so from Norton to the bottom of Broadway hill where we enter the rich Vale of Evesham. From the top of Broadway Hill the view is most extensive and grand. You see up the whole Vale of Evesham, the Malvern Abberly and Breedon Hills &c. Arrive at Pershore at 7 P.M. The Vale of Evesham is cultivated in a very peculiar manner: the district is very flat & level. The ridges of land are made consequently remarkably high and wide for the purpose of draining the water off. They make one land very wide and then a narrow one betwixt[123]. Stay the night at Pershore at Mr Barnbrook's.

Monday Morning June 22
[Pershore to Burford]

Rise at 4. Walk to Worcester[124]. Take a place by Mail[125] from latter place home. Miss Emma Reynolds of Pershore meets me there to come by Abberly to new House[126]. Get home by 1 Clock, after having been absent just a fortnight. Thus ends the first tour of any distance from home I ever made and with which I have been highly gratified.

Notes

1. Dean Park, Burford, Shropshire.
2. About eight miles – for distances and modes of travel generally, see Appendix 1.
3. The Alert ran every other day (Sundays excepted) from Hereford to Shrewsbury, calling at the Angel & Crown, Ludlow at 8.30 a.m.
4. L'Hirondelle ran daily between Cheltenham and Liverpool, calling at the Lion Hotel, Shrewsbury, at 12.30 p.m. It was one of the fastest coaches on the road at this time, the golden age of coaching: two years before, it had covered the 136-mile Liverpool to Cheltenham journey in 9½ hours, a speed of 14 mph including stoppages.
5. Using the retail price index as the comparison, £1 in 1835 is equivalent to slightly more than £86 today. So, 18 shillings is about £78 in today's money.
6. Shrewsbury is 30 miles from Ludlow. Assuming the Alert started on time from Ludlow, it therefore travelled at just under 10 mph – somewhat slower than L'Hirondelle.
7. Dr John Broad, the Secretary of the British Agricultural History Society, has provided much helpful information. Notes on the agricultural context are his unless stated otherwise. Light gravelly soils were ideal for growing grain crops, and therefore the classic crop rotations of the period, which frequently used turnips. Turnips had two functions: first, to provide a break crop instead of a fallow, and one that did not take nutrition from the soil in the way that grain crops did; and secondly to provide winter feed for cattle and sheep. High Farming, as it developed towards 1850, was based on having the right mix of grain growing and livestock keeping, with the livestock eating the turnips and often some of the grain, and in return producing large amounts of manure, which was the main fertiliser that kept up the yields of the grain crops. The stiff clays would have been in the area that concentrated upon dairy farming. The Cheshire cheese farming country, and its southward extension into Shropshire, was one of the most commercialised cheese-making areas of the country at the time the diary was written.
8. The horse-drawn drill had been 'invented' by Jethro Tull (1674–1741) about 100 years earlier, but it was not perfected and widely used until 1800 or soon after. Using drills to plant seed had the advantage of better controlling the amount of seed sown, and of ensuring it was planted in regular rows.
9. Potatoes only became widely grown in the first half of the nineteenth century in England; before 1800 they were largely a garden crop grown by individual cottagers rather than commercially produced by farmers. North-west England was the earliest area to adopt the potato widely, so it is unsurprising that a young travelling farmer should remark on the methods that have been developed – basically growing the crop on a raised bed, with drainage ditches between the beds – in an area with the longest history of using the crop.
10. Shrewsbury to Wrexham: 29 miles – covered in 2½ hours.
11. Dale Street was one of Liverpool's earliest and most important streets, the principal location for the large packhorse and coaching inns, which provided lodgings and board for travellers and changes of horse for the coaches.
12. Today Liverpool's largest hotel, the Britannia Adelphi (in a building which dates from 1914) is situated in Ranelagh Place at the East end of Ranelagh Street. The original Adelphi Hotel dates back to nine years before Peter Davis' visit.
13. Its architect was John Foster junior, *c*. 1787–1846, who was influenced by his travels in Greece: his Custom House was bombed in the Second World War and subsequently demolished – generally thought to be a tragic loss to Liverpool's heritage.
14. It has been shown that the number of American ships visiting Liverpool (bigger and more efficiently run than their British counterparts) was an important feature of the port's trade until the American Civil War, 1861–1865, after which that part of the trade declined.
15. In Bold Street, known as 'the Bond Street of the North', the News Room, which was also Europe's first lending library, was housed in a neoclassical building dating from about 35 years before Peter Davis' visit.
16. Its architect was the same John Foster junior as later built the Custom House (see above). His commission was to design and lay out (in a disused stone quarry) a cemetery along the same lines as Père Lachaise in Paris, which dates from some 20 years earlier. £20,000 was raised for the purpose by public subscription.

17. John Foster senior, 1758–1827, was the Exchange's architect, based on James Wyatt's designs. It was completed in 1809. In the words of a contemporary, 'The Exchange buildings form with the town-hall three sides of a quadrangular area, which is used by the merchants of Liverpool as an Exchange. This quadrangle is 197 feet long from north to south, and 178 feet wide; it therefore contains 35,066 square feet, which is more than twice the size of the recently destroyed Royal Exchange of London. The buildings which form the west side of the area are occupied as offices by merchants while the east side comprises a news-room, 94 feet by 52 feet, which is frequented by the merchants and brokers, and an underwriters room above, of somewhat smaller dimensions. The architecture of the two wings harmonises with that of the town-hall. In the centre of the area is a monument, erected in honour of Lord Nelson'. See photograph on page 37.

18. Opened on 16 September 1830, it was described as consisting 'of a principal dock, 250 yards long, 135 yards broad at the north end, and 111 yards broad at the south end with a Basin 160 yards by 100 yards between it and the river, furnished with gates by means of which vessels may be admitted inwards and outwards at half-tide.'

19. An American visitor to Liverpool in 1832 wrote that 'it is smoky and black, and extends two miles or more along the river, and an equal distance inland … The boast of the port is its spacious and magnificent docks … immense basins of massive stonework.'

20. The first Liverpool Zoological Garden had only been opened in 1832: located in West Derby Road, its site was a series of disused clay pits. The founder, Thomas Atkins, used it to house his travelling menagerie: this included a male and female elephant, kept together – apparently unusual at that time.

21. The journey was from Crown Street Station, Liverpool, to Liverpool Road Station, Manchester. Stephenson's *Rocket* had won the Rainhill trials in October 1829; following that, the passenger service opened on 17 September 1830, two days after *Rocket* had caused the world's first railway casualty, the death of William Huskisson MP. Soon the Planet class of steam locomotive came into operation on the service. 'It was the success of the Planet class that in reality lifted the Stephensons into the millionaire bracket and led to their acceptance as the true originators of rail transport.' (Chant)

22. The only Liverpool Royal Hotel nowadays is in the suburbs.

23. The *Manchester Trade Directory* for 1836 lists four Mosely Arms in Manchester, three under the heading Taverns and Public Houses. The one under Inns and Hotels – namely at 13, Piccadilly – seems best to fit Peter Davis' description.

24. The Town Hall, located in King Street at the corner of Cross Street, was designed by Francis Goodwin and constructed during 1822–25, much of it by David Bellhouse. The building was designed in the Grecian style, Goodwin being strongly influenced by his patron John Soane.

25. Then situated in Piccadilly Gardens.

26. It was a further 11 or so miles from Bolton to Chorley.

27. Chorley to Preston was another 11 or so miles.

28. To Lancaster from Preston is 21 miles.

29. The River Lune, after which Lancaster is named.

30. The Castle, which now houses the town prison, has twelfth-century origins, but was built on the site of three Roman forts.

31. Lancaster Priory (mainly fifteenth-century), the prominent church adjacent to the Castle, has always had a tower rather than a steeple! A rare slip.

32. There has been a Royal Oak public house on Main Street since at least 1889.

33. Burton-in-Kendal.

34. Slyne.

35. There were farmers who deliberately grew seed crops of all kinds, and seed merchants were well known by 1800. Farmers grew grass seeds for sowing when ploughed land was put down to grass. This was one aspect of improving farming, important in the early nineteenth century: if land was deliberately sown with grass seed, the grass was of much better quality – that is, it would feed more animals and make more hay – than if the land was simply left to turn to grass naturally.

36. Bolton-le-Sands.

37. It is not clear what Peter Davis means by this – or the slightly different ploughing description he gives later in the same paragraph.

38. The Royal Oak in Burton-in-Kendal is now the Royal Hotel in the main street. In Edith Howard Freer's transcription of the diary – see Introduction – '(About time I should think! GLF)' is inserted here. Gertrude Louisa Freer was Peter Davis' eldest daughter and Edith's mother.

39. Farleton Knott is one of the lesser known areas of limestone pavement in the north of England: now in woodland, it remains clearly visible from the road.

40. The obelisk was erected on Bowling Fell in 1788.

41. Kendal Castle was the ancestral home of the Parr family and birthplace of Henry VIII's last wife, Catherine Parr (in about 1512). It fell into ruin not long afterwards, but remains imposing.

42. From Kendal to Bowness is nearly 9 miles, making the distance from Burton 20 miles, and upwards of 30 miles walked in the day. (No wonder Peter Davis was tired.)

43. The Crown Inn (located between Brantfell Road and Kendal Road) has now been converted into flats. The White Lion (now the Royal Hotel) gets a mention in Book 2 of Wordsworth's 'The Prelude':

> Upon the Eastern Shore of Windermere,
> Above the crescent of a pleasant Bay,
> There stood an Inn, no homely-featured Shed,
> Brother of the surrounding Cottages,
> But 'twas a splendid place, the door beset
> With Chaises, Grooms, and Liveries, and within
> Decanters, Glasses, and the blood-red Wine.
> In ancient times, or ere the Hall was built
> On the large Island, had this Dwelling been
> More worthy of a Poet's love, a Hut,
> Proud of its one bright fire, and sycamore shade.
> But though the rhymes were gone which once inscribed
> The threshold, and large golden characters
> On the blue-frosted Signboard had usurp'd
> The place of the old Lion, in contempt
> And mockery of the rustic painter's hand,
> Yet to this hour the spot to me is dear
> With all its foolish pomp.

44. Calgarth Park.

45. Belle Isle House.

46. Now the Low Wood Hotel.

47. 'Once seen, never forgotten' wrote Alfred Wainwright. The two main pikes of Harrison Stickle (2,414 feet) and Pike of Stickle (2,326 feet) form a rugged and distinctive profile. The Langdale Pikes are visible on the skyline from many miles away when approaching from the south.

48. James Brancker of Clappersgate.

49. A seventeenth-century establishment, a mile from the lake, now a three-star hotel (part of the Best Western group).

50. The route would have taken Peter Davis over Kirkstone Pass, 1,481 feet above sea level.

51. It seems that Peter Davis' pony took him only as far as Glenridding on Ullswater, about 10 miles north of Ambleside and 8 miles south of Pooley Bridge. As Glenridding is at the head of the lake, he would actually have been rowing down Ullswater. (Subsequently, he describes the journey correctly.)

52. Patterdale Hall.

53. The Sun is still in business, as it has been for some 250 years.

54. Penrith is some 6 miles north of Pooley Bridge, a two-hour walk.

55. The River Eamont marks the border between what were then the two counties of Westmorland, to the south, and Cumberland, to the north. The village, though more or less

a suburb of Penrith, still contains a number of fine houses, including the Mansion House of 1686 – a Grade II*, five-bay, three-storey house, now offices.

56. There was an inn of that name in Scotch Street, Carlisle. (There is no longer a 'Blue Bell' in Carlisle itself.)

57. The court buildings are located close to what is now the railway station: English Street passes through the separate parts.

58. Peter Davis is probably referring to Carlisle Castle: Queen Mary's Tower was once within the inner bailey.

59. From Carlisle to Longtown is a little over 8 miles.

60. The *Farmer's Journal* began publication in 1808.

61. From Longtown to Langholm is 11 miles.

62. From Langholm to Edinburgh is over 70 miles, making a total of some 90 miles covered during the day.

63. The Lothians were arguably some of the most advanced farming country in the United Kingdom, with very large farms and progressive methods even in 1835.

64. Most large towns had market-garden areas close at hand.

65. There is still a Black Bull at 12 Grassmarket, one of the oldest pubs in the city, but rebuilt since 1835. Today, however, there is no trace of any Armstrong's Tavern opposite. (Coincidentally, at the other end of Grassmarket, No. 83, there is an Armstrong's vintage clothing shop, established in 1840.)

66. Built to commemorate Nelson's victory at Trafalgar in 1805, it was designed (by Robert Burn) to look like an upturned telescope.

67. There are in fact two observatories on Calton Hill: the Old Observatory, designed by New Town architect James Craig in 1792; and the City Observatory, built in 1818.

68. The National Monument – as it was indeed originally named – is a prominent feature on the Edinburgh skyline. Started in 1816, a year after Napoleon's defeat at Waterloo, it was meant to be a replica of the Parthenon in Athens (confused by Peter Davis with Rome's Pantheon), and a memorial to those who had died in the Napoleonic Wars. Funds, however, ran dry and its Edinburgh architect William Henry Playfair (1790–1857) only saw a facade of his building completed.

69. Does this perhaps mean both Old and New Testaments in separate volumes?

70. Peter Davis is referring to St Stephen's church, located in the New Town at the bottom of St Vincent Street. It was completed in 1828, also to a design by W. H. Playfair.

71. Peter Davis no doubt refers to the High Kirk of Edinburgh, commonly known as St Giles' Cathedral. (As a cathedral, it is rather smaller than average.)

72. Now St Mary's Metropolitan Cathedral, the then chapel was built just off Leith Street in 1813 by James Gillespie Graham (1776–1855). This was the first new Roman Catholic chapel to be consecrated in Edinburgh since the Reformation. The site was chosen in 1801 by the bishop of the time who had seen his chapel in Blackfriars' Wynd burned by a mob. The Catholic Relief Act 1829 was the culmination of the process of Catholic Emancipation in the United Kingdom.

73. Parliament only enacted Sunday closing laws for Scotland in 1853.

74. In fact, it is in St David Street nearby.

75. Kippered haddock: admission is now £3 (no kipper included).

76. Mary Queen of Scots.

77. Charles II never entered Edinburgh. Peter Davis must have meant to refer to his father: Charles I stayed at Holyrood in 1633, the night before his coronation as King of Scots in the adjoining abbey.

78. The work of James Smith, the statue was in fact erected in 1685. It shows Charles II dressed as a Roman emperor, and is the oldest lead-cast statue in Britain. (Why did Peter Davis describe the statue as 'new'?)

79. Peter Davis' experiences here and also in Liverpool (the Exchange) on the previous Tuesday were undoubtedly the trigger for his efforts to establish a reading room in Tenbury: see 1836/7 Diary, entries for 10 March 1837 and subsequently.

80. Walter Dickson 'had a very fine nursery in Leith Walk at Edinburgh, once considered the best and most extensive in Scotland' – according to Mark Lawley, who has researched the

life of Walter's more celebrated brother James Dickson (1738–1822), plant collector and one of the founders of the Linnean Society.

81. About 2 miles.

82. Situated in Parliament Square, to the south of St Giles' in the Royal Mile, Parliament House was built in the 1630s, with new frontages added in 1803. It was home to the Scottish Parliament until the Act of Union between England and Scotland in 1707 made it redundant for that purpose. It is now the centre of the Scottish legal system, housing the Court of Session and Court of Criminal Appeal as well as the Advocates' Library, founded in 1682.

83. Finished in 1822 to a design by the architect Robert Reid.

84. The Dome bar and restaurant now occupies the site (14 George Street) where James Craig's Physicians' Hall of 1775 originally stood, until it was demolished in 1844.

85. Tranent.

86. From the wording it seems unlikely, but this visit may possibly have come about through an introduction by the Hopes of Netley, Shropshire, Peter Davis' father's landlords – see Appendix 5. A Mr George Hope's farm (Fenton Barns, Drem, Haddingtonshire: Drem is about 9 miles east of Tranent) is referred to as an example of advanced mechanisation in the *Journal of the Royal Agricultural Society of England*, 2nd Series, Vol. III, published in 1867. This same volume contains a lengthy appreciation of Peter Davis' own modern methods at Bickmarsh Hall, Warwickshire. (See Introduction, page 24.)

87. Northern England and southern Scotland adopted large, fixed equipment for threshing grain from the eighteenth century onwards, building 'wheel-houses' as they were called. In many cases the power for these machines came from horses being harnessed up and made to walk round and round inside the wheelhouses, turning a geared wheel. In the nineteenth century, these large facilities were easily adapted to steam power. Southern England tended to adopt small, portable, machines for threshing grain. However, the Davis family farm at Dean Park in 1835 would probably either have threshed by hand, or used relatively simple hand-powered machinery.

88. The horse hoe (another of the contributions Jethro Tull made towards the Agricultural Revolution) was a device to increase productivity on the farm by turning the soil between rows of crops (wheat, turnips, beans) to prevent weeds proliferating and throttling the crops. Its effectiveness depended on the crop being planted regularly and precisely, for instance by a drilling machine.

89. This was one of three coaching inns in Berwick-on-Tweed. There is a Red Lion public house in Castlegate, Berwick, today, but the building hardly seems important enough to have been a coaching inn.

90. It is now in England!

91. Newcastle is 61 miles south of Berwick.

92. 'Elsureth' seems to be exactly the word used, though no trace of it exists. Nor is it clear why it is described as a country house.

93. Lambton Hall was demolished half a century before Peter Davis' tour, but its name continued to be associated with the newer (eighteenth-century) Lambton Castle, built with proceeds from mining the surrounding land for coal. By 1835, 'Radical Jack Lambton' (1792–1840) had just been created (1st) Earl of Durham.

94. Built in the fourteenth century, it is now a hotel (and the romantic backdrop of Durham County Cricket Club's Riverside ground).

95. This must have been the inn known as the Wheatsheaf in the village of Rushyford, which, in the early 1800s, was located on the Great North Road in Windlestone township. In Charles Harper's words, '... Rushyford Bridge, a pretty scene, where a little tributary of the Skerne prattles over its stony bed and disappears under the road beside that old-time posting-house and inn, the Wheatsheaf. The old house still stands and faces down the road; but it has long since ceased to be an inn.'

96. Tadcaster is 11 miles south-west of York.

97. Teasels and woad were both much used in the Yorkshire woollen industries nearby.

98. Sherburn-in-Elmet.

99. Lucerne was a fodder crop, grown instead of hay to feed animals, and often referred to as an 'artificial grass'. One of its attributes, like clover, was that it 'fixed' atmospheric

nitrogen, thus actually increasing the available nutrition in the soil when the crop was ploughed up and grain later grown.

100. Flax was a major crop and the raw material for the linen industry, but it used up soil fertility very quickly.

101. Opening only nine months prior to Peter Davis' journey, this was one of Britain's first main lines, and the first to be built in Yorkshire. It ran from the growing industrial city of Leeds to the quays at Selby. The new railway revolutionised travel between the two places: summer stagecoach traffic previously consisted of about 400 people per week, but throughout the summer of 1835 the railway carried a weekly average of 3,500 passengers.

102. From Tadcaster to Ferrybridge is 13 miles (about), and from Ferrybridge to Doncaster 17 miles.

103. The same applies to sainfoin as to lucerne: see note 99.

104. The main route from London to York was (and is) via Ferrybridge, with its important crossing of the River Aire. The opening of the Aire and Calder Navigation in the early eighteenth century brought with it cheap transport for the lime business. Lime was a major part of agriculture in the eighteenth and nineteenth century. Where the soils were acid, addition of lime in large amounts enabled much higher yields of crops afterwards, and agriculturalists advocated regular dressing of the soil with lime A chaldron was a dry English measure, only introduced in 1826.

105. Tickhill is some 7 miles south of Doncaster. Tickhill to Nottingham is 36 miles.

106. The Worksop Manor Estate was purchased by the Duke of Newcastle from the Duke of Norfolk at a price of £370,000. The manor at the time was an eighteenth-century building, but was changed out of all recognition in the 1840s: it is now a stud.

107. The Greendale Oak arch was measured in 1790: 10 ft 3 in high by 6 ft 3 in wide. It was created by the 1st Duke of Portland (1682–1726), who won a bet by driving a coach and six through it. He had the ancient tree hollowed out for the purpose, killing it in the process. A cabinet was made for the Countess of Oxford with oak taken from the tree's heart. Apparently a stump is still left today.

108. Clumber House in 1835 was the seat of the 4th Duke of Newcastle. Much of it was destroyed by fire in 1879: it was then rebuilt, but, following another fire, it was demolished in 1938. Its parkland now belongs to the National Trust.

109. The original eighteenth-century Thoresby House was occupied in 1835 by the 2nd Earl Manvers, who had served in the Navy with Nelson. It burnt down in 1845.

110. Manvers.

111. There had been five ducal seats: Bestwood Park (St Albans); Clumber (Newcastle); Thoresby (Kingston – this title became extinct in 1773); Welbeck (Portland) and Worksop (Norfolk).

112. Sherwood Forest is famous through its historical association with the legend of Robin Hood. The forest of today (and even of 1835) is but a remnant of a much larger royal hunting forest.

113. There no longer appears to be an inn of this name there.

114. Leicester to Northampton: 31 miles or so.

115. The traditional alternative to drilling was 'broadcasting' seed: the labourer walked across the land in a straight line, regularly taking a handful of seed out of a bag he carried and throwing it in as uniform a way as possible to allow the crop to grow evenly – but much less so than drilled seed.

116. The 112-mile-long railway line between London and Birmingham (engineered by Robert Stephenson, son of the more celebrated George and co-responsible with him for *Rocket* – see note 21) was, when it opened in 1838, one of the first inter-city railway lines in the world, and the first to be built into London. It survives to the present day, as the southern section of the West Coast Main Line.

117. Henry Davis married Isabella Henderson on 20 June 1835 at St Mary's church, Edge Hill, Lancashire. (At least from this point on, the diary must have been written up from notes following the end of the tour.)

118. 103 High Street, Brackley.

119. Farthinghoe – a village 4 miles from Brackley and 6 from Banbury.
120. Vetches are another kind of fodder crop planted to feed animals. Store sheep mean lean sheep which need keeping for some months before sending to slaughter when they are fat. The word 'crache' is a mystery.
121. Banbury to Chipping Norton: 13 miles.
122. The London to Worcester coach, after calling at Chipping Norton, passed through Moreton and Bengeworth, just north of Evesham.
123. Even in 1835 the Vale of Evesham was noted for its fruit growing and market gardening. It is also prone to floods, so drainage ditches would be interspersed with raised areas to grow the crops.
124. Pershore to Worcester: 9 miles.
125. The Royal Mail departed every morning at 10 o'clock from the Star and Garter, calling at Tenbury on its way to Ludlow. From Worcester to Tenbury via Abberley is 24 miles.
126. New House, Heightington, in the parish of Rock, is a little way to the north of Abberley. Its occupants were Peter Davis' uncle, Joseph Reynolds, his wife Mary Ann and his father (and Peter Davis' grandfather), Peter Reynolds.

Peter Davis' Life in Shropshire: 1836/7

1836

Jany. 26
Fair and very mild. Go to the surgeon's (Mr. H. Davis[1]) and get the aching tooth drawn, a new thing to me, never having had one drawn before. Aunt Maria and Mary Partridge arrive home from visiting their friends at Burcott &c.[2]. They walk from new house[3] the mail being loaded.

27
Small frost – dry fine day. Go to Park[4] and stay all day and night. William goes to a dinner party at Mr. Wm. Myttons[5]. Father to Mr. Collin's dinner party.

Jany. 28
Stormy – keen west wind. William goes to an afternoon party at Boraston (Sayer's). Still at Park myself. Send a lot of Apple & Pear trees to Lydia Chambers to plant a garden – about 16 of them.

29
Very rough winterly day. Snow, rain &c. Rose[6] being round Park shooting, calls and dines there. I go to a Dinner Party at Mr. Home's 4 clock, a Jovial party of us keep it up till nearly 3 clock in the morning – and then obliged to wish the set good morning – no one else attempting to move.

30th
Stormy and wind still high, snow disappears. Go to Park and remain all day there.

31st Jany.
Rained A.M. Fair in afternoon. Eliza and I go to Mr. Edwards[7] to invite him and Mrs. E to tea on Wednesday. A Miss Boden there. William also drops in.

22. The first page of the 1836/7 diary.

Feby. 1
Cold west wind and slight storms of rain. Go to Park and return to Burford in afternoon. Wm. also comes down to look at the wethers[8] before offering them for sale.

Feby. 2nd
Piercing cold wind from the east. Go to Park whilst William attends a sale at Clater Park, Couchers – buys nothing. He returns and goes to the oyster club at Swan[9].

Feby. 3rd
Most miserable day, snow, rain &c. all day. Have a small party to tea and supper viz Mr. & Mrs. Collins, Mr. & Mrs. Edwards, &c.

4th
Another stormy unpleasant day. Go to Park and send Wm. to Burford with his gun to meet Messrs. Edwards and Williams on the plea to shoot Rabbits but really to get his name as one of the stewards for Grove's assembly

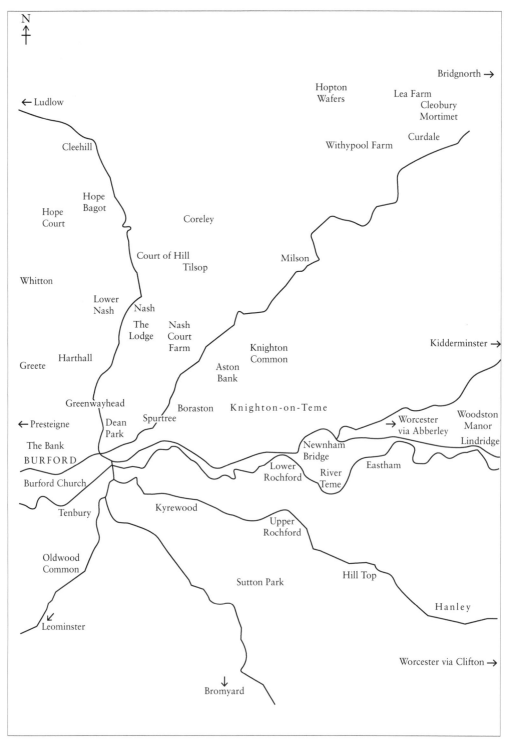

Map 9. Burford and district.

which is fixed to take place on 25th inst. William complies. Grove comes to Park in the evening to see him concerning it. Stays tea. Jim Pearman also comes to Park to stay the night and proceed to Presteign tomorrow. Messrs. Edwards, Williams and brother William meet at Collins's who treats them with a <u>grill</u>; after which they go to my Father's and drink Gin till 11 at night. Manage about a bottle each!

5 Feby.
Beautiful day. Fair & sun shiny. William goes to Trumper's[10] dinner party – I stay at Park and sleep there – Mr. Partridge[11] calls in evening and takes Mary home with him – after supper.

6th
Same weather. Go to Nash to get part of an oat rick in – Mr. Partridge and Mary come to spend the evening. Mary stays the night. Mr. Nicholls of Kyrewood drops in.

Feby. 7th
Mists A.M. Sunday. Mr. Turrall of Kidderminster comes over to visit us. Arrives just after dinner – stays all night.

8th
Fair and mild. Father and William go to Ludlow fair. I stay at home and spend the day with Mr. Turrall. They get home to dinner. Miss Giles's of Tenbury call in afternoon. Mr. Turrall leaves to go home at ½ past 10 P.M.

9
Delightfully fine and mild day. Write again to Saml.[12] requesting him to tell us when he intends coming to Burford. The Miss Wilkinsons come to tea and spend the evening.

Feby. 10th
Fair A.M. Rains P.M. Eliza and I drink Tea with our neighbours – the Jones's[13].

11th
Small frost and a very cold wind. William goes to Kidderminster Market. Leaves Father and I at Park to amuse old Cooke late of Orleton with a course for his dogs – start 5 Hares and Kill one – 4 of them being put off the upper white leasow[14]. Rose, Coleman and Williams join us. A dinner party at Mr. Cooke's Tenbury. Father goes.

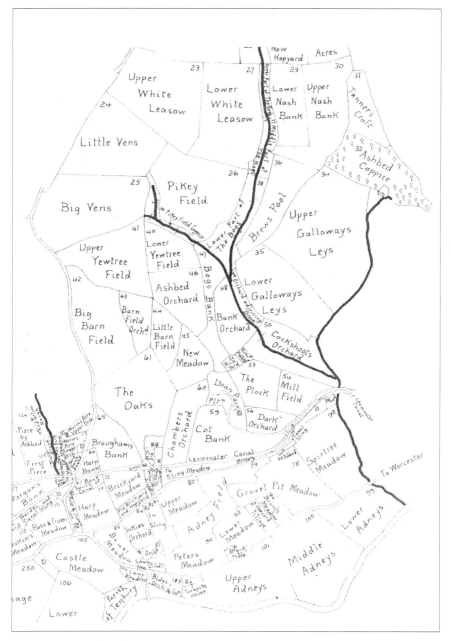

Map 10. Part of Burford Township, around 1840: many of the fields named were farmed by the Davis family.

23. View *c.* 1780 of Tenbury over the River Teme, from *Collections for the History of Worcestershire* by Dr Treadway Russell Nash, DD.

12
Fair. Mr. Rose comes to catch the rabbits. We net 3 couples. Dines with us

Feby. 13
Haze, coldish wind. William goes to Worcester Market. I attend at Park the while. Mr. & Mrs. Jones drink Tea at Burford. Mrs. H. Davis expected but did not come.

14
Most delightfully fine, sunshiny day, Sunday. Mr. Rushout faltered very much in performing the service. His eyesight and the use of his limbs seem to fail him. Write a letter to Samuel acquainting him of it and desiring him to come over as soon as possible to Take the duty. Father dines at Mr. Evan's, the [*word illegible*]. Eliza and I call at Vicarage and I drink Tea at Mr. H. Davis's.

15th
Same weather. Go to Eastham[15] to see the men setting ash quick[16] – then back to Park – remain there the night. William goes to Eardiston in afternoon and Father goes to Ludlow Market and buys for William a lot of seed Barley.

16
Cold. Haze. Go to Worcester to deliver and receive for William's lot of clover seed. Get home to Tea and sleep at Park.

17th
Very cold wind. Stay at Park and getting on William's pony mare to go to Tenbury, she plunges and falls backwards over – did not much hurt me, however.

Feby. 18th
Very cold north wind: fair – stay at Park whilst William goes to Kidderminster Market.

19th
Frost. Cold day. Mrs. H. Davis and Mr. & Mrs. Jones drink Tea and spend the evening with us. Mr. Davis also comes in after Tea.

20
Very sharp frost. Beautiful day. Go to Park and thence to Nash. Weigh a load of wheat. Remain at Park the night. Yesterday Maria at Park brews a Barrel of Ale for my Father, holding about 42 Gallons – 5 Bushels of malt used.

21 Feby.
Fair and fine. Sunday – Misses Sayer sit with us at church. Geo Winton and William Mytton dine at Park. Father and I spend the afternoon there.

22nd
Same weather. Eliza gets a letter from Samuel fixing Friday week 4th March as the day for coming home.

23
Same weather. Mr. Wheeler of Eardiston calls going from Tenbury – dines and stays Tea with us at Park – Mr. Wm. Mytton also calls and he and Wm. go to the oyster club at Swan. Mytton returns and takes a bed.

Feby. 24
Rain and snow in the afternoon – in very large flakes. Miss Hotchkiss arrives at Park to attend the Tenbury ball tomorrow night. Mr. Good of Knighton Common, calls and buys William's fat gilt[17] at £6.13s.od. Mary Partridge remains all night at Park.

25th
Severe frost, snow nearly all goes. A ball held at the Swan. Brother William one of the stewards. Very thin attendance. Four ladies go from Park viz – Two Partridges, Miss Burton & Miss Hotchkiss. Eliza and I go from Mr. H. Davis's.

24. Dean Park, Burford: photographed in 2009, it would no doubt still be recognisable by Peter Davis as his family home.

Feby. 26th
Frost. Snow P.M. Go to Park to breakfast and spend the day there along with the Ball ladies &c. Two young Giles's of Hope call in the forenoon. Also Robert Sayer who stays dinner and evening – Willliam Lowe, Greenwayhead[18] also spends the evening. Get down home to sleep.

27
Frost. Snow and rain. The Ball ladies leave the Park after dinner. I remain at Park the day and night.

Feby. 28
Little frost, and snow and rain. Sunday – Old Mrs. Edwards of the Farm breathes her last. Eliza and I drink Tea at the vicarage, Tenbury. Miss Wilkinson very unwell[19].

29
Fair and rather mild. Good bye fair twenty-ninth for another four years. Father and William go to Ludlow Market. I am now generally stationary at Park again.

March 1st
Heavy rain. Tenbury March fair[20].

2nd
Fair and very fine day with however a little rain at night. Father and I go to
Eastham on business – to settle with Merrick for digging the ashbed, setting
the quick, &c. and also for repairing the pool head which he finishes today.
Thomas Davis takes the ground (young ashbed) at 4£ a year for 2 years and
pays the first year's rent in advance which of course Father turns over to Mr.
Nott[21]. Call at the "Dingle"[22] in going, and on the road between there and
Eastham, Father's old Mare comes down with him and breaks her knees
shockingly. When we get home to Burford find Miss S. Cooke there – she
goes home again at night. Miss Nicholls calls. Mrs. H. Davis drinks Tea and
Mr. D. sups with us. Old Mrs. Edwards of Farm buried at Burford.

March 3rd
Fair and very fine. Remove my "traps"[23] from Burford to Park again to
make lodging room for Samuel whom we expect early tomorrow. Begin
reading the second volume of Southey's life of Cowper[24].

4
Frost. Fog, fine till night, then rains. Samuel arrives home from Culmstock
to take charge of the Burford flock, being appointed curate or rather
engaged as one by Mr. Rushout. Mary Partridge stays the night here.

5
Fair A.M., heavy storms in afternoon.

6
Heavy storms of rain all day, wind E. & cold. Samuel enters upon his duties
as Curate at Burford. Reads prayers & Mr. Rushout preaches. Whilst at
Church the boy, Wm. Phillips, who stayed away unknowingly to us, robs
Eliza's purse of 22/-. He confesses it afterwards and discovers the money
hid in the house. The same fellow that stole silver teaspoons of his former
master, Mr. Hall and once robbed Eliza's purse of 1/- before.

Feby. [*error, for 'March'*] 7
Small frost. Mr. & Mrs. H. Davis and Mr. Trumper come here (the Park)
to Tea and taste Miss Reynolds Piclets[25]. She being famous for making
prime ones as indeed she is for doing everything else in the way of cookery
&c. They stay supper. We play at whist, myself being most singularly
unfortunate losing more than I ever did in one evening before at the game
viz about £4. So much for gaming. However there's one consolation
– if one did not sometimes see and feel the evil consequences of vice the
practice of virtue would not appear so delightful.

8th Feby. [*error, for 'March'*]
Frosty and fine day.

9th
Frost, but very cold and rainy afternoon.

10th
Fair but cloudy A.M. Rain P.M. Go to Kidderminster to receive cash for 60 bags of wheat of Mr. Lloyd the quaker being the first deal we have had with him. Tak a sample of Wm.'s Barley but could not sell any. Get home to Tea and find Samuel there who takes Wm.'s horse down with him to ride to Worcester tomorrow.

11th
Very blusterous, stormy and windy day throughout. The newly brewed barrel of ale goes down to Burford[26].

March 12th
Stormy and wind still high. Assist Samuel in unpacking his books – a considerable quantity of them he has already collected.

13
Highish west wind and slight storms of hail and rain. Mr. Rushout continues preaching the sermon at Burford & brother Samuel reads the prayers. Maria goes to Lodge[27] to dinner.

14
Same weather. Go across to Kyrewood to Tea. Call at Vicarage going to tell Mr. H.[28] that Father had oats to part with at Nash, his man having come here for some this morning and William having none to sell.

March 15
Heavy rain and snow A.M. Storms and wind P.M. Father goes to Leominster Fair and rides William's horse. Teme[29] nearly bank full <u>with us</u> – so great the quantity of rain and snow fallen that the water has not been so high or the ground so wet for many months past[30].

16
Very bright fine day, drying wind – west.

17
Quantity of rain in the night and early this morning. Fair and fine

afterwards. William goes to old Yapp's sale and buys a cow and Calf for Father.

March 18
Fair and mild. Samuel rides William's horse to Ludlow. Bring the old desk up again from Burford. Finish reading the first volume of Hume's History of England[31], having borrowed the work of Samuel for that purpose.

19
Most delightful day, very mild. William goes to Aston and buys a barren cow of Mr. Good for Father at 11£10/-. Brings the last No. of *Athenaeum*[32] from Mr. G. for myself to read. Saml. drinks Tea here.

March 20th
Same weather. Samuel goes to preach at Boraston this afternoon for Mr. Stewart. Mr. & Mrs. E. Edwards drink Tea here this evening as well as Father & Eliza.

21
Beautiful day but not quite so warm as yesterday. Samuel rides William's horse to Worcester to attend a sale of furniture.

22nd
Rain, wind in all quarters. Samuel dines at Burford House[33]. The Young Honourable[34] over. Uncle Reynolds Teas here.

March 23rd
Gloomy, cloudy day, inclined to rain. Dine at Burford along with Mr. Nott from Eastham, who comes to pay his half year's rent[35].

24
Stormy, hail and rain. Father and William go to Bromyard Fair. Maria and myself go to Lodge to spend the evening and eat an oyster supper.

25th
Rain early, then fine, then snow and cold wind in the evening. William attends the parish meeting at Burford and is appointed overseer[36].

March 26
Storms of snow, very cold wind. Samuel and Eliza drink Tea here.

27

Severe frost. Heavy storms of hail, snow &c. Evening service begins at Burford Ch. Saml. takes the whole evening duty.

28

Most miserable day – rain, snow, cold wind. The poney and I have another tumble over together. After failing to throw me off by plunging, she fell forwards and came over, I lighting on my head with great force in the road. My head and neck much hurt.

March 29

Cold wind, slight storms. Father and William go to Ludlow Fair. Mr. Mortimer Buckingham from Devonshire comes to Burford on a visit to Samuel.

30th

Hard rain all forenoon. Fine P.M.

31st

Very high wind, west, slight storms of snow. Go to Kidderminster Market. Take sample wheat of Father's and one of Barley of William's, sell a load of Barley at 4s/6d per bushell. Return to Tea. Afterwards walk to Burford where I meet with Mr. & Mrs. H. Davis, Miss Simpson, Miss A. Davis, Miss Sayer, Mr. Buckingham, &c. – part before supper.

April 1st

Frost, begins snowing at 11 clock and continues all day. <u>Good Friday</u>. Attend church and dine & spend the afternoon at Burford. Find Mr. Williams at Park when I get home.

2nd

More snow and rain, a little frost into the bargain.

3

Drying north wind. Easter Sunday. Receive the sacrament. Mr. Rushout taken unwell in preaching and obliged to leave the pulpit for a short time. Attend the evening service – a large congregation. Samuel takes the duty and gives us a good discourse.

April 4

Sharp frost and very beautiful day. Take a ride to Woodson[37] to take a leisurely survey of the farm. Mr. Adams offering to let it but wants too

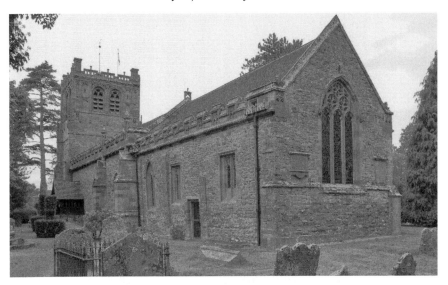

25. St Mary's, Burford, built of red sandstone; the tower top and embattled side are late nineteenth-century additions to the essentially medieval church of Peter Davis' day.

much. Return and dine at Burford. Saml. and Young Buckingham ride to Milson to call on Mr. Edwards. They return by Park to Tea.

5th
Slow rain all day. Go to Tenbury Market[38]. Meet with Mr. James Adams and try to treat with him for Woodson Farm but he wants too much – 320£ a year rent for 189 acres besides Tithes which are high and all other expenses. Mr. A. walks up to Burford. Father bids him 280£, a bold stroke! in my judgement.

April 6th
Rain, sun, rain again. Samuel and Young Buckingham go to Mr. Edwards's, Milson to dine. William goes to Coney-gren[39] to stay the night for Kidderminster Market tomorrow.

April 7th
Stormy, mild. William at Kidderminster Market. Oyster dinner at Swan.

8
Solid rainy day. Another great flood. When will it cease? Such a rainy spring surely was never known before. Had another conference with Adams about the Farm but he wouldn't come low enough.

9
Stormy. Samuel and Mr. Buckingham return from Mr. Stewarts having gone to dine with him yesterday. They afterwards ride to Ludlow.

10th April
Cold wind. Some sun. Sunday. Samuel performs all the morning service and gives a lecture nearly 50 ms. long. Mr. Mytton, Deptcroft[40] and Mr. Partridge drop in in the afternoon.

11
Small frost, most delightfully fine & mild. Young Buckingham leaves Burford for Rugby by the Birmingham (Red Rover) coach[41].

12
Cloudy and not so mild. John Nott of Eastham calls and buys William's horse of him. Leaves his own here to tack.

13
High west wind and stormy. Miss Cooke of Hill Top[42] pays a visit to Burford, also Mrs. H. Davis there at Tea.

14
Slight storms A.M., very fine afterwards. William goes to Kidderminster Market along with Mr. Edwards in his gig.

15
Very warm & fine. Maria goes to Nash[43] to Tea.

16
Fair and mild. Old Mr. Nott of Eastham dines here on his way from Hartall[44] home.

17
Dry cold morning. Warm afternoon. Sunday. Maria and I drink tea at Lodge.

April 18
Dry fine day. William goes to Netherwood[45] sale. Father and Samuel to Ludlow.

19th
Mild, mists of rain. News comes of the first opening of the new Islington

26. Broncroft Lodge Farm, Diddlebury, in the Corve Valley, north of Ludlow, where Peter Davis farmed in the early 1840s.

Market at London which has been in building since 1833 and cost the proprietor (Mr. Perkins) 100,000£[46].

20th
Stormy, wind. Mr. Williams calls to look at some cattle, sheep, &c. Buys none. Dines with us.

April 21st
Fair. Wind. Father & William go to Cleobury Fair.

22
Mild. Slight storms. A party of Gents dine with us from Tenbury Fair viz Wm. and Edward Mytton, J. Smith, James Adams, E. Edwards, Mr. Partridge & Geo. Winton.

23
Same weather. William goes to Orleton Fair.

24
Cold. East wind and rain. Snow on the Clee Hill. Sunday. Call on Mr. Williams and drink Tea with Mr. E. Edwards.

April 25th

Very severe frost. Go to Ludlow Market to meet with a Mr. Smith, steward for Mr. Johnson who we had heard had a farm to let at The Lodge near Diddlebury[47] but he was not there. Saw however his wife who informs us that the farm will not be let this year.

26

Fine day but a sharp storm at night,

27

Cold gales of wind from the north and slight storm of snow, rain, &c.

28

Another sharp frost, cold wind and stormy. Take a trip up into Corvedale to look at a farm at the Lodge belonging to Mr. Johnson advertised a short time back to be let. Call on Mr. Bowen of the Hill House and dine there.

April 29

Extremely cold north wind and storms of snow.

30th

Very severe frost, fine afterwards, but cold in the evening. Go to Burford to horse-hoe the winter beans[48]. Send a letter to Mr. Johnstone who is at Borthnoy in North Wales to inquire about the rent &c. of the farm at Lodge.

May 1st

Very cold wind from the north. Slight storms. Sunday. Mr. Pearman & James from Tennall call – the one going to Ludlow and the other Leominster Fair. Go with them to Burford and call on Mr. Edwards. Mr. John Benbow there.

2nd

Dry, some sun, but very cold wind. Go to Ludlow Fair and buy a nag of Mr. Evan Price of Ackel near Presteign[49] for 20£. A real roadster or cob[50] about 14½ hands, colour grey.

3

Clear & windy. William goes to Bromyard Fair.

May 4

Dry windy day. Get a letter from Mr. Johnstone in reply to mine, stating his intention of not letting the Lodge farm this year.

27. The former New House, Heightington, home of Peter Davis' uncle, Joseph Reynolds, at the time of the diary.

5
High E. Wind & violent storms of rain.

6
Wind & storms of rain. Ride down to New House and stay the night ready for Worcester tomorrow.

7
Small frost, very mild fine day. Proceed on to Worcester from New House. Take some cash and do some business at the bank. Meet with Mr. Turnall there. Dine with him along with a few more at the Hopmarket Inn[51]. On returning home between Eardiston and Lindridge meet with a chaise containing the new married couple Mr. J. Smith & Late Miss Mytton, the ceremony having taken place at Lindridge this day[52]. Revd. Mr. Powell, the officiating clergyman, got quite mellow as well as some of the other company.

May 8
Wind still in the north and cold morning and night but fine and warm day. Sunday. Spend the evening at Lodge, Maria & myself. Samuel does duty at Tenbury in the evening at 6, Mr. Hall being unwell.

9

Mild & fine. Samuel starts off to Mr. Dakin's sale at Drayton house to buy furniture.

10th

Severe frost, hot day. Miss D. Sayer & Robert & Miss M. Giles of Hope call going from Boraston to Tenbury. William Lowe of Sutton comes to buy some hop poles of William which he does at 7/6 per hundred (small ones). Edward Smith also calls in the afternoon. Father, Samuel and Eliza dine at Burford House.

May 11th

Fair and very warm. Take Mr. Good of Aston his *Athenaeum* and stay tea with him.

12

Frost, very warm. William goes to Kiddermister Fair. Calls to breakfast along with new married couple (Mr. & Mrs. J. Smith, Coneygreen) and stays to dine with Mr. Turrall. Mr. & Mrs. Partridge, Mary, Mrs. Reynolds & Mrs. Smith drink tea here. Mrs. P stays all night.

13th May

Frost & extremely warm day. Pass the day at Burford hoeing the winter beans &c. The grey nag gets his fore-leg strained at the fetlock. Poultice and bleed him.

May 14

Very small frost & hot day. William goes to Droitwich to buy a horse for Samuel which he does of a person of the name of Robinson for --- [*a blank is left here*] and returns by Worcester home. Mr. Partridge comes to Tea & John Nott calls afterwards.

15

Fine warm day. Charity sermon preached at Tenbury by Mr. Hall. Eliza, Father & I go. Mr. Partridge dines here along with Mrs. P. The sun in eclipse from a little before 2 till nearly 4 clock – easily observed with the naked eye – the sun resembling a being in the form of a half moon and the country quite darkened as though a thunderstorm were coming on[53].

16

Very hot day. Father goes to Ludlow Market.

17th
Same weather.

18
Warm. Some tempest. Go to Stanford[54] to see after the sheep-shearers
(Stintons) to come to shear the sheep which they promise to do on Tuesday
next. Call on Mr. Davis at Orleton and stay dinner there. Mr. & Mrs.
Downes of Hope and two Miss Bayliss's from Ledbury there: chat Tom
Davis in afternoon[55].

19
Cloudy A.M. fine and warm P.M. Call on the new married folks at the
Bank, Mr. & Mrs. Jones, late Butler and Ladies Maid at Burford House.
Mr. G Nicholls buried at Rochford.

May 20th
Morning hot. Tempest and slight storm in afternoon.

21st
Wind. fair & warm. Father and I go to Eastham to meet a man who was to
come to buy some ash timber but he came not. Call at Kyrewood in going,
Mrs. Nicholls having told Eliza yesterday if I wanted a Farm, Lambswick
may, she thought, be had and taken to immediately. Mr. Lambert of moment
being out, nothing further could be known. Maria & Ellen Partridge start
off after Tea to Mrs. Bayliss's, Bockleton.

22
Fair and very fine. Cool air. Sunday. All partake of the sacrament[56]
except myself who had not prepared. Dine at Burford. Go to Oldwood
in afternoon to see my Father's brother Edwd. Davis who is unwell and
leave him a ticket to be admitted to the dispensary. Get to Mr. Nicholls at
Kyrewood to Tea. Mr. Lambert was gone to Lambswick, and consequently
got no further intelligence about the farm. Maria returns.

May 23rd
Cold, east wind. Fair. Mr. Nicholls and I meet with Mr. Lambert at
Lambswick. The answer I get concerning the Farm (Lambswick) is that
Mr. L. has not finally made up his mind with regard to it but promises to
send word in a few days. William sheep-shearing at Mr. Edwards' Burford.
Father goes to Bromyard Fair and buys a pair of oxen for working. Revd.
& Mrs. Stewart, brother Samuel & Miss Sayer take Tea here. Mr. B. Sayer
drops in after.

May 24th
Fine warm day. Sheep-shearing at Park. Mr. B. Edwards and Mr. Partridge come to assist. B. Sayer drops in in afternoon.

25
Sharp frost, clear warm day. Had a right hard day's sheep-shearing. Five of us shore nearly 157 (all large ones). Mr. Edwards not here. Mr. Partridge comes in afternoon, it being Ludlow Fair.

26
Wind, clear & fine. William & Matthias Trumper start off on an excursion to London. Willm.'s first visit.

May 27th
Small frost, very clear & fine day.

28
Same weather exactly. Miss Wilkinsons call at Park after Tea.

29
Morning cold, very fine & milder P.M. Sunday. Maria goes to Lodge to dinner. Eliza and myself at home.

30
Clear, windy & mild! John Nott of Eastham drops in to dinner having come to take the colts from tack. Uncle Reynolds brings his flock of sheep to wash and stays tea. Samuel goes off on horseback to Burcott, Badger &c. Eliza goes to Tea at Mr. Giles', Church house, to meet the Miss Giles's of Hope. Barker comes to repair the grate in Hall and also puts a new back and bonnet to it.

May 31
Fair & warm. Mr. Lambert informs me of his intention of continuing the farm til Lady Day and says his brother has the refuse of it[57] and intends coming to live at it. Mr. Wheeler (the landlord)[58] says not so.

June 1
Fair & warm. Samuel returns from Burcott and brings Mrs. Reynolds[59] with him in her carriage with his own horse. Maria goes to dine at Lodge and tea at Boraston.

28. Boraston House, built for Edward Mytton *c.* 1800.

2nd

Fair A.M. little rain P.M. Father goes to Kidderminster market. Mrs. Reynolds, Eliza and I inspect Mr. Stewart's new house and call on old Mr. Mytton & Mrs. Smith[60] at Boraston.

June 3rd
Storms all day.

4
Slight storms. Samuel returns from buying a four-wheeled carriage at Birmingham.

5
Stormy. Sunday. Mrs. Reynolds accompanies us to Burford Church and stays dinner at Burford. I come home and find William returned from town quite delighted with his journey.

June 6th
Fair, windy P.M. Samuel starts off into Devonshire. Mrs. Reynolds (Burcott) leaves us for the Lodge, Nash, &c. Eliza and I ride over to Hill Top[61] in afternoon and find a party dining there. Father goes to Ludlow Market.

29. Hill Top, Rochford, home of the Cooke family at the time of the diary.

7th
Rain A.M. Fair P.M. mild. Dine at Nash Court[62]. Return home & find Mr. Good of Aston. Ben. Sayer drops in afterwards and they stay supper.

June 8th
Slight storms. Mild. Ride up to High house Turnpike[63] to see after the shearers to come to shear the Lambs. On returning meet with the Cooke's, Miss Hursts & Ben. Giles going to Hanley to look through the pleasure grounds shrubberies, &c. &c. Accompany them and return to Hill Top to Tea & home.

9
Fair A.M. rain at night. Go to Kidderminster market. No business to be done. Dine with Turrall. Mrs. Reynolds (of Burcott) accompanies Eliza from Lodge party to stay the night here.

June 10th
Stormy, shearing lambs all day.

11th
Slight storms – mild. Father & I go to Eastham to sell to and measure some ash Timber &c. for Weaver of Breem Turnpike[64]. The ash at 1/6 per foot.

30. View of Bridgnorth.

Mrs. Reynolds and Eliza go for a ride in carriage to Ludlow. Mr. Trumper calls, stays Tea and supper.

12th June
Stormy. Sunday. Mrs. Reynolds & Eliza go to Nash to Chapel and stay dinner at Mr. Reynolds's. Father & William return home with them. I tea at Lodge. Mr. E. Edwards calls on parish business for William.

13
Very fine and warm. Put Samuel's Horse to Mrs. Reynolds' carriage and take her home to Burcott. Get there to dinner. In the afternoon Mrs. R. and two female neighbours of hers (Mrs. & Miss Hardwick) go to see Devenport house[65], the seat of the Devenport Family which has been lately fitted up for the present proprietor who is a clergyman[66]. Was very much pleased with it altogether: its situation is beautiful, the views from the upper apartments most splendid, avenues opening in different directions through the trees very much add to its effect. Return to Burcott to sleep.

14th June
Fine and warm. Mrs. Reynolds & I go in her carriage to Bridgnorth. First visit the china showrooms in the town and also the mill for grinding & preparing the bones & flint for making it, which is from thence sent to Colport[67] to be manufactured. Call at Mr. Jones's, a wine & spirit merchant. Walk round the town and see most of it: a very curious place[68]. Return to Burcott to dine. Mr. & Mrs. Powell & the Hardwicks drink Tea with us.

June 15th
Fine & very warm. Get an early breakfast and start off to Badger. Find Mr. & Mrs. Green at home (the first time of seeing the latter). Walk about along with Mr. G. till 11 viewing his farm and the alterations and improvements going on upon it and also the house. Proceed to Wolverhampton market with Mr. G. in his gig. Walk over the town and stand the corn market with him. Wheat worth 8/6 a bushel being 7 or 8d more than at Kidderminster. We dine at the ordinary[69] at New Hotel – a most respectable company stay till six, and back to Badger to Tea. Go from thence on horseback to Kemberton to visit my Uncle Peter Reynolds. Stay the night there.

June 16th
Fair but not so warm. Walk about Kemberton till Dinner which being over I start off homeward, and get to Mr. Lowe's of Lea[70] to Tea. Meet with young Wheeler of Eardiston there. On arriving at home find Robert and Miss Sayer and Mr. Trumper here. They stay supper. Father goes to Kidderminster Market and sells a load of wheat for William.

June 17
Fine clear day. William goes to Ludlow to settle some business about the county rates.

June 18th
Fine A.M. Tempest & storms in afternoon. Mrs. Nurse & Mrs. Bright[71] arrive here from New house having come from Abberly in Nott's cart, the coach being loaded[72]. Father comes up here to help William and I to shear his stock of Lambs.

19
Fine day. Sunday. Eliza & I dine with Father at Burford. In the afternoon I visit my uncle[73] at Mr. Potts's who was taken ill a few days since and is still in the same state – a kind of stroke has come over him which has made him almost insensible. Call and drink Tea at Kyrewood coming home. Meet there the two Miss Witts from Mount, Mrs. Smith from Birmingham & William Wheeler.

June 20th
Fair & fine day. Father & I go to Kidderminster Fair. Take the three years old Hackney filley to offer for sale – she returns. Call at the Coney-green coming home to pay the wedding visit to Mr. & Mrs. John Smith. Willm. Wheeler gets there to Tea and we return together and sup at the White house.

31. Kyrewood, home of the Nicholls family at the time of the diary.

21

Stormy. Miss Wigly's coachman comes to look at the filley but goes away without making the purchase. I take a ride to Milson for some Turnip seed. Mr. Minton however sent it all the way home. William Wheeler comes to stay the night for Brampton Brian Fair.

22nd

Stormy. William and Young Wheeler start off for Brampton Brian. Wheeler buys a poney mare. William comes back as he went. The three ladies, Mrs. Nurse, Mrs. Bright & Maria go to Nash Court to dine.

23rd June

Fair, some wind. Eliza and I pay the wedding visit to Mr. & Mrs. Willm. Mytton at Lindridge[74].

24

Rain. Mr. & Mrs. Wm. Reynolds and aunt Partridge dine with us. Father comes back to the Park. Another wedding! Saml brings his wife home out of Devonshire. A Miss Buckingham daughter of a Revd. Gent residing at Burrington[75].

June 25th

Stormy. Eliza and I go down to pay the wedding visit. Much pleased with Samuel's choice. She appears a very sensible and well disposed person: rather good looking into the bargain.

26

Slight storms. Father and Eliza dine at Burford along with Samuel and his bride.

27

Fair & warm. Dine with the Adams's at Eardiston having gone down to have a leisurely peep over George Adams's Farm at Upper Woodson[76]. Mrs. Nurse and Mrs. Bright leave Park for the Lodge. Mr. & Mrs. Henry Davis & Miss Henderson from Liverpool[77] call in the evening.

28

Same weather.

29th

Very warm & fine. Samuel and his bride call this afternoon – Mr. Lowe, Greenwayhead, after Tea.

June 30th

Excessively hot. Go to Ludlow Races, being the second day. Only three races to be run for and for these we have 2 heats, the oakly Park[78] being walked over for and the handicap decided at one heat. How sadly fallen off and just no company into the bargain. Father goes to Kidderminster Market. James Adams comes to Tea and have another word with regard to Woodson but could not treat. Asks now 300 guineas, bid the 280£ again.

July 1st

Very warm & fine. Father and William go to pay rent to and dine with Mr. Rushout. Maria goes to spend the evening at Nash. I go to an evening party at Mr. H. Davis's. We play at cards, dance, eat supper &c. till 2 clock.

2nd

Same weather

July 3rd

Very hot (Sunday) Go twice to Church and call at Vicarage Tenbury & stay supper. Mr. Hall has been successful in his Tithe suit with the parishioners, having won the trial establishing his claim to the privy or vicarial tithes in Tenbury parish. Lost his suit with regard to the large &c. tithes on Sutton Park, as also the Large in Tenbury district[79].

July 4th
Excessively hot. Father goes to Ludlow Market and pays the rent for Court of Hill land &c.

5th
Still hotter if anything, with thunder & lightening this morning and also during the night.

6th
Very fine clear day. Mrs. Nurse & Mrs. Bright come here to stay the night from Lodge. Mr. Edwards calls.

July 7
Clear & fine till evening, then slight rain. Mrs. Nurse and Mrs. Bright start off by coach to new house[80].

8
Beautifully clear & warm day. Go to assist Father carrying hay at Burford in afternoon and tea with Samuel & Mrs. Davis. Eliza goes to Mr. Reynolds's, Nash to stay a day or two.

9 July
Same weather.

10th
Weather delightful, very warm at times. Sunday. Attend Boraston chapel in afternoon. Mr. Stewart christens his own child (the 2nd). Tea at Boraston.

11th
Very clear & warm with some wind.

12
Little rain early, fine and clear afterwards.

13
Clear morning. Haze in afternoon with considerable wind.

July 14th.
Clear fine day. Go to Kidderminster Market.

15th
Tempest. Heavy storms of rain.

16
Clear windy day – last of hay-making.

17
Same weather. Sunday. At church morning & afternoon. William goes to
Lindridge and Eliza to Boraston Chapel in afternoon.

18
Same weather. Little warmer. Go to Worcester – the assizes going on.
Commission opened on 16th. Call at Lindridge on way home and stay
supper along with Miss Sayer & the host & hostess.

19th
Rain A.M. & wind high, clear P.M. Two Miss Wilkinsons call this
evening.

20
Steady rain, clear but cool in the evening. Tenbury races[81]. Captn.
Winnington, Steward. A good race in the morning for the maiden plate. 3
heats won by Mr. Patrick[82]. The Sweepstakes and hack race very poor, the
former won by Nelle Gwynne, the latter by Mr. Dunn's horse, Jewstone[83].
Some friends dine with us, Uncle Peter from Kemberton, Joseph from New
house[84], Mr. Baylis, Mr. Edwards, Partridges, &c. Mr. P. Reynolds returns
and stays the night with us.

21st
Stormy. Two Mr. Partridges call to take Mr. P. Reynolds back to Lodge to
Dinner, but he was at Tenbury staying to see the fight between two scamps
for a subscription prize, viz Turner off the Hill[85] and a sweep.

July 22nd
Slight storms, some sun, but not warm. Father & I go to the Furlongs to
measure a stick of oak Timber which he bot of Mr. Edwards last year,
but no go. The right stick was cut off and being fobbed off with another
would not do. John Nott calls and takes tea. Chooses another yearling
Ram in turn of the one he bot. last year of us.

July 23rd
Clear warm day. Call, spend the afternoon and drink Coffee at Burford with Samuel & Mrs. Davis. The Stewarts and Mrs. Lawson call upon them.

24th
Rain A.M. Clear fine afternoon. All at home to dine. William goes to Mr. Edwards's in afternoon and Maria along.

25
Fair, little cloudy. Dine at Burford along with Mr. & Mrs. S.D. Spend a very pleasant afternoon with them. Mr. & Mrs. Collins call on them in afternoon. Father goes to Bewdley Fair.

July 26
Cloudy, warm at intervals. Aunt & Uncle Reynolds call and take Tea going from Tenbury Market. Samuel & his wife also call and drink Tea afterwards. Mr. Jones from bank[86] calls to talk to William concerning the gamekeepership for the Mr. Hope's at Greete and Berrington[87]. Willm. having recommended Mr. J. to them when they applied to him. The poor law commissioner (Mr. Head) comes to the Swan to form a union of Parishes under the new poor law act[88]. William attends as overseer at Burford.

27
Fair & warm towards evening. Mr. Cooke, Hill-Top, calls and dines with us. Comes with the intention of attending the meeting at Swan of the rate-payers for the union that is to be formed under the poor law act. I go with him but we were too late. The commissioner (Mr. Head) having begun at 2 and explained it all to them before we arrived. Go to Lodge to Tea and return home with Maria, where was Mr. E. Edwards, who came to know about the meeting &c.

28th
Fair & warm. Begins to rain at 9 at night. William goes to Kidderminster Market. Aunt Partridge comes here to stay the night.

July 29th
Good deal of rain last night & some storms in the day. Aunt Partridge & I go to Burford in afternoon, she to pay the wedding visit[89], stay Tea.

30
High wind, slight storms A.M. Father goes to attend the funeral of his late brother from Mr. Potts's Oldwood to Tenbury Church. Miss Sayer drinks Tea here, also Mr. Partridge who comes to fetch his wife home, she having been staying here for 2 or 3 days.

July 31st
Clear & fine. Sunday. Father and Eliza dine at Burford. Attend church morning and evening. William goes to Boraston in afternoon.

Aug. 1st
Clear. Rather cold at morning & night. William goes to Bromyard Downs to order a new cider mill, Runner &c. which he does and is to cost 15 guineas and to be made on the new construction – the runner being wider and cut in a sloping fashion instead of being upright[90]. Father goes to Ludlow Market. Mr. & Mrs. H. Davis & Miss Henderson call after Tea to invite us down to the concert at Swan on Thursday night.

Aug. 2nd
Fair and very warm day.

3
Same weather. Go across to the Lea to see Mr. Wm. Lowe & also call on Sarah Pugh to get her to hire some hop-pickers if they be had in that neighbourhood. Call at Milson in going and dine there along with the old Gent & Lady[91] and Son William after which we all start off together for the Lea.

4th
Mild little rain. Sleep at Lea last night and get home to Breakfast. William, Maria and the two Miss Partridges go to the concert at Swan, the Fredrick Family, as they term themselves, the performers. They go (except William) to Mr. H. Davis to Tea. Mr. Hall & two Miss Wilkinson's call here tonight.

Aug. 5th
No rain but dull hazy day. Mr. Mytton of Boraston and Mrs. Smith come to dine with us. Mr. M. goes down to look at Burford hopyards along with Father before dinner. Mr. Williams and Ben. Sayer also dine here. Mr. & Mrs. Reynolds come to Tea.

Aug. 6th
Fair and warm day. Dine with Samuel and his wife at Burford and stay Tea.

7th
Fog, hot at times. Maria and I go to Nash Chapel and dine at Lodge. I Tea along with Aunt & Uncle Reynolds at Nash.

8th
Fair and very warm. Father goes to Ludlow Market. Eliza leaves the Park after Tea and goes to stay at Nash all night.

9th
Fair and very warm. Eliza and Mr. Trumper are married at the Nash Chapel. Matthias Trumper calls here and accompanies William and I up to Mr. Wm. Reynolds, Nash court where the wedding is kept. William gave her away and Miss Sayer acted as brides maid. Aunt and uncle Reynolds, Aunt Partridge, Matthias Trumper and myself also accompanyed them to church[92]. We all breakfast together as soon as the ceremony is over, and at a little after 10 the couple start off in a chaise to Worcester to proceed onwards tomorrow on an excursion somewhere but where I know not. In addition to the company mentioned, Old Mytton, Ben. & R. Sayer, Mrs. Smith, two Miss Partridges &c. dine with us at Nash. We keep it up til between one & two o'clock and leave a lot of them about to sit down to whist. So much for the first wedding I ever attended.

Aug. 10
Fair and hot day. Miss Partridges tea here.

11th
Same weather. Father goes to the Clee hill to hire hop pickers – gets 14. Calls on Mr. Bishop of Lowe to pay for the cheeses, William goes to Kidderminster Market.

12
Strong fog and very warm afterwards. Take Tea at Burford along with Saml. and his bride, a truly affectionate and estimable person.

13th
Same weather

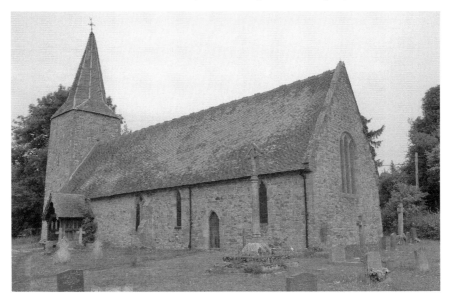

32. St John the Baptist church, Nash, which dates from the early fourteenth century; Eliza Davis and William Trumper were married there on 9 August 1836.

14th

Tempest and storm in the night and again at evening. Storm in the day. Warm. Sunday. Dine at Burford and stay evening service.

15th

Slight Tempest accompanied with light storm. Very hot. William goes to Ludlow Market. Samuel & his wife drop in to Tea with us.

16th

Fair, hot day.

17th

Same weather.

Aug. 18

Stormy, high west wind. Mr. Trumper and his wife return home.

19

Windy, clear day.

20

Storms, colder.

21
Very fine clear day. Sunday. William goes to Tenbury to accompany Mr. & Mrs. Trumper to church, dine &c.

22nd
Rain in morning and again a good deal in the evening. Father goes to Ludlow Fair. Miss Partridges call here going from Tenbury and on account of the rain stay all night.

Aug. 23
Rains nearly all day. Make the wedding visit to Mr. & Mrs. Trumper. Tea with them and leave along with Mr. Reynolds, Mr. Partridge, Wm. Mytton &c.

24
Dry clear day.

25
Sharp frost. Fine warm day. Wm. goes to Kidderminster Market.

Aug. 26th
Fine clear day. Mrs. Partridge calls here and Maria accompanies her to Tenbury to pay the wedding visit to Mr. & Mrs. Trumper. I take Tea with Revd. Mr. Jones at Burford and call on Mr. Hall coming home. He had just parted with his tithe valuer (a Mr. Fowler) who is making a valuation of the small Tithe &c. gained by Mr. H. in the late suit.

27
Rain, high wind. Mrs. Partridge stays with us and goes home this afternoon.

Aug. 28th
Fine & warm day. <u>Sunday</u>. Go down to Eastham Church and thence to the Hill Top to dinner[93]. Stay the whole afternoon with them. Nobody but themselves except a Mrs. Bennett.

29
Same weather. The guardians of the poor for the Tenbury Union are elected. The meeting took place in the national school-room. Mr. Grove & my brother William chosen for Burford Township. The number of Guardians in all is 22, viz 3 for Tenbury, 2 for Burford and 1 for each of

the other Parishes included in the union. Mr. Head, one of the assistant Commissioners, was present[94].

Aug. 30th
Hazy at times. John Nott from Eastham comes to look at the hopyard. Mr. & Mrs. David Jones come to Tea.

Aug. 31st
Fine warm day. Go to Bromyard Down to order a stone bed for the cider-press to come along with the mill and runner which William is going to have of Mr. Milton the owner of the Quarry there. From thence get across the country for Orleton where I arrive in time for Dinner[95]. Find Mr. H. Davis and Mrs. Davis[96] only at home. We go to see Mr. Strafford's hopyard, which is a very good one, particularly some young ground the first year of polling and which (for the first year) is most extraordinary. From thence we go through Mr. D.'s own hopyard which also is very good but small. Then to Mr. Davis the Fall farm[97] to see a new hop-kiln built upon a new, and as some say an improved plan, being in a circular form with an open top and roofed with zinc. The bed of the kiln is placed at a considerable elevation above the fire. It is a Kentish scheme and several planters are building upon the same plan.

Sepr. 1st
Storm A.M. Wind. Clear fine afternoon. Rose & Son come to Breakfast. William turns out with them shooting. They bag 6 brace by luncheon time. William & Rose's Son kill most of them. Send 4 Brace to Mr. Rushout, the rest left here. William then goes to Kidderminster market and sells 150 Bags of wheat viz 100 of his own and 50 of Father's.

Sepr. 2
Same weather. Cold wind at night.

Sepr. 3rd
Fair. Wind. William goes to Nash to the two Mr. Hope's shooting. They have engaged Mr. Jones of the Bank to act as gamekeeper both at Berrington and on these Farms.

4th
Stormy. Mild. Sunday. William & I go for a walk to see the Rey's hopyard and call at Trumpers as we go through the Town. The hopyard pretty good on lower side but thin on upper. Call & drink Tea along with the Nicholls's.

5 Sepr
Slight storms in evening. Fair A.M.

6th
Stormy A.M. Fair P.M. Begin hoppicking, Father and I been at it all day.

7th
Very fine warm day.

8th
Same weather. Ned. Mytton comes to us and stays all night.

9
Rain A.M. Warm. Confirmation held at Tenbury.

10
Stormy, Mild.

Sepr. 11th
Mild morning, cold wind in afternoon. Sunday. Dine with them at Burford and stay evening service and Tea. Mrs. & Miss Hanbury at Church with the Burford Family.

12th
Fine, warm day.

13th
Same weather.

14
Storm of rain. Mild.

15
Fine warm day. William goes to Kidderminster market.

16
Fair morning, misty in the afternoon.

17 Sepr.
Hot. Showery & an hard storm.

18th
Fair, cool wind. Sunday. Mr. Partridge & Mr. Williams call in afternoon.

19
Fair & warm. Father goes to Worcester fair. Mr. H. Davis and Matthias Trumper call this evening and sup.

20
Warm. Showers. William as one of the Guardians of the poor for the Tenbury Poor law union elected along with Mr. Grove to act for Burford township attends the meeting today to appoint officers &c. Mr. Cooke & Mr. H. Davis to be the surgeons. Mr. Collins one of the relieving officers[98].

Sepr. 21st
Frost. Fair & very warm day. Samuel goes to Hereford to see the Bishop concerning taking priests orders, the Bishop having refused to ordain him a priest in consequence of not letting him know when he first came to serve in his diocese.

22nd Sepr.
Fair and mild. Begins to rain a little at night. Samuel starts off by coach into Devonshire at 10 clock this morning. Father remains at Burford to sleep in Saml.'s absence. Take Tea at Burford along with Miss Starr, Mrs. D. & Father.

Sepr. 23rd
Hard storm of rain. Very mild.

24
Very warm, fair A.M. Slight showers P.M. William goes to Worcester market and Father to dine at Burford along with a party at 6 clock.

25
Beautiful day, very warm. Sunday. At church twice and take Tea at Mr. Trumper's.

26
Same weather. Finish hop-picking. A meeting of the guardians &c. of the Tenbury union. A fair at Tenbury & a Dinner at the Oak[99] at which William staid – 46 sat down. After paying the hoppickers we have a dance amongst them on the green by moonlight. Robert Sayer calls and sups.

33. The Royal Oak Hotel, Market Street, Tenbury.

Sepr. 27
Warm and fair till evening then begins raining. Mr. Giles[100] & his son come to purchase the Hops. They leave and the Old Gent comes back to close the bargain and stays Dinner.

Sep 28
Showers all day, mild. Father & William go to Ludlow Fair. I stay at home and sup with the Trumper's at night.

29th
Stormy. Mild.

30
Showers, Mr. J. Nott comes to pay the Eastham rent. Dines. William goes to Bromyard Down having sent the teams for a cider mill, ordered of Mr. Milton.

Octr. 1
Great deal of rain A.M. Wind P.M. Go to Worcester Market along with Mr. Edwards in his Gig. Make a purchase of a new Mackintosh Top coat of the best quality for 89/-.

2nd

Storms and wind. Sunday. Sacrament administered. William and Father stay. Mr. Grove and Mr. Bangham call about the Parish union business.

Octr. 3rd

Great deal of rain last night. Wind and slight storms today. William goes to Ludlow Market. William Wheeler of Eardiston married to Miss Nicholls of Kyrewood at Tenbury Church. No end to the weddings this year in this neighbourhood!

Octr. 4th

Sharp frost and fine warm day. Go to Cleobury for William to receive cash for 50 bags of Wheat of Mr. Wheeler the miller.

5th

Sharp frost. Warm. Storm in the afternoon. Go along with the teams to Stourport or rather after them to weigh the Hops. Stay to see the market out and go to Coney-green to dinner. Meet with Mrs. Smith from Boraston and Mrs. Winton there. Bring a note from Mr. Giles[101] to Tenbury – call at Trumper's – thence to Burford to see Samuel who is just arrived out of Devonshire having obtained not his end there, the Bishop refusing to ordain him priest when preaching out of his own Diocese.

Octr. 6

Strong fog. Fair & warm afterwards. William's party come to celebrate his birth day[102]. Mr. Winton, Wm. & Edd. Mytton, Mr. Reynolds[103] Mrs. Partridge, P. Reynolds from Kemberton, M. Trumper, Mrs. Trumper – all to dinner. Some more drop in afterwards.

7th

Stormy. Mild. Father & I start off for the Sale as soon as Dinner is over accompanied by Peter Reynolds & Edward Mytton, the latter to Lindridge the former to the New house. They both slept here. Mr. Whitcombe's farm bot. in at the reserve bidding 10,500. Mr. Trumper, the last bidder (for Mr. Whitcome) at 9,500£. The other estate (Mr. Pheysey's) sold very high, Mr. Trumper the purchaser for him at 8,025£ – 150 acres. This stretch in price was caused by Mr. Wheeler[104], the opposition bidder, who imagined Trumper was bidding for us! Thus showing his good feeling towards us. Go from thence to the new house and stay all night. Father returns along with Mr. Godson.

Octr. 8ᵗʰ

Good deal of rain in night but fine mild day. Start from new house after Breakfast. Call and leave the horse at Coney-green and walk to Stourport[105] to see the two loads of Hops weighed. Back to Coney-green. Thence to Bewdley along with John Smith, where I go to inquire about the Sutton farm by Kidderminster belonging to Mr. Skey of Spring grove. Tom Rea accompanies me to speak to Old Baker who at present holds the refuse. Am to know finally after Monday next whether he will take it. Dine at the "George"[106] along with a party of them, Tom Rea, Baker, J. Smith &c. &c.

Octr. 9ᵗʰ

Stormy, Sunday. Mr. Rushout does the whole duty. Evening service omitted for the first time.

10ᵗʰ Octr.

Stormy. Father goes to Ludlow Market. Mr. Williams comes to tea and buy some pigs, &c.

11ᵗʰ

Very blustrous night. Stormy day. Father & I go to Stourport fair, partly on purpose to inquire about the Sutton farm. Call at Coneygreen to lunch, then to Bewdley where we meet with Mr. Baker who informs us that Mr. Boraston still holds the refuse of it[107].

12

Wind still high with storms towards evening. Mr. & Mrs. Trumper visit the Park together for the first time. Father here and become sociable with them – a step gained! John Pheysey refuses to have his farm at the rate Mr. T. bt. it.

Octr. 13

Extraordinary high wind last night – fine clear day. Many trees blown down, bows separated &c. &c. William goes along with Mr. Trumper to look over Mr. Pheysey's Farm at Rochford. Mr. P. having employed Mr. T as agent to buy the estate for him & he having done so, Pheysey turns round upon him and won't have it. A dinner party at Trumper's. William goes. Maria to Tea.

Octr. 14ᵗʰ

Great deal of rain last night. Clear fine day.

15ᵗʰ

Rain in morning, fine afterwards.

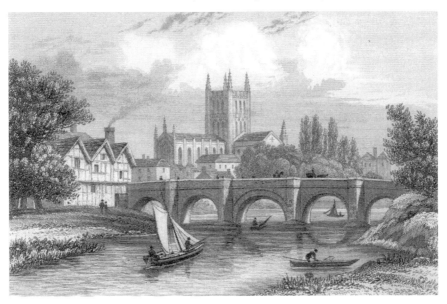

34. The River Wye at Hereford, with the medieval bridge and cathedral, as drawn and engraved for Dugdale's *England & Wales* (1846).

16

Fog, fair & warm. Sunday. Mr. Cooke of Hill Top, Miss S. Cooke and a party come from Hill Top to Burford Church thinking to hear Samuel do duty but were of course disappointed on acct. of his misunderstanding with the Bishop. Drink Tea at Mr. Trumper's.

Octr. 17th

Fog – fair & warm. This the day fixed for agreeing for Mr. Whitcombe's farm at Eastham between himself and the gent Mr. Berry at Bewdley. Mr. Trumper (Whitcombe's attorney) goes along with him, but they could not make the bargain. Mr. W. bids 10,000£ but they hold off for more.

18

Mists A.M. Very mild. William goes to the evening party at Hill Top. The poor law guardians meet but do not fix about the situation for the workhouse.

Octr. 19

Fine & warm day. Father & I start off for Hereford, partly on purpose to see the agricultural show and also to meet with Sir J. Cottrill about a farm which Mr. Court had informed us he would have to let. Got no decisive answer from Sir J. Father returned home after dinner. I stay all night and dine at the Swan and go afterwards to hear the prizes awarded at the agricultural dinner.

Octr. 20th

Fog, fine after and warm. Sleep last night at the Oak Inn, no bed to be obtained at the Swan[108] for less than 5/- although hired. Stay the fair which in proportion to former Hereford Octr. fairs was not large. Get home to Tea.

21

Fair & very mild. Mr. Langley & Edward Mytton call and Tea with us.

Octr. 22nd

Most beautiful day. William goes to Worcester market.

23rd

Same weather. Sunday. Father & I dine at Burford – home to Tea.

24th

Same weather. Go to Ludlow market & home to Tea. William goes to Uncle Reynolds's birth day[109] party at Nash.

25

Mist and Fog A.M. – clear & fine afternoon. Go to Maynston to see Young Johnstone about the farm at Broncroft[110]. The place[111] is situated on the Hereford Road from Ledbury, 3½ miles from the latter & 12 from the former. It is about 12 miles beyond Bromyard. A meeting of the board of guardians at Tenbury determined to build the workhouse at the brickyard having bot. the land of Mr. Turner for 100£[112].

26

Very fine mild day. Whilst at Burford this evening Samuel comes home from Hereford having gone to see the Bishop who still persists to refuse to allow him to preach in his diocese until he has been made a priest 12 months. So much for neglect in not having given notice at his first coming. Call on Mr. Rushout to see the Shrewsbury paper to ascertain the day of the revision of the votes for Burford, which happens to be past, being on 24th, William (who is the Burford overseer) having neglected to attend[113].

27th

Stormy – cold wind. Meet Mr. Johnstone of Maynston at Ludlow & get the final refuse of the farm.

28th

Very cold, snow &c. Father & I go to Broncroft to look over the Lodge Farm but could not agree for it. The farm is 322 acres, the price put 420£ a year. We bid the 400£ and parted. Feel very angry with my Father for not closing upon it, the farm being not only a good one but in a good state and the buildings &c. all very complete or to be made so in a short time.

29

Still excessively cold with snow, sleet &c. Repent and ride to Broncroft again about the farm but too late being let last night after we left to a Mr. Matthews from Mongomeryshire. William is obliged to go to Stretton[114] to meet with the revising barristers to have the Burford list of voters revised, he having neglected to attend at Ludlow on Monday last, the day fixed at Ludlow.

Octr. 30th

Sharp frost, fair but cold. Sunday. Mr. H. Davis of Orleton comes up to dine here. Mr. Edwards & R. Sayer also & Matts. Trumper.

Octr. 31st

Very severe frost. Fair. Father goes to Ludlow Market.

Novr. 1st

Little frost. Milder & fair. Mrs. Reynolds, Mrs. Smith, Miss Sayer, Ellen Partridge, Mr. Partridge, & Uncle Reynolds call here to Tea and supper, most of them on their way from Tenbury market.

2nd

Very mild again & fair. Mr. Edwards calls.

Novr. 3

Rain. Wind P.M. Go to Kidderminster market & call at Eardiston on way home to pay the wedding visit to Mr. & Mrs. Wm. Wheeler. Mr. & Mrs. J. Strafford also drop in.

4th

Mild. little rain. Father goes to Withypool & Curdell[115] about buying some casks of Mr. Beddoe but did not finally agree for them.

5th

Hard rain in morning. Mild and clear afterwards. Mr. Trumper goes to Bewdley to see Mr. Berry about the Rochford Estate but Mr. B. was absent in London.

Novr. 6th
Frost, cold air. Little snow or sleet. Maria & I go to Nash Chapel and Dine at the Lodge. Mr. & Mrs. Reynolds come to Tea after which we soon return.

7th
Frost, clear fine day. Father & I go to look at Rochford Farm & back to Dinner.

Novr. 8th
Hard frost – fine & warm afterwards. Wm. goes to Leominster fair.

9
Great deal of rain. Go to see Mr. Hall at the Vicarage and drink Tea with him. Meet with Leadinton[116], a workman of Mr. Reynolds, Nash, coming home bearing a large prop which the fellow says he had out of the rickyard at Boraston. Mr. Trumper gives him a reprimand and makes him promise to bear it back again.

Novr. 10
Hard storm of rain at noon. Father goes to call on Mr. Mytton of Boraston and they afterwards go together to dine with the Sayers. William goes to Cleobury to sell Mr. Lawley some cider which he does, 4 hogsheads and at 65/- per hogshead[117]. Also buys some Timber of him to build a new broadwheeled waggon. Mary Partridge calls here going from Tenbury and stays dinner.

11th Novr.
Good deal more rain – mild. Mr. Williams comes to buys some sheep, pigs, &c. and lunches with us. I take Tea at Nash Court. Mr. & Mrs. Bayliss[118] being there where they had gone from the Lodge and to which place we return to sup.

12th
Mild and fair day.

13
Rain most of the day. Sunday.

14
Small frost – fine. Start off early[119] for Badger and get there by 10. Find that the farm at Badger belonging to Mrs. Browne (occupied by Mr.

Bacon) is to be kept in their own hands, so that is done with at once. Dine with Mr. & Mrs. Green and take a ride with Mr. G. in the afternoon to enquire about another farm at Hilton[120] belonging to a Mrs. Smith there. Find the refuse given to someone else. The rent asked is 2£ pr. acre. Turnip and barley soil. 4½ miles on the Wolverhampton road from Bridgnorth. Return to Badger and stay all night.

Novr. 15
Small frost – some drizling rain. Start from Badger little past 10. Get to Mr. Reynolds's, Burcott, to lunch – then for home. Call at Milson to Tea. Find the old Gent (Mr. Lowe) laid up with the Gout in bed. Reach home between 7 & 8[121].

16
Mild, fine day. Mr. Wm. Good calls – dines and stays Tea. Mr. Collins also calls.

17th Novr.
Rain in night – fair & mild day. Mr. Bishop of the Lowe[122] comes for a load of fruit. Ride to Milson in the evening and stay Tea and Supper. Mrs. & Miss Cooke staying there from Hill Top. Mr. Lowe sitting up stairs with gout.

18th
Fine morning. Snow Rain &c. in afternoon. Dine with Mr. & Mrs. Samuel at Burford. Tea at Mr. Trumper's.

Novr. 19th
Frost & cold wind accompanied with storms during the day. Two Miss Partridges dine here. Father takes Tea with Samuel at Burford. Mr. & Mrs. D. Jones there also. Thos. Phillips puts 10£ out for use in Father's hands in addition to the sum before advanced[123].

20th
Small frost & very fine day. Sunday. William dines at Burford. Maria and I go to spend the afternoon at Mr. Edwards's of Burford. Mrs. Lloyd there.

21st Novr.
Sharp frost – strong fog & rain at night. Father & I dine at Burford. Meet Revd. D & Mrs. Jones & Mrs. Trumper. Father was also at Ludlow market.

22nd

Small frost – strong fog and rain at night. Go for William to Mr. Hearman to get the rate signed by him. Lunch with Mr. Rawlings and pay his lime bill for him to Mr. Lewis at Swan in afternoon.

23rd

Very high & rather cold wind. Maria & I go to Lodge to dine. Meet Uncle & Aunt Reynolds there. Stay the evening and Supper. Robert Sayer also drops in.

24th

Little frost. Hard storm of hail, sleet &c.

25

Sharp frost succeded by fog and snow, rain &c. at night. Spend the evening at Mr. H. Davis's along with the vicar (Mr. Hall), Miss Wilkinsons and themselves.

Novr. 26

Very rough day. Rains nearly the whole. Mr. & Mrs. Wm. Reynolds, Mr. Partridge & Mr. & Mrs. H. Davis come to Tea and supper, also Ellen Partridge who stays the night.

27th

Very mild & fair till night when it begins to rain. Sunday. Father & I dine at Burford. I afterwards drink Tea & sup with Mr. Hall at the Vicarage.

Novr. 28th

Mild morning then very severe storm of rain. Mild evening. Go to Ludlow market. Do nothing except receiving the cash for a load of wheat of Mr. Whatmore.

29

Excessively heavy rain all night as well as day. The quantity of rain fallen of late is immense. For several years we have not had such a flood in Teme. Reaches half way up both the Adneys[124] and covers nearly the whole of the lower one. Mr. Wheeler's reys hopyard completely inundated and the greater part of the reys meadow. We put a fox out of the cot in orchard at Burford and the dog runs him into the river. 9 o'clock at night. Just returned from saving a lot of nine sheep from being drowned in the middle adneys, the water having risen so rapidly since the edge of night as to cover nearly the whole of the meadow. Find the sheep in the middle of the meadow surrounded by water entirely. Bring cattle and all into Spurtree meadow. Get a fall from the horse beginning to plunge whilst in the water amongst the ditches. Very vivid flashes of lightening. The deepest flood that has been for a number of years.

Novr. 30
Little rain A.M. Very mild fine afternoon. Father goes to Cleobury on business for William. Rides my horse and gets a fall off him in mounting – not hurt. Flood going down very fast. Aunt Reynolds's birthday[125]. Only Maria & I go. Keep it up till 1 clock. Although the Father of the flock (Mr. Mytton), Mr. & Mrs. J. Smith, Mr. Langley and a few others were absent, we were a pretty large party.

Decr. 1st
Frost & very mild, fine day. Mr. Reynolds, Mr. Winton &c. bring their dogs to have a course or two upon our ground. They kill 3 here and 1 on Lodge . The Swan Ball takes place. The two Miss Partridges go along with us. A very pleasant party – not overcrowded but still sufficient for the room. Only two of the Stewards, Mr. E. Good & Mr. C. Price attend, young Walker of Burton (the other) absent .

2
Rain & wind. The Partridges stay all day with us.

3
Rain in night – fair & mild day. Ride to Milson to offer Mr. Lowe a Sample of Barley for William, but could not deal for it. The Miss Partridges leave us.

4
Mild & fair. Sunday. Father dines at Burford and accompanies Samuel to Boraston chapel.

Decr. 5th
Some rain. Mild. William goes to Worcester fair. Father to Ludlow market but partly on purpose to get the rate book signed for William. This is the first rate entered in the new books under the authority of the poor law union[126]. Take tea & supper with Mr. & Mrs. Trumper & Mr. Sayer at Tenbury.

Decr. 6th
Same weather. Father & William go to Ludlow fair. William returns to dinner with Mr. Cooke of Hill Top – Mr. James Adams, James Pearman &

Mr. Hodgets of Hales Owen[127], the two latter having come to try to buy William's 4 fat cows & 2 Bullocks.

7th
Very heavy rain. James Pearman, Mr. Hodgets & I start off together. Get to Tennall to Dinner.

Decr. 8
Rain. Go to Birmingham market along with the Pearman's. Nothing particular going on there. Get home to Tea to Tennall.

Decr. 9
Mild, little rain. Jim Pearman & I go to Birmingham in afternoon. Visit the Museum in Paradise Street & go to the theatre at night. Nothing but the Arab tumblers worthy of notice.

Decr. 10th
Frost, snow, rain &c. Leave Tennall after Breakfast and get home by ½ past 3 P.M. Bait[128] at Bewdley.

11
Froze a little but rain in morning part – mild. Sunday. Father & I dine at Burford. I take Tea at Mr. Trumpers.

Decr. 12th
Frost at beginning of the night, then rain, snow &c. William goes to Bewdley fair and Father to Ludlow market. I tea & sup with Mr. Hall at the Vicarage.

13
Some rain, mild.

14
Slight storms, mild. Father goes along with the teams to Ludlow intending to proceed on to Netly to night to see his landlord Mr. Hope. William and Maria dine at Burford along with a party there.

15
Fair & mild. Dine at Burford & tea & spend the evening at Mr. Hall's at the vicarage. A Mr. Wybrough[129] from Hereford calls at Burford about the curacy. Mr. Pinhorn accompanies him. Father returns home from Netley.

16

Same weather. William goes to Leominster fair.

17

Mild, rains all the afternoon. Wm. goes to Worcester market.

Decr. 18

Fair & very mild. Sunday. Dine at home. Boraston chapel in afternoon and Tea at Burford. Call on Mr. Jones (the Revd.).

19th

Same weather. Father goes to Ludlow market. Wishing to see old Mr. Lowe of Milson who has been of late laid up with the gout, I take a walk there and finding him & Mrs. L. gone to the Lea, I follow them there and stay the night, being rather <u>too far</u> to walk back again without a rest[130].

20th Decr.

Frost and most beautiful day. Get home from Lea to Dinner.

21

Fair & mild. Mr. H. Hope comes to the Swan to receive the Rents. Father & I go to settle and Father dines with them. Mr. Hope leaves them to dine by themselves with 5/- each for Dinner & all!

Decr. 22nd

Beautiful day, fair & mild. A party come to dine with us. The Trumper's, Miss & Robert Sayer, Mr. Davis of Leominster the new auditor &c.

23rd

Very cold east wind. Little snow at night and freezing sharp. Robert Sayer & Edward Smith call & spend the evening.

24

Frost, snow & very cold wind. Ellen Partridge leaves us.

25th

Same weather. Sunday & Christmas day. Father & myself stay the sacrament. Samuel assists in administering it. Home to dinner and attend the evening service at Tenbury church.

26

Frost more severe. Wind very cutting from NW. Little snow.

27th

The same intense weather continues. Walk across to Stoke to take Mr. Rawlings his lime Bill which I paid for him at the Swan a short time back. <u>Dine</u> there. Mr. R. sends 10/- to be given away in Bread at Burford church[131]. Come by Tenbury home. Call on Mr. H. Davis. Geo Adams accompanies me to the Park to Tea. William had a party to partake of a Turbot which was sent him by Mr. Trumper.

Decr. 28th

Weather become milder with a small fall of Snow. Aunt & Ellen Partridge leave us this afternoon.

29th

Same weather. Mr. & Mrs. Reynolds dine at Burford. Father goes to meet them. Having called in at Mr. Trumper's I stay to join in a barrel of oysters sent him by Mr. Blakeway.

Decr. 30th

Frost & snow still continue. Ride down to Eardiston on William's mare. Go from there along with the two Mr. Adams's in their carriage to the Hundred House[132] to answer an information against Mr. G. Adams charging him with trespassing, shooting without a certificate on the first of Octr. last which Charge he completely overturned & proved very satisfactorily that he was not out shooting on that day and also produced his certificate. Return to Eardiston to Dinner. The two Mr. Adams and two Mr. Strafford's accompany me as far up the road as Lindridge to attend an Oyster Supper at Mr. Myttons. I get home to Tea.

31st

Same weather.

1837

Jany. 1st

Very sharp frost & beautiful day. Some sun. Sunday. Brother Samuel reads prayers for Mr. Rushout who is unwell. Could not myself go to church in consequence of having a cold and sore throat. Wm. & Maria go to Lodge to spend the afternoon.

35. The Peacock Inn, Boraston.

Jany. 2
Snow & frost going away very mildly. Yesterday the 1st being Sunday, Mr. Rushout holds his Rent & Tithe Audit today as also does Rev. Mr. Stewart his tithe Audit at the Peacock[133]. Father & Wm. go to Burford, I to Mr. Stewarts. Fuller (who gets beastly drunk before dinner) the receiver assisted by his new partener in the law Mr. Preston. A good dinner prepared by Mrs. Smallman. Uncle Reynolds, B. Sayer, & I leave together and go to spend the evening at Boraston where we meet the Sayers, Mrs. Reynolds &c. and stay playing at cards till between two & 3 o'clock.

Jany. 3rd
Most delightful day. Sun shining all day. The auditing of the accounts of the overseers in the Tenbury union was begun yesterday by Mr. Davis of Leominster, the new elected auditor. William passed his today after some inconvenience having introduced them yesterday and being obliged to recopy most of them. Samuel & his wife dine here being the first time the Lady ever favoured the Park with her Company at Dinner.

4 Jany.
Very mild & fine. A meeting holden at Burford to appoint a new Clerk in the room of Mr. Gent, resigned. Mr. G. wished to come in again but the

office fell upon Mr. Wm. Jones the Blacksmith. Receive a note of invitation to dine at hill Top but could not accept it for two reasons, first engagement to spend the evening at Mr. Sayers and 2nd having a very bad cold which prevents me accepting either.

Jany. 5th
Some wind, colder. A young cart Horse at Nash from a hurt in the bottom of the foot like to die – so much for neglect. Wm. goes to dine at Mr. Trumper's.

6th
Rain in the night. Fair & fine day – Sun. Father goes along with Mr. Jordan of Greet to look at a farm at or near Acton Beauchamp belonging to Mr. Hemming of Kingsland. A party at Lodge. Willm. goes.

Jany. 7th
Fair & fine – wind. Go to Worcester on business of the bank for Wm. & Father. Put up and dine at the rein deer[134]. Ride Wm.'s mare.

8th
Frost, very fine. Sunday. Samuel reads the Prayers. William Jones the new clerk enters upon his office and makes a rather promising beginning.

9th
Fair. Set off by the Red Rover[135] to Kidderminster having heard from Mr. Turrall last Saturday at Worcester that Mr. Lavender of Wolverly wished to let his Farm. Call on Mr. L. find he has no such intention. Return to Mr. Turrall's, stay the night with him.

10th
Fair. Kidderminster. Get on the coach at Lion[136] and proceed on to Wolverhampton. Peep in at the new Hotel and get amongst the Travelers it being a commercial inn. Sleep there. A deer place.

Jany. 11th
Sharp frost. Wolverhampton market. Meet with Mr. John Green of Badger. After the market which by the bye was a flat one we dine at the ordinary at New Hotel. Mr. Green very politely invites me to take part of his Gig to Badger which I accept. Get there to Tea and stay the night with them.

12
Frosty night, after which it turns to snow which continues nearly all day. Pass the day at Badger. Having yesterday heard at Wolverhampton of a

Farm to be let of Sir G. Pigots called Burnall Green. Mr. J. Green and myself walk over it this morning. A large concern with much good land upon it and fields 30 & 40 acres a piece. Mr. G. & I get an interview with Sir G. Pigot in the afternoon. Find from him that two persons had before been looking over it with the intention of taking it and who had not yet done with it. Get the next refuse and come away. Stay at Badger all night again. A young Bauton, a neighbour, comes to spend the evening with us.

13 Jany.
Some rain, dreary unpleasant day. Frost all gone. Get on Mr. Green's gig horse and Ride to Burcott. Find Mr. & Mrs. Reynolds at home. Lunch with them and proceed on Mr. G.'s horse to Trysull[137] to see Mr. Thos. Lowe who had given me the invitation at Wolverhampton and had also told me of a farm to be let under Sir John Wrothesley[138], his own landlord. Stay the night with Mr. L. at Trysull which is a village about 5 miles from Wolverhampton.

Jany. 14
Frost and very pleasant day. Accompany Mr. Lowe over the whole of his Farm which lies a good way apart, being in two or three places on both sides the village. Very good land of Turnip and Barley soil the greater part of it keen upon Gravel. Tithe free, and rented at 36/- per acre. Call on Captain Dickens at Trysull a person who has in part the letting of Sir J.'s farms. Get the refuse of the farm called Wrottesley Lodge, provided Sir John had not already promised it. Situate on the road between Wolverhampton and Shiffnal, and only 3 miles from the former place which is reputed one of the best markets in the Kingdom for agricultural produce. Get on Mr. Green's horse and Ride him home to Badger. Get there before dinner and find Mr. G. out shooting along with a neighbour, Mr. Eakin[139]. We dine at four. Spend the evening with them and contrary to my intention the night also.

Jany. 15th
Sharp frost. Sunday. Get to Burcott on foot time enough to go to Wourfield[140] Church along with Mr. & Mrs. Reynolds. The most comfortable and at the same time best fitted up country church I ever was in. Mr. Broadbent the clergyman. Dine & spend the remainder of the day at Burcott & sleep there.

16 Jany.
Froze at the beginning of the night but turns to thaw in the morning and the frost nearly all out of the ground by night. Thought of starting home but the frost disappearing prevented me. Walk to Bridgenorth and back to dinner. A Miss Hardwick comes to Tea with us and spends the evening.

36. The Church of St John the Baptist, Kinlet, where Peter Davis' mother was baptised.

Jany. 17th
Misty morning – clearer in afternoon. Start off from Burcott for home.
Mr. Reynolds lends me his horse to ride part of the way. Bring him as far
as Kinlet[141] and walk the rest of the way. Call at Mr. Lowe's, Milson. Take
some refreshment there and home to Tea, pretty well fatigued being very
bad walking from the frost leaving us.

Jany. 18th
Fair and mild for the season. Ellen Partridge comes to Tea & William
accompanies her to Tenbury at 8 clock to see some performance at the
Oak, Tenbury[142].

19th
Misty day – very cold air. A dinner party at Nash Court. Although all
invited, none of us go to dine but William goes in afternoon.

20th
Little frost & snow – misty unpleasant day. The Nash Party come coursing
here; kill three hares.

21st
Some rain, sleet & cold wind.

22nd

Rain A.M. Fair P.M. Sunday. Samuel does the whole duty at Burford in the morning and the same for Mr. Stewart at Boraston in afternoon. Father & myself dine at Burford.

Jany. 23rd

Good deal of Rain – very mild. Father goes to Ludlow market.

24th

Beautiful day – very mild. John Nott from Eastham comes here and stays dinner. I dine at Burford, Samuel & his wife having invited Rev. Mr. Pinhorn & Lady & Mr. & Mrs. H. Davis – all come.

25

Great deal of rain. Cold east wind – flood.

26

Same weather exactly. The flood increased to an alarming extent. Very nearly as high as the last in Novr. last.

27th

Cold wind – very little rain. Send a part of the drawing room furniture from Burford in cart to Leominster to meet Revd. Mr. Edwards who

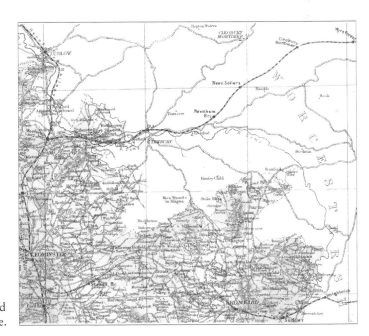

Map 11. Extract from a map of Herefordshire of the 1880s, showing the north-east part of the county, and its boundaries with Shropshire and Worcestershire.

purchased it – consisting of two Tables, couch & 6 chairs – all rosewood.

28th

Some little snow – very cold wind. Having received a letter from Mr. Blashill dated the 25th stating that Sir J. Cotterill had a farm to offer, William & I start off this morning to see it and get to Garnons (the seat of Sir John) by nine. Find that the old tenant (Mr. Prichard) was under arrest and had not quitted having got into arrear for Rent to the amount of 1000£ & upwards. The fact of his having begun to remove his goods alone it seems drove Sir John to arrest him. The estate not a good one from the appearance of it – quantity 320 acres. Mr. Blashill promises to write on Monday again. Return through Weobly (a nearer way).

Jany. 29

Frost & snow. Sunday. Mr. Rushout does the whole duty. Samuel goes to do duty at Whitton in afternoon for Mr. Lawson in the absence of Mr. Jones who is gone into Leicestershire to officiate for Mr. Lawson there. Father & Samuel give away ten shillings worth of bread each at Burford church. Mr. Edwards of Burford comes here in afternoon. I dine at Burford.

Jany. 30th

Frost & snow which goes away in afternoon – beginning to rain. Call to see Aunt Partridge who is very unwell. Mr. & Mrs. James Partridge there. Mr. John Green of Badger comes here in afternoon having given me the promise when I left Badger to come. Got the final refuse of Sir G. Pigot's farm through him.

31st

Some rain. Milder. Samuel dines along with us and Mr. Green. Mr. G. Stays the night.

Feby. 1st

Very mild. Mr. Green, Father & myself start off for Badger this morning as soon as breakfast is over & get there to Tea having called at Burcott to dine.

2nd

Same weather. Breakfast at Badger. Mr. Green then accompanies us to look over the Farm of Sir Geo. Pigots called Burnill Green & Snowdon[143]. A most excellent farm altogether. Good land; all Tithe free except 40 acres, the farm being 440 acres. The Rent required by Sir G. was 2£ pr. acre. We

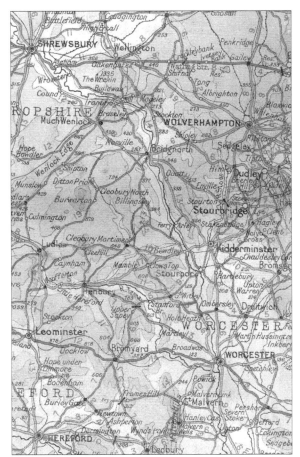

Map 12. Map showing parts of Shropshire, Worcestershire and Herefordshire, and some of the towns and larger villages referred to in the 1836/7 diary; it shows in particular the Grand Junction Railway, referred to in the entry for 25 May 1837.

give him a good bidding viz 800£ which he refuses after which we bid him good by and a better offer & return to Badger to Dinner and then return home.

Feby. 3rd
Rain A.M. Fair & mild afternoon. Samuel sends off his luggage to Worcester by Yapp's wagon. Mr. Partridge and his brother James Partridge (who with his wife is staying at the Lodge) accompanies him. They leave before Tea, a message having come from Lodge stating that a letter had been recd. from Devonshire bringing an account of the death of one of the family of Mrs. Partridge there.

4th Feby.
Very fine day. Go to Worcester on business for my Father & Wm. Buy a lot of hawthorn & ash quick &c. &c.

Feby. 5th

Little Rain, air cool. Mr. Rodmell the newly appointed curate of Burford, reads prayers the first time there. Mr. R. comes from Kinlet and has agreed to board along with one of us (which ever goes) at the Rectory House at Burford[144].

6th

Very mild & fine day. Take a ride to Suckly about 4 or 5 miles beyond Bromyard to look at a farm there now occupied by Mr. Lightband called upper Suckley Court, the proprietor being a Mrs. Collis of Stourbridge. The said farm was advertized in the Worcester papers of last week to be let & having enquired of Mr. France, the attorney at Worcester on Saturday last the particulars I agreed to look at it today; but the person who was to show it did not come. There is at present an execution in the house for half a years rent only, & which only became due on Candlemas day[145] – and the the tenant not under notice to quit so that the object appears to be only to get out of the tenant. The farm not suitable if to be had. Good deal of Hop land upon it, some orcharding, and good deal of ordinary Tillage – Rent 1£ an acre. Mr. James Partridge and Ellen from Lodge come to Park in afternoon and spend the evening. Mr. Lowe of Trysull & Edward Smith call coming from Ludlow fair and stay Tea. Father also at Ludlow.

Feby. 7th

Most delightful day – quite mild. William goes to attend the meeting of the guardians at Tenbury.

8th

Mild, some gentle rain. Walker & his hounds bring a fox which they had unbagged on old wood across the Kyrewood covers, through Teme & the Canal[146] by Boraston through ashbed and unto culvet on our bank below the hawthorns – dig him out and kill the gentleman before many yards. Samuel and his wife leave Burford for Mr. Pinhorns to start off by coach tomorrow morning for Devonshire. Goodbye.

Feby. 9th

Most beautiful day – very warm. By my Father's desire I am come to reside at Burford – again. Mr. Rodmell the new curate to have part of the House and we the other part. The agreement with Mr. R. being that he will pay 50£ a year for his board, including the house and premises which being 15£ brings it down to 35£. Mr. R. to find his own grocery, meat, wine, Linen, washing &c. His horse to be kept for 4/- pr. week the summer half

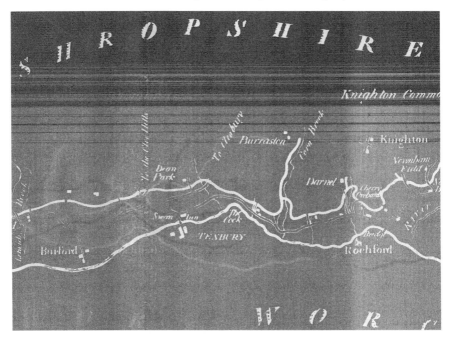

37. Extract from the 1791 plan of the proposed canal between Kington and the River Severn near Stourport.

year and 5/- pr. week the winter half year[147]. A maid servant here upon trial, Elizabeth Angel.

10th
Fair & mild A.M. Rain P.M. & wind. Father goes to Sivington[148] to value some poles for Mr. Jordan of Greet upon the farm he has taken there.

11
Great deal of rain A.M. Fair afternoon. Mr. Rodmell reaches here having been absent all the week in London.

Feby. 12th
Clear day, cool wind. Sunday. Father dines with me here after which Mr. Rodmell goes to do duty at Boraston for Mr. Stewart who lies ill in bed. Mr. R. returns and dines at 5.

13
Some rain. Mild. Go to Ludlow market & Father to Leominster fair which were both very flat concerns.

14th
Most delightful day – quite warm.

Feby. 15th
Sharp frost, fine & warm afterwards.

16
Very mild fine day. We this day celebrate the return of Mr. G. Rushout as member for Evesham[149] by giving an Ox & sheep away – the sheep roasted and the ox given away uncooked. Slaughtered and managed by Mr. Williams. First parade Tenbury, with the train then to Burford where we make the exhibition before the house. Drink the honourable members health and a dance takes place whilst the Ox is cut up and prepared for distribution in the barn. About 250 of the poor of Burford & Tenbury partook of the Beef & Bread the latter being in three penny loaves. Mr. Rose of the Harpfields gave an hogshead of old cider which was a very necessary addition to the entertainment and proved sufficient. Our worthy Landlord (Mr. Rushout) and two Miss Rushouts were present during the whole ceremony and were very much interested and pleased with the marks of respect shown to the young member. The "favours" were prepared by the Miss R.'s and directed to the different individuals who subscribed. Cider, Ale &c. was liberally served out to the bearers, musicians & at the different houses in Tenbury where the procession halted. At Burford House also the supply was liberal and we all drank the members health with a loud three times three to the end of it. When all was over Mr. Rushout entertained the Tenants and other more respectable part of the company with a hot lunch &c. Altogether the day went off very pleasantly and no accident happened.

Feby. 17
Most delightful day. Very mild. Father & I go to the dinner at the Crown[150], Tenbury to celebrate the return of Mr. Rushout Jnr. as member for Evesham. The number who dined 19 – including Mr. V. Wheeler, Mr. J. Nott of Hallow, Mr. Turner of Brockmanton and a few of Mr. Rushout's principal Tenants with Mr. Godson as president and Mr. Fuller as vice. The Dinner good but the wine terrible.

Feby. 18th
Wind and heavy rain in afternoon. Father goes to Worcester market to buy ash quick &c. About ¼ past 10 at night we discovered the Aurora Borealis in the form of a broad, red and fiery belt, which extended from east to west across the welkin[151], the moon shining brilliantly at the same time. This the most beautiful and striking appearance of the Aurora I ever

beheld. By 11 clock this awful meteorous phenomenon had disappeared. M. Libos attributes the aurora to the decomposition of the two airs which compose the atmosphere, oxygen and nitrogen, in the polar regions by an accumulation of the electric fluid there. This explanation is supported by a very accurate attention to the chemical phenomena produced in the atmosphere by electricity, which decomposes it and forms nitrous gas. At what time this meteor was first observed is not known; none are recorded in the English annals till the remarkable one which hapened on the 30 Jany. 1560[152]: another very brilliant one appeared in 1760.

Feby. 19th
Very rainy, unpleasant day. Sunday. Father dines with me at Burford & we both drink Tea at Park. Mr. E. Edwards also drops in after Tea – there.

Feby. 20th
Fine windy day. Father goes to Ludlow market. Mr. Rodmell dines with Mr. Rushout.

21st
Fine day with however some slight storms. Send a letter to Sir G. Pigott to ask him if he thinks my bidding for his farm now worth accepting. Mr. Edwards of Burford dines with me. Mr. Rodmell goes out again to dinner somewhere.

22
Very fine windy day.

Feby. 23
Good deal of rain A.M. Stormy P.M. accompanied with wind. Take Tea with Mr. & Mrs. D. Jones. Call at Mr. Trumpers to decline the invitation there tomorrow.

24
Storms of snow, hail &c. Cold wind. Father unwell with a cold. Rev. D. Jones and myself drink Tea with Mr. Hall at the Vicarage, Tenbury.

25th Feby.
Little snow & frost. Fair day. Get a letter from Sir George Pigott, stating that he had let his farm to a respectable tenant at the rate he offered it me, viz 40/- pr. acre. Good luck with it to him, say I. Call & drink tea with Mr. Edwards at Burford.

26th
Sharp frost – snow in evening. Sunday. Mr. Edwards dines with me. Brother William comes in in afternoon.

27 Feby.
Misty. Mild. Bottle off 19 Bottles of Perry from barrel in Pantry – made of Longhas[153] and very prime.

28th
Fair and pleasant day.

March 1st
Frost, cold. East wind. Mr. Williams calls to look at the cows and buys them. Mr. Trumper also calls having been along with William to wait on Mr. Rushout concerning the Title of the land at Tenbury given by Mr. R. to build the new workhouse upon. Mr. Rushout finally gives them the land and all the papers &c. belonging to it[154]. The sale as advertized of the lands, mill, House &c. at Boraston belonging to the Gills takes place at the Swan. Not one lot sold. The reserve bidding for Mill & land being 1650£ and for House and little land (about 2 acres, 1200£) very much above the value as were all the other lots besides. Ann Price comes here to be under Servant on trial.

March 2nd
Sharp frost, fine day but begins to rain a little at night. Begin gardening. Cowdell set some Peas, Beans, Potatoes, Cabbages, Lettuces & Radishes. Take a walk to Tenbury after tea for the new books & stay supper with Mr. Home.

3rd March
Small frost. Fair with rather cold wind. Mr. Rodmell returns the remainder of things come in a cart.

4
Dry & pleasant day. The Barrel of Ale and small Beer come from Park.

5th
Frost, cold day – rains a little at night. Stay at home and dine by myself. Call on Mr. Edwards in the afternoon. The spare money in subscription by buying the Ox, Sheep, Bread & given away on the occasion of Mr. G. Rushout's return for Evesham, given away at Burford Church. How much better this than spending the money (and a good deal more with it) in roasting the meat and spoiling the greater part of it.

March 6th
Very mild, fine day. Write to Mr. Green of Badger again in reply to his last favour to me. Wm. goes to Ludlow market. Maria from Park and Mary Partridge call and Tea with me.

7th
Small frost & fine & very mild day. Father calls here to Breakfast and goes on my Horse to Leominster fair. Tenbury fair also – I attend that and make a purchase of a barren cow – very small fair. Mr. Jones calls and drinks Tea with me – the Revd. I mean.

8th
Sharp frost, delightful day.

9th
Mild. Some rain.

March 10th
Mild & fine A.M. Some wind & Rain P.M. Call on Eliza at Tenbury this morning, who comes to drink Tea with me in the afternoon. Take her home and call at the Swan on return for the purpose of asking Mr. Grove if he had a room in the House he could spare for a reading room[155], myself and some others proposing to establish such a thing at Tenbury. Get permission for the new room in front – a very suitable one.

11th March
Little snow in the morning – fine & mild afterwards. Send a letter to Bewdley to get the rules and regulations of the reading room there.

12th
Some frost. Dry & fair, coldish wind. Sunday. Father stays Dinner with me. Mr. Rodmell goes to do duty at Boraston in the afternoon. Take a walk up to Nash & call at Lodge to Tea.

March 13th
Frost, cold wind. Go to Ludlow market. Dine at Feathers[156] & home to Tea. Mr. Edwards calls afterwards.

14th
Sharp frost, fair – cold wind. Go to Tenbury market. Call & Tea at Mr. H. Davis's, then to the Park and stay supper, where were Mr. Partridge, Wm. Low & Miss Lowe of Weston.

38. The Feathers, Bull
Ring, Ludlow, described
by *The New York Times*
as 'the most handsome
inn in the world'.

15
Same weather. Poor Old Frank Kinnersly buried at Burford. Meet with
Mr. Wm. Lowe of Weston at Tenbury, who tells me he lost 2 five pound
notes out of his pocket at Park last night: it appears he pulled them out
when taking some silver from the pocket. The girl (Susan Davis) finds the
money on floor this morning, pockets it, gives the one to the other girl.
Susan's mother swears to picking them up between Park & Tenbury!! Mr.
L. has the notes again. So much for dishonesty.

March 16th
Take a ride to Ludlow partly to attend the sale of furniture at Mr. Garrett's
but forgot to put the purse in my pocket and was obliged consequently to
return without making any purchases which perhaps was not unfortunate
as the articles were all sold high.

17th
Most delightful day, very warm P.M. Ann Price goes home ill & her Sister
Sally comes. Smith[157] very unwell.

18 March
Small frost, very cold east wind. Go to Worcester market along with Mr. Edwards, and take coach from Hundred House and back. Dine with Mr. Hall and the Spirit merchant.

19th
Same weather. Sunday. Father stays dinner with me. The spare money collected on the occasion of celebrating Mr. Rushout's return as M.P. for Evesham given away in Bread at Burford Church.

March 20th
Very sharp frost. Cold east wind, some little snow.

21
Very severe frost & extremely cold day, some snow. Go to Ludlow Fair, return to dinner.

22
Considerable quantity of snow fallen – very cold along with it.

23
Very heavy fall of snow – such that is seldom seen at this season of the year. Freezing sharp[158]. In the evening young Taylor is here in Smith's (the grooms) place – came yesterday.

24th March
Good Friday, and such an one that I never saw before. Snow nearly knee deep – and freezing very sharp at night. Mr. G Rushout Junr., the new member of Pl. for Evesham at Church having come over during the recess. Mr. Edwards and I take a ride to the Park in afternoon, I having suggested to Mr. Edwards the propriety of inviting Mr. Rushout to a public dinner being the first occasion of his coming home since his return took place. We confer with William & Father about it and agree to see Mr. Rushout himself about it in the morning. The housekeeper very ill.

March 25th
A most severe frost, perhaps more so than has occurred during the whole winter past. The annual parish meeting[159] takes place at Burford, Mr. Hearman appointed overseer & Mr. E. Edwards churchwarden. Mr. Grove & William agree to be elected guardians for Burford for the year ensuing. Mr. Edwards & William sound the young gent Mr. R. Junr. about giving

him a public dinner but he declines on account of being obliged to leave in a day or two. Aunt Partridge & Mrs. James Partridge come here for a short stay – fetch them in the carriage.

March 26th
Sharp frost. Some snow and sun. We all go to church & Father, Maria & Mrs. Partridge stay sacrament. Mrs. Trumper also here. Mr. Partridge comes to dinner here along with Mrs. P. and Mrs. James P. First day we have service in the afternoon. Mr. Rodmell does the whole duty morning & afternoon, Mr. Rushout being absent from church.

27 March
Sharp frost, fine day – begins to snow at night. Mrs. Trumper calls. Mr. & Mrs. Jones and William drink Tea and spend the evening with us. Mr. Edwards calls after Tea.

March 28th
Snow, rain and very unpleasant day. Mr. Revis comes from Ludlow to make a proposal for establishing a news-room at Tenbury that is supplying us with papers. Says he can let us have two London Daily and six provincial papers for 20 guineas. That is 20 subscribers at £1.1s.- each supposing the rent of the room be no more than 8£[160]. We drink tea with the Jones's, our neighbours.

March 29
Slight storms A.M. Fine & bright P.M. Two Mrs. Partridges & myself drink Tea with Mr. & Mrs. E. Edwards.

30th
Sharp frost and very fine bright day. Go to Deep Croft[161] to weigh a load of Hay and back to Breakfast. Aunt Maria, Ellen Partridge & William come here to Tea.

March 31st
Sharp frost & fine warm day afterwards. Father goes to attend the funeral of Mr. Salwey of the Lodge, his Landlord. Young Revis calls here and takes Tea. Afterwards I call on Mr. Hall to talk with him about the projected reading room. Stay Supper with him.

April 1st
Same weather. Mr. Revis calls here about news-room. Nothing done.

April 2nd
Sharp frost and cold wind in afternoon. Sunday. Aunt Maria & Father stay dinner with the two Mrs. Partridges and myself. Mr. Edwards also comes in to Tea.

3rd April
Some snow, very cold wind.

4th
Sharp frost, cold east wind. Spend greater part of Day at Tenbury trying to start the news room. Mrs. Grove asks 25£ for the room including fire & candle! Which of course wouldn't do. Meet tomorrow if we can[162]. Mrs. James Partridge leaves along with Mary P. who comes down in the morning. Mr. Rodmell goes to Mr. Moore's, Corely to Dine and stay all night.

April 5th
Sharp frost and very cutting wind. Mr. Trumper calls here on his way from Burford House.

April 6th
Sharp frost and very cold wind accompanied with storms of hail & snow. Aunt Partridge and I drink tea with Mr. & Mrs. Jones.

April 7th
Sharp frost again, indeed very severe – little rain at night. Mr. & Mrs. Trumper to Tea. Also Miss Reynolds and Ellen Partridge. Mr. & Mrs. E. Edwards drop in after and stay supper. Ellen stays all night along with her mother.

8th April
Frost, storms of snow in afternoon. Take Aunt Partridge back home again in the carriage and Ellen along with her. Stay Tea.

9
Severe frost again, very cold east wind accompanied with storms of snow, hail &c. Sunday. Dine & spend the evening alone: go to church twice like a good boy.

10th
Very severe frost and cold east wind. Father goes to Ludlow market and calls here on his return.

11ᵗʰ
Same weather accompanied with snow at night.

12
Heavy fall of snow in the night and continued at intervals during the day with a very cold east wind. Father attends a meeting of the commissioners at Swan. Revd. D. Jones takes his son Saml. off to London (Chts. Hospital[163]) to school.

13ᵗʰ
Slight fall of snow & very cold wind. A meeting of the road commissioners at Swan to appoint another Clerk and other business.

14
Very small frost, fair & considerably warmer. Go for a ride to Orleton in the afternoon and take Tea with Mr. Davis.

15
Another sharp frost. Some Rain & sleet in afternoon.

16ᵗʰ
Sharp frost with very cold wind and little snow in afternoon. Sunday. Dine at Park. Aunt Partridge and Mrs. James Partridge staying there. Mary P. also comes dinner.

17ᵗʰ
Severe frost. Fine day, some sun. Go to Ludlow market. Sell William's clover seed and hire a cook &c. (Mrs. Griffiths) at 8£/10s.- a year who was with us before. Call on Mr. Mason, Blethewood[164].

18
Very severe frost. Fair & very warm afterwards. Mr. Partridge dines with me on his way from Mr. Rushout.

19
Sharp frost. Very warm in middle of Day. Get a letter from Mr. Lavender about the Bury Hall Farm he having it now to let[165].

20ᵗʰ
Some rain, sleet &c. Mr. H. Davis of Orleton comes to take a valuation of the stock, crop, implements &c. upon Burford & Nash between Father & myself including Furniture. Every thing valued to me excepting two lots

of wheat the one at Nash the other in Burford Granery, and two Beds, bedsteads &c. viz the Bed and all belonging to it in White room without a counterpaine, the bed in my room and the steads &c. in Study room[166].

April 21st
Storms of rain, hail &c. nearly all day – mild. Father goes to Cleobury Fair. I dine at Lodge and Tea at Park on way home from Nash. Get a letter from Mr. John Green, giving a description of Sir G. Pigot as a landlord, he having been liberal enough to take all the chairs away from the incoming Tenant at Burnhill Green, Mr. Cleveley.

22nd April
Little rain, mild. Go to Orleton fair & home to dinner without doing any thing. Walk to Park after Tea and meet with Mr. Robinson from Mr. Trumper's there. First time I have met with him.

23
Good deal of rain. Sunday. Tea at Park, Father having dined with me at Burford.

April 24th
Rain, mild. Go to Bewdley fair. Buy a lot of Barren Cows and Bullock. Dine at George with Mr. Trumper and return with him in his gig, his servant, Gent riding my horse. William goes to Orleton fair but buys nothing.

25
Frost, fair A.M. Rain P.M. Father & William go to measure timber at aston bank.

26th April
Fair & warm.

27
Mild, storms of rain. Mr. Jones comes in to Tea. Father also stays Tea.

28th
Mild, slight rain A.M. Go in afternoon and look at the furniture in the late Mr. Robinson's[167] house which is now to be sold. Tea at Revd. Mr. Jones. Meet with Mr. Lewis the preacher from Tenbury there.

April 29th
Rain A.M. Fair & Mild P.M.

30th
Same weather with however a brisk wind P.M. Sunday.

May 1st
Mild, some small storms of rain. Go to Ludlow fair. Dine with Mr. Tinson
& home to Tea. Part with the lad and girl, Taylor & Price, and hire another
lad at Ludlow, James Russell – for £2.12s.

2 May
Fine & very warm day. Attend a sale of furniture at the late Mr.
Robinson's Tenbury. Buy a dining table for £3.15s.0d and other small
articles. Things sold rather high in general although mine is considered
a cheap purchase. Susan Davis here to be waiting, parlour & chamber
maid at 5£ the year.

3rd May
Sharp frost, warm. Some rain. Go to Bromyard Fair and come home
without doing any business for a certain reason which I will not record
here[168]. Attend the second days sale of furniture at Mr. Robinson's which
sold in general very dear. The lad comes whom I hired on Monday last as
groom – James Russell. Mrs. Griffiths, housekeeper, comes.

May 4th
Mild. Rain in afternoon. Go to the sale again and purchase several small
articles. Home to Tea.

5th
Small frost. Slight shower P.M. Mild. Go to Bleathwood to weigh the lot
of Hops. Mr. Edwards calls after Tea & stays supper.

May 6th
Sharp frost, warm and fine afterwards.

7th
Cooler, rain. Sunday. Charity sermon preached at Tenbury church by
Revd. J. Pearson and subscription at Door. No service at Burford A.M. On
that acc't. go to hear it. An excellent discourse. Mrs. & the Miss Pearsons
there. They all appear at Burford in afternoon.

8th May
Mild, good deal of rain. Go to Nacker Hole[169] to a sale of timber &c.
advertized but come away without purchasing being nothing worth

staying for. Mr. Rodmell goes to dine and stay the night with Mr. Holland of Stoke Bliss.

9
Cool east wind. Slight storms. Mr. Rodmell returns.

10th May
Very severe frost. Cold E. Wind. Go to a Tea Party at Lodge. Leave there before Supper along with Eliza & Mr. Trumper. Call on Mr. Hall in the afternoon.

11th
Small frost. Milder, fine day. Old Mr. Giles[170] drops in in afternoon, Father also having come along with Starmisher the cutler.

12 May
Some more rain, mild. William goes to Ledbury Fair to buy working oxon.

13th
Same weather.

14
Wind in the east, some heavy rain. Sunday. Father dines with me and stays afternoon service & Tea.

15th
Mild fine day. Mr. Edwards calls on me to lunch. We then ride up to Nash – he goes to Court of Hill and back to Lodge. I call there also after going to Hopton[171] to see Hatton about making a new broad wheeled waggon. We go to Morgans of Nash to see a two years old colt which I buy of him at 12£ warranted sound and got by Tuton – back to Lodge to Tea and call at Park on our way home.

May 16th
Small frost, very warm fine day. Being Wit Tuesday the Club have their annual feast[172] at Rose & Crown, having first attended divine service at the church.

17
Frost, very warm and fair. All go to Ludlow fair which was but a small one for cattle. Call on Mr. Hotchkiss – lunch with him.

39. The Rose & Crown, Burford.

May 18th
Little rain A.M. Fair P.M. with cool wind.

19
Very cold wind. Go to Hereford Fair and return to Tea. Find Mr. Rodmell with his poney unwell – something of the colic, bleed him, throw up a clyster[173] &c.

20
Same weather. Maria & Ellen Partridge Tea here. Mr. Rose comes in afterwards.

21st May
Little rain, cold wind. Sunday. At Park to Tea and call at Trumper's in returning home.

22nd
Fair, cold wind. Aunt Maria and I start about ½ past eleven A.M. in Samuel's carriage and get to Burcott to Tea after which I borrow Mr. Reynolds's saddle and bridle and ride to Trysull[174]. Mr. Lowe gone to Cleobury fair, does not come home. His eldest sister Miss Lowe there keeping house for him. Stay all night at Trysull.

May 23
Fair & warm. After breakfast start off from Trysull to Albrighton Fair.
Go through Pattingham by Wrottesley. Meet with Mr. T. Lowe & Uncle
Peter Reynolds at the fair. Stay a short time and then go for Badger where
I arrive before dinner. Dine, spend the afternoon with Mr. Green who by
the by lately met with a misfortune, his horse having fallen with him in
going home from Bridgnorth Fair on the 1st inst. – put his shoulder out
and otherwise hurt him – now however doing well. After Tea go from
Badger to Burcott and stay the night there.

May 24th
Fair, warm A.M. Cool P.M. Aunt & I start from Burcott and get to Shiffnall
to Lunch (at Mr. Reynolds's)[175]. Stay dinner there. We then proceed on to
Teddesley going a cross-country road through Penkridge. Find Mr. Bright
at home suffering from an head ache. Mrs. B. gone out but returns at
night. Her sister Miss Reynolds from Shiffnall[176] staying there. This estate
of Lord Hatherton's (Teddesley) is a rather extensive concern. A large tract
of land by the house is held in their own hands, under the management
of Mr. Bright who appears to understand the business of farming both
scientifically and practically and applies his knowledge. His farming is
excellent. A Stock of 30 short horn cows kept of the purest blood. They
are both large & handsome.

May 25th
Cold wind: some little rain. Take a ride out with Mr. Bright round the
Teddesley estate and Park. Call at Penkridge and go as far as the railway
to speak to the engineer. This railway from Wolverhampton to Liverpool[177]
is nearly completed. Proceed on to the farm they (the proprietors) occupy
and then to Teddesley to Dinner. A Mr. Stubbs and his sister, new Tenant
to Lord H. come to Tea, after which we all go to Teddesley hall to view
the house, pleasure grounds &c. The house[178] built of brick about 60 or
70 years back and painted stone culour – very substantial – pleasantly
situated having a commanding view of the whole country round for many
miles. The pleasure grounds are extensive and well laid out.

26 May
Cool wind early, afterwards warm with a little drizzling rain at night.
Rise at ½ past 5, have a look round the cattle yards, stables &c. The 30
beautiful short horn cows tied up, milked, the calves being taken all by
hand and fed first with their mother's milk – then gradually weaned till
wey and meal only is allowed till grass. The greatest order prevails in
regard to every thing and every operation upon the farm. Go with Mr.

Bright to take the level for a drain to bring the water from one quarter to bring the water from the Reservoir which is intended to supply the wheel for driving the threshing machine, the water being nearly all collected from such drains for the purpose. The wheel 9 feet in circumference is being made at Teddesley, wood and iron used in it. The tunnel for taking the water from the wheel is now being made and is upwards of 20 feet below the surface. It will convey the water to the meadows below which are intended to be floated with it. The cost of the Tunnel and wheel Mr. B. says will be 500£. Take breakfast and then go for a ride with Mr. Taylor, one of the office clerks, to Mr. Stubbs's – lunch there and back to dinner, after which the ladies go to Ridgley[179] in the carriage and Mr. Bright and myself take a walk over a part of the estate I had not visited before. A high hill called Cannock Chase[180] forms the boundary of the property on the east side. From here we have an extensive view of the country for many miles. Return to Tea.

27th
Dry and pleasant day – not too warm. After breakfasting and buying a mare of Mr. Bright (of the right stamp) we start for home. Bait at Wolverhampton, and get to Kidderminster to dinner. Home between seven & eight. The journey has afforded me a great deal of pleasure and instruction. The superior manner in which the farming and whole concern at Teddesley is carried on is well worth the notice of any one, more particularly of those who like good farming. The estate is upwards of 12000 acres, the Park alone more than 1200, & the latter with seven or eight hundred acres more is all under the management of Mr. Bright.

May 28
Fair, mild day some nice rain at night. Sunday. Mr. Mytton of Deptcroft comes to the Park to pay his rent – go there to Tea. Robinson, Mr. Trumper's clerk there also.

29th
Mild. Storms of rain. Father goes to Ludlow market. Call on uncle Reynolds and bespeak some swede seed of him.

30th
Some slight storms of rain – wind. Go to Park in afternoon to get the flock of Sheep washed, stay Tea.

May 31st
Fair – wind. William commences his sheep-shearing at Park.

June 1ˢᵗ

Slight storm early – fair afterwards. Go to Kidderminster Market, partly on purpose to meet a mare from Teddesley which I purchased of Mr. Bright, but she was not sent on acct. of some slight distemper which she had taken. Mr. B.'s young man (Mr. Taylor) meets me at Kidderminster.

2ⁿᵈ

Beautiful day, milder. Mr. Rodmell goes to Worcester.

3 June

Little rain A.M. – mild.

4ᵗʰ

Beautiful day, mild. Rain at night. Mr. Trumper's clerk (Mr. Robinson) calls on me and goes to church. Stays dinner along with Father and Aunt Maria from Park. Mr. R. stays Tea and supper. We go to see Mr. E. Edwards.

5ᵗʰ

Delightful day, very warm. A busy day, drilling[181] swedes.

June 6ᵗʰ

Fair, very warm P.M.

June 7ᵗʰ

Same weather. Sheep shearing day here. Mr. B. Edwards, Mr. Partridge, Mr. Jones, Bank, and William come to assist. Stintons never came. Mr. E. Edwards comes in at Suppertime. Mr. Rodmell has his grass seed sown in garden.

8ᵗʰ

Cool wind, sun. Go to Nash and call at Lodge, Mr. Partridge being shearing his sheep, stay and assist. Mr. Edwards and Two Mr. Lowe's there[182].

June 9ᵗʰ

Mild. Good deal of rain in the afternoon. Mr. B. Edwards, Mr. Wm. Lowe and Mr. Jones, Bank with myself make a finish of the sheep-shearing having shorn the lambs today, 41 in number. Father also drops in: with the company of Mr. Wall the rat-catcher we were also favoured who caught <u>five</u> only. Leaves me one of his Terriers, "<u>Busy</u>". All go before supper.

Jun 10
Continual storms of rain.

11
Slight storms, quite mild. Sunday. Go to Nash Chapel to hear a missionary sermon preached by Rev. Davis of Worcester. Text from 5th of 2nd Cor. 14th verse[183]. Good discourse and well delivered. Dine with Uncle & Aunt Reynolds. Then to Boraston chapel where we hear another sermon by the same man not so good as the morning one but very tolerable. Collection at Nash £4.12s.6d. Do. Boraston £2.7s.7d. Mr. Stewart (who still remains in the North of England very ill) sent 1£ to each place. Tea at Boraston with Mr. Mytton. Call at Sayers and home.

12th
Stormy. Mild. Sup at Trumpers.

13
Same weather. Dine at Park. J. Nott there. Miss Burton & Ellen Partridge also.

Jun 14th
Most delightful day, very mild. Sadlers come to do the old Geering up. Mr. Wade & two men. Mr. & Mrs. Trumper call. Mr. M. Trumper comes to shoot rabbits – kills two couples. Stays supper. Mr. Rodmell comes home having been away since yesterday morning.

15th
Same weather. After coming from Nash, go to help William and his company (Edwards, Jones & James Lowe[184]) to shear the Lambs at Park – 115 of them. Finished before 5 clock. Merrick comes to cut and nail the garden trees.

16th
Very warm, fair A.M. Tremendous thunder storm in afternoon. Dine at Lodge. Send Curran with the cloak & bonnet on mounted on the mare (just broke in) to Boreston to take the whip home and exhibit himself in female attire[185]. Mr. Rodmell has a friend to see him and stay.

June 17
Showers of rain. A.M. fair. P.M. mild. Mr. Edwards sends down for me to go to help to shear his sheep which I accordingly do. Mr. Rodmell & his brother[186] borrow the carriage to go to Ludlow but the poney wouldn't go.

18th June
Little rain early, delightful day. Sunday. Mr. & Mrs. Reynolds, Mrs. Smith, Miss Sayer & the people from Park come to church and stay dinner with me. Mrs. Edwards comes to Tea.

19th
Fair & warm. Father goes to Ludlow market[187]. Having occasion to go to Tenbury, I call on Mr. Hall to borrow his Tithe commutation act[188] which he lends me with another book on the revenues of the Church. Two more of his Nieces (Wilkinsons) from the North over at Tenbury – younger ones.

June 20
Beautiful day: fair and warm. William brot. me the mare down which I bot. of Mr. Bright of Teddesley and which came to Park last night.

21st
Mild. Showers. When at Nash take a ride as far as Hopton to visit Mr. Hatton who is about making a new broad-wheeled waggon for me, but has not yet begun it. Mr. Parker the coachman late Master of the Worcestershire Foxhounds along with another call on me to look at a horse and mare which I have to sell but buy neither. Father comes down and stays Tea.

June 22nd
Frost[189]. Very warm fine day. Go to Brampton Brian Fair. Take the grey horse and sell him for 24£ to Mr. Pye. Flat fair generally. Return with Mr. Edwards in his gig to Tea. Find Father at Burford very unwell. News comes of the King's (Wm. IV) death which took place at Windsor on Tuesday the 20th inst. The princess Victoria of course proclaimed[190].

23
Exceedingly fair and warm day. Father taken violently ill in the afternoon. Fell down in a fainting state, afterwards vomited a large quantity of blood. The surgeon Mr. Davis sent for and about ½ past 8 I start off to Ludlow for Dr. Lloyd who comes and prescribes for him. Mr. & Mrs. Trumper come to see him and Mrs. Trumper remains with him.

June 24th
Very fine warm day. Father passed a pretty good night and was a little better this morning. Go to Deptcroft about the timber. Call on Courtney

for his rent then to the Nash and home to Dinner. Mr. Giles, Mr. Partridge, Mr. Trumper, Mr. & Mrs. D. Jones and Mr. H. Davis the surgeon all call during the afternoon to see my Father. Mrs. Trumper goes home to night.

June 25th
Delightful day. Sunday. Father had a bad night. Better afterwards. Mr. Davis writes for Doctor Lloyd again but he couldn't come <u>today</u>. Mrs. Trumper comes and stays all day. William comes in the afternoon and we all receive the sacrament together from Mr. Rodmell. Wm. stays Tea. Mr. Trumper comes to fetch Mrs. T. home.

26th
Fair & warm. Go to Ludlow market. Sell some wheat for Father to Mr. Jones. Mr. B. Edwards calls in afternoon and stays supper.

27th
Very hot. The Queen Victoria proclaimed at Tenbury by Mr. H. Davis of Orleton – high constable.

28th
Still hotter. Two or three of the parishoners of the Nash Township meet to agree about mending the by roads – nothing agreed upon. Return to Dinner. Mr. & Mrs. Partridge, Mr. C. Williams & Mr. Trumper call to see Father – Mrs. T. goes home – continues very ill.

June 29th
Excessively hot. Father's illness less severe. The Doctor only calls once. Mr. Reynolds & Mr. B. Giles call – as well as Mr. & Mrs. Jones. Call at Lodge. Cousin Emma[191] from Pershore over & a Miss Lunn.

30th June
Fair & warm but not so hot as yesterday. Attend a meeting to appoint a road surveyor for Nash Township. Mr. Pugh chosen and appointed, Myself refused it. Mr. & Mrs. Trumper & young Parson Jones to Tea. Father better.

July 1st
Same weather. William & I attend Mr. Rushout's rent audit.

July 2nd
Most delightful day. Sunday. Father comes down stairs for the first time

since Friday week, the day he was taken so violently ill – his complaint arising from a bad state of the stomach and vomiting blood therefrom.

3rd
Fair & very warm. Go to Ludlow Market and pay Rent for Court of Hill ground for my Father to Mr. Dansey. Dine at Angel[192] with the other Tenants, Mr. Dansey presiding. Canvassing going forward at Ludlow for M.P.'s. No less than four candidates in the field viz the two sitting members (Lord Clive and Charlton) Mr. Salwey (brother to our Landlord) and a Mr. Alcock[193].

4th
Same weather. Go to Nash to get in a rick – back to Dinner. Mr. F. Davis to Tea. Mr. Jordan also calls.

July 5th
Slight, but very slight storms of rain, very warm. Send down to Mr. Trumper the Rosewood Chiffoneer and he sends back the bookcase and a card Table (bot. at Robinsons sale) by way of exchange.

6th
Fair and very hot in the afternoon. Go to Deptcroft to see about the building for Father who had projected to go along in the carriage but found himself unable to do so.

7th July
Fair and exceedingly hot day. Ellen Partridge brings Emma Reynolds and Miss Lunn here to Tea. Eliza drops in after, also Mr. Wm. Jones to tea. Miss R. looses her Frill going home.

July 8th
Fair and <u>very hot day</u>. Haymaking going on at a rapid pace. Call at Lodge and lunch.

9th
Fair & most delightful day. Sunday. The Lodge people Misses Reynolds, Lunn & Partridge come to Burford Church and go to Park to Dinner. Maria from Park taken ill in Church and obliged to leave. Call at Park in afternoon and stay Tea with them.

10th July
Fair, very hot day.

11th
Same weather. Haymaking day. Go to Tenbury after Tea. The Harp
Meadow knocked down at 620£ to Mr. Godson. Terrills not sold.

July 12th
Fair and very hot day.

13
Little rain in the night. Fair & hot day. Father worse again. Mrs. Trumper
been here twice. Mr. T. once. Miss Reynolds and Miss Lunn in the
forenoon.

14
Slight showers, very warm. My Father had a very bad night and is much
worse again, a considerable quantity more blood passed both ways. Mr. M.
Trumper goes for Dr. Lloyd again. Meet Mr. Hope Junr. at Swan in forenoon
to pay the Nash Rent. Meet him again in the afternoon at Greete – he rides
along with me to Nash on my Mare to look at the repairs &c. wanting to
be done, back again to Greete and home with him. Agree with Mr. H. to do
what was absolutely necessary & to get an estimate of the rest. Mr. Rodmell
has another nag horse brot. for him from his brothers in Yorkshire.

July 15th
Warm. Tempest – severe storms, hail in some places. Dr. Lloyd comes again
to see my Father – gets no better. Aunt Partridge comes down and stays the
whole day & night.

July 16th
Fair, cool breeze of wind. Sunday. Mr. Trumper, Mrs. Partridge and Wm.
dine with us. Aunt & Uncle Reynolds come in afternoon. Father a little
easier.

July 17, 1837
Stormy, mild. Dr. Hastings sent for from Worcester to attend my Father.
Comes at 6 clock this afternoon. Dr. Lloyd and Mr. Davis meet him. Mr.
Hastings gives a somewhat different acct. of the complaint than the others.
Mr. Reynolds of Nash also consults about his legs.

July 18th
Slight storms. Mild. Father still continues in the same state – nearly as ill
as possible and be alive.

19

Mild fine day. Had a full day's hay making (at Nash). Father's illness still no better – been [*word illegible*][194] twice today.

20th

Mild with slight storms. Tenbury Races take place but none of us attend.

July 21st

Very fine and pretty warm. Hay making at Nash. Father they say is worse this afternoon; gets weaker.

July 22nd

Very warm. Storm in the evening. Go to Worcester market and return with Mr. Edwards. The City candidates nominated at Worcester viz Bailey[195], Davies[196] & Robinson[197]. Robinson gives up the contest and the other two were of course elected.

23rd

Mild. Little rain in evening. Sunday. Mr. & Mrs. Trumper come to dinner and Willm. Mr. Partridge calls in afternoon.

24th July

Hot. Hard storm at Dinner Time, wh. did the hay (out) no good! Aunt Partridge comes to Burford again to be along with my Father who is since Saturday better.

July 25th 1837

Very warm. Storms of rain. Father getting better somewhat rapidly.

26th

Warm. Stormy. Nomination day at Ludlow. News comes of the return of Mr. Godson[198] for Kidderminster and Mr. Borthwick[199] and Mr. Rushout Junr. for Evesham all conservatives – so far so good.

27th July

Very warm and fine day. Had another full days Hay and Clover carrying at Nash. Mr. Lowe of Milson, Mr. E. Edwards, Miss E. Partridge and Mr. Trumper have been callers here. The latter has been at Ludlow these two Days at the election. They have he says returned Lord Clive & Mr. Salwey (our Landlord's brother)[200].

July 28th

Fair clear & warm day. Mr. Rushout Junr. leaves Burford again having come yesterday from Evesham after being returned their member. Miss Sayer takes Tea here. Mrs. Trumper and the latter go to Tenbury together.

29

Great deal of rain comes in storms. High wind. Write again to Saml. in reply to his to Father[201].

30th

Fair & warm. Sunday. Aunt Partridge & Maria dine at Burford. I at Tenbury with Mr. & Mrs. Trumper, Miss Sayer and Matthias. Aunt Partridge goes home after Tea.

31

Stormy. Mr. Rodmell has the Masons, carpenters &c. here – [*word illegible*] Stable & making a window.

Aug. 1st

Warm fine day.

2nd

Very hard rain early in the morning and continued hard storms the whole of the day. Eliza and uncle Reynolds call to see Father. Take Tea with Mr. Edwards along with Mr. Shenton, Mr. Lowe and Mr. Benbow.

3

Stormy. Warm. Matthias Trumper and I go to Orleton to take a Glimps of the farm now occupied by Mrs. Green in the event of its being let again. Mr. Partridge comes to see Father and stays Tea. Mr. Rushout also comes to see him. Mr. & Mrs. Trumper call at night.

4th

Fine clear day, slight shower A.M. Call at Court of Hill to see Mr. Baker about repairing the road there.

5th Aug.

Fine day. Go the Clifton way to Worcester. Call at Wichenford to look at a small Estate "the Hucks" belonging to Mr. Collis. A compact thing according to the size 133 acres, but being too small and the rent too high and having no time given to consider the matter I return without taking

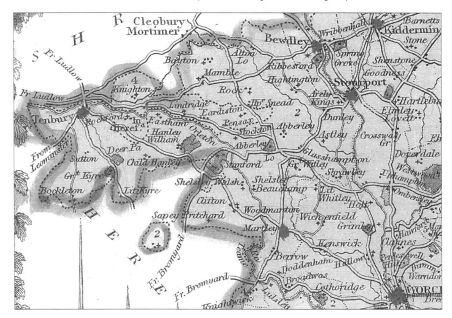

Map 13. Extract from the 1837 map of Worcestershire by Thomas Moule.

it[202]. Dine at the Bell[203] along with Mr. & Mrs. Trumper, Brother Willm. and Wm. Mytton of Lindridge.

Aug. 6th
Clear dry – cold wind at night. Sunday. Mr. Baker preaches his farewell sermon at Nash, being about to remove to Devonshire where he has a living given to him nr. Barnstaple.

7th
Beautiful day – very warm, cold night.

8
Same weather. H. Davis, of Orleton, J. Nott, Eastham and brother Wm. here to Tea. Mrs. Trumper dines with us.

Aug. 9th
Fair & warm, some wind also. H. Davis of Orleton comes to value the wheat crop at Nash[204]. A Dinner at the Swan to Captn. Winnington on his return for West Worcestershire[205]. Don't go. Get a meeting at Nash to agree concerning the road rate.

40. The former Swan Hotel, Burford.

10th Aug.
Exceedingly hot day. Go to Kidderminster market. Return with uncle Reynolds. Tea at Milson. Exceedingly flat market – could do nothing.

11
Dull morning – little rain, warm. Aunt Partridge leaves us again on account of Maria & Ellen going to New house tomorrow.

Aug. 12th
Very warm, slight storms. Visit Hatton at Hopton who is making a waggon for me.

13
Same weather. Sunday. Mr. H. Davis dines with me. Mr. & Mrs. Trumper to Tea.

14
Fair & very warm. Go to Nash and stay all day. Breakfast at Lodge. Send a sample of wheat by Mr. Reynolds to Ludlow market but sells none.

Aug. 15th
Very fine warm day. Aunt Partridge comes back to us. Mr. Jordan dines here.

16
Same weather.

Aug. 17th
Very warm, slight storm of rain. B. Edwards dines here. Old Trumper[206] & Eliza from Tenbury come to see Father and stay Tea. Mr. Hotchkiss also calls to see him.

18th Aug.
Very warm fine day. Mr. Partridge and Maria from Park to Tea. Mrs. Edwards, Burford calls to see my Father who is today a little worse.

19th Aug.
Same weather. Mr. E. Good calls here along with Mr. Trumper and brother Willm. this morning. Sup at Mr. Trumpers – Matthias & Mr. T. Senr., come home top heavy rather.

20th
Same weather. Sunday. Aunt Partridge and I dine by ourselves. Ellen Partridge and Maria form Park come to Tea.

Aug. 21
Stormy, warm. Go to Ludlow. Take a hackney mare (Miss Downes) to sell, but could not get quite enough. 13£ the most that was bid. Mr. Rodmell has party to breakfast with him and go to see the Clee hill.

22nd
Mild. Good deal of rain, most in afternoon. Mr. G. Adams comes to look at Mr. Rodmell's poney to buy him but Mr. R. was gone out to dinner. Write a letter to Samuel acquainting him of the dangerous state my Father lies in at present.

23rd
Mild – great deal more rain. Go to Cleobury Market in the afternoon. Could do no business. Call at Milson on my return home.

24
Cold east wind – rain in morning, warm and fair afterwards. Write to Mr. G. Adams concerning Mr. Rodmell's horse. Also write to Mr. H. Davis of Orleton on some private business. Mr. & Mrs. Trumper call after Tea to see my Father who lies now in a very precarious state.

Aug. 25th
Fair & fine day. Begin harvesting the grain at Nash. Excise-man calls to take the hop entry.

Aug. 26
Dreadful tempest and severe storms in the forenoon. My father getting worse very fast – no hopes left. Mrs. Trumper comes to stay the night. Mr. Partridge to Tea.

27th
Fair and fine day. Sunday. Mrs. Trumper stays the night. Ellen Partridge and Miss Elizabeth Partridge come here to Tea.

28th Aug.
Exceedingly fine and warm day. Go to Nash harvesting grain and stay the whole day. Get a letter from Saml. respecting my poor Father and his illness. Expects to arrive at Burford tomorrow.

29
Storms of rain all day – very hard rain at night.

30
Warm clear day. This morning about ¼ to 5 o'clock my poor dear Father departed this life without a struggle having bourn a lingering illness of nearly 3 months. In the 69th year of his age. May the Lord have mercy upon the soul of my best friend upon earth. All the family present besides Samuel who arrived at Park by this day's Mail. Aunt Partridge goes home to return tomorrow. Mr. Trumper comes to Tea and takes Eliza home with him.

31st
Slight frost – slight storms of rain with a heavy onset at night. Uncle Reynolds and I take a walk through the court of hill Lawn[207] – see Mr. Baker and take it of him till Lady Day next at 25/- an acre 16 acres.

1st Sepr.
Continual storms of rain – one of hail (partial). Saml. & Mr. Trumper call here this forenoon and make some more arrangements respecting the funeral.

Sepr. 2nd
Slight storms A.M. Fine afternoon. The funeral day of my poor dear Father. The chief mourners, my brothers William & Saml., Mrs. Trumper

41. Court of Hill, from 'the Lawn'.

and myself. The Pall bearers, eight in number, viz Mr. Wm. Reynolds, Mr. Partridge, Mr. B. Edwards, Mr. E. Edwards, Mr. B. Giles, Mr. C. Williams, Mr. J. Nott of Eastham & Mr. Wm. Mytton of Deepcroft. The under bearers 6 of the workmen viz Thos. Phillips, James Porton, John Davis, John Jones, Wm. Bayliss & Thos. Peade. Mr. Rushout & Mr. Rodmell, the clergymen – the former performed the burial service. Also present Mr. H. Davis, the surgeon, & Mr. Anderson the Attorney who prepared the will, Morgan the coffin Maker, Mills the Tomb builder. The pall bearers wore hatbands and scarfs, the workmen hatbands and gloves with 5/ each in money. All the rest of workmen at Park, Nash and Burford who were not bearers, Gloves and 5/ each in money. Mr. Russell the Undertaker. On returning home Mr. Anderson read the will. Only Saml. & Aunt Partridge stay dinner with me. The Executors – my two brothers and myself. The trustee for my Sister Mr. Wm. Reynolds. All passes off in the quietest and pleasantest manner possible – and may the Lord have mercy on the soul of the departed. A better Father, a better husband or a more upright and honest man never was in existence.

Sepr. 3rd
Fair & warm A.M. Rain in the afternoon. Sunday. None belonging to us except Samuel go to church, he twice. Samuel and aunt Partridge stay

42. The tomb of Elizabeth, Caroline and Samuel Davis, in St Mary's churchyard, Burford, placed as near as was possible to the south wall of the church's chancel and with the simplest of inscriptions.

dinner, the former leaves for home before Tea. The latter stays till after. Both Mr. Rushout & Mr. Rodmell in their sermons alluded to the late melancholy event wh. has lately befallen us.

Sepr. 4th
Fine warm day. William goes to Ludlow market. Sells a load of wheat for me, some for himself. Takes a draft of agreement for Saml. to Mr. Anderson to prepare between Mr. Mytton of Deptcroft and himself for renting that Estate, the draft furnished by me. Samuel dines with me after calling at Burford House. First day of Hoppicking with us.

5th
Same weather. Mr. Trumper sends me a Brace of Birds. The first I had ever presented to me.

6th
Same weather. Mr. Rodney Anderson comes to Burford to prove the will which was done by commission. Mr. D. Jones[208] the acting commissioner. Personal effects that remain sworn under 2000£. Mr. A. stays and dines accompanied by his sister who also stays dinner. Saml. with them.

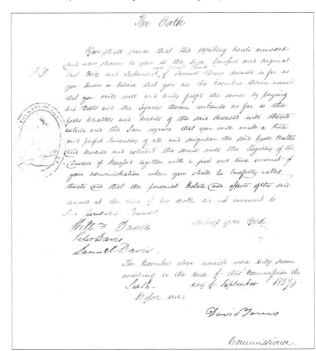

43. Oath of the executors of the will of Samuel Davis senior, administered by the Revd David Jones of Burford.

7th Sepr.

Warm, little rain at Night. Samuel comes to stay the night and brings his horse and carriage.

8th

Very warm, fine day. Samuel starts off from here with his carriage and horse for Dawlish, proposing to get as far as Monmouth[209] tonight.

9

Warm, fair A.M. Some rain in the evening. I acknowledge by my signature at Mr. Collins's the registrars the death of my poor Father.

10th Sepr.

Fair and rather mild. Sunday. Aunt and Uncle Partridge come to go to church with Willm., Eliza & I. All stay dinner & all go to Park to Tea except Eliza who returns home.

11th

High wind in the morning and great quantity of rain falls in the afternoon beginning about middle day and continuing till nearly 6 in Torrents. Wm. goes to Ludlow market, rides my mare and gets a good soaking.

12th
Warm. Some slight storms of rain in the afternoon.

13th
A great deal of rain last night. Slight storms in day – mild.

14
Slight storms. Mrs. Trumper & Miss Sayer Come to Tea. Wm. goes to Kidderminster market and rides Trumper's horse.

15th Sepr.
Frost, fine windy day.

16
Rainy almost all the forenoon: fair P.M. and mild all day. Mr. Rodmell returns from his journey.

17th Sepr.
Fair & mild. Sunday. Miss Elizabeth and Ellen Partridge At Burford church. Return to Park to Dinner with them. Mr. E. Edwards calls there in the afternoon and we come home together.

18th
Mild but rainy. Go to Ludlow market. Return over the Hill by Nash. Tea at Park having brot. some money from Mr. Harding for William viz 23£ on acct. as well as the 27£ for my own wheat.

Sepr. 19th
Fair & mild. Mr. Rodmell had two Friends come here last night on a visit to him to stay a few days. William goes to Worcester Fair.

20th
Fair and very warm.

Sepr. 21st
Fog. Fair and warm

22
Very fine warm day. Return by Park from Nash and take Tea there. [Mr. Rodmell's one friend leaves him[210].

23rd

Same weather. Instead of going yesterday Mr. Rodmell's friend leaves this morning.

Sepr. 24th

Delightful day, brisk east wind. Two strange clergymen do duty at Burford viz Mr. Rodmell's friend in the afternoon and a person from Burford house in the morning.

25th

Sharp frost. Very fine warm day. Mr. Rodmell and his friend Mr. Upton start off on their tour. I go to Ludlow market, appeal against the charge made upon Mr. Rodmell for a horse above 13 hands kept before Lady Day successfully. Sell a load of Beans to Mr. Hand. Get the refuse of Euston House & the land near provided it be not sold.

Sepr. 26th

Dry, cold east wind in the morning. Fine and very warm afterwards. Finish hop picking. Give the pickers their dinner of Plum pudding and Mutton Pasty. Being so fine a day we lay the Tables in the green before the house and all seemed delighted with the entertainment.

Sepr. 27

Cold east wind. Mists of Rain. Send Mr. Trumper his bottles back again full of Perry bottled some time back. Call at Park coming from Nash and take Tea there along with my sister, Ellen Partridge and Mr. James Adams.

28

Cold wind still. Wm. rides my mare to Ludlow Fair. Miss Reynolds and Ellen Partridge come to Tea.

29 Sepr.

Most delightful day. Very warm in the afternoon. Call at Court of Hill to speak to Mr. Baker on business. Go to Park to Tea and assist Wm. in settling with his hoppickers.

30th

Fair & very warm forenoon. Rain in the evening. Call at Court of Hill again about the things to be taken to before the family goes to Devonshire[211] – agree for 2 cows.

44. The Lodge (or Dean Lodge), Nash, the former home of Peter Davis' aunt, Eleanor, and her husband, William Partridge.

Octr. 1st
A good deal of rain this morning – warm and fair afternoon. Sunday. Mr. Rushout does the whole duty in the absence of Mr. Rodmell who is at present from home along with his friend, Mr. Upton. Call on brother William in the afternoon and go from thence to the Lodge to Tea and return by Park along with Aunt Maria.

2nd
Fair and very mild day. Call on Mrs. Baker again and acquaint her that Mr. Reynolds & Mr. Pugh had agreed to be at Court of Hill on Friday next to value the rick of Hay to me. Ellen Partridge comes here to Tea and it being too late for her to go home she stays the night at Burford.

Octr. 3rd
Mild – good deal of rain in evening.

4th
Fair & warm.

5th
Same weather.

6th

Same weather, with however some very slight storms. Mr. Reynolds & I go to Court of Hill to meet Mr. Pugh, but we could not agree for Mr. Baker's Hay stack. Buy the cart for 5£, geers 2£ for William (the latter).

Octr. 7

Fair and very mild. Call on Mrs. Baker again – the hay to remain till Mr. Baker's return.

8th

Very warm with some slight showers. Sunday. Mr. Rodmell & Mr. Rushout administer the sacrament. William and myself stay. Take a walk to Kyrewood to see Mr. Nicholls who has had the small bone of his leg broken by a colt.

9th

Frost, very warm & fine. Go to Ludlow market – home to Dinner and accompany my sister who was at Burford home[212] and stay Tea and supper. Lunch with Mr. Jones, the veterinary surgeon at Ludlow.

10th

Most beautiful day, very mild. Go to Nash and stay there farming all day.

11th Octr.

Same weather and same occupation.

12th

Same weather. Sup at Trumper's with Price & Cooke.

13th

Same weather. Go to Nash to drill wheat. Call on Mr. Baker about the Hay rick at Court of Hill but could not deal, he wanting 100£ for it, much more than the worth (19 Ton).

14 Octr.

Sharp frost – very warm and fine afterwards. At Nash all day again drilling wheat.

15th

Fine, warm day. Sunday. Got a violent cold yesterday or day before. Home all day.

16
Same weather.

17 Octr.
Warm day little rain in the afternoon. Go to Mr. Child's sale at the Grange along with Mr. Williams. Purchase two cows and stay till nearly 11 o'clock before we start to come home.

18
Fine & very warm. Go to Nash to finish the wheat sowing.

19th Octr.
Same weather. Meet with Mr. Edwards by Nash who rides through Lawn with me and down thro' Nash ground home. Mr. Rodmell returns from Hereford. Mr. Edwards calls and sups with me.

20
Same weather.

Octr. 21st
Same weather. Go to Worcester market. Meet with Mr. Giles on the road, going. Return with Mr. B. Edwards.

22nd
Same weather. Sunday. Dine at Park with the Trumpers. Sup at Tenbury. Spend very pleasant afternoon.

23rd Octr.
Mild, rain in the afternoon. Go to Ludlow market, sell the load of Wheat to Mr. Jones and return to Dinner.

24th
AM mild. Hard Storms of hail and Rain. Attend the court leet and court Baron of the lord of the Manor at Rose and Crown as a juryman[213] – Mr. Godson, Mr. Rushout's agent.

Octr. 25
Cold wind. Snow on the hills. William & I ride together to Nash and call on Uncle and aunt Reynolds. I go there afterwards to Dinner being the day after his birthday. Call at the Church House, Mr. Giles's in the evening and it happening to be the wedding day[214] of Mr. Wm. Lowe there was a party of them.

26 Octr.
Wind, little rain. Go to Bromyard Fair and return along with Mr. Wm. Lowe to Sutton to dinner. Meet with his brother from Trysull there and stay supper.

27
Hard rain A.M. Fair afternoon. Stay at home nearly all day excepting going to Tenbury to look at the Hops at Mr. Trumper's.

Octr. 28th
Storms, mild. The Trumpers and William go to Worcester Market.

29
Frost. Rain in afternoon. Mr. Rushout is unwell in Church and obliged to go home. Dine along with Mr. & Mrs. Trumper at Tenbury and spend the evening. Wm. calls there in the afternoon.

30th Octr.
Rain and high wind in afternoon. Go to Ludlow and return to Dinner. Eliza calls in afternoon and stays Tea. Mr. & Mrs. Cooke of hill top come to Burford to engage Miss Jones[215] as a governess for their own family.

31
Continual storms of rain. Mild.

Novr. 1
Very hard rain down to 4 P.M. as well as the greater part of last night.

2nd
Rain all the forenoon. Fair P.M. William comes along with me to Wofferton[216] to look at two colts at Mr. Wards, a cart colt and hack Do. both coming two. By the hack at 16£ and bid 20£ for the cart which is one of the finest I ever put my eyes on for his age.

3rd
Sharp frost, fine and fair with the exception of a shower or two.

4
Mild, slight showers A.M.

Novr. 5th

Fair. Sunday. The church service very much lengthened by Sunday falling on this memorable day[217]. Mr. & Mrs. Trumper, Mr. M.T.[218], Miss Reynolds and Wm. from Park dine along with me and spend the evening. Mr. Edwards also drops in in the evening.

6th

Fair & most beautiful day. Wm. & Matthias Trumper go to Nash to kill a brace of birds. Captain[219] meets with a hare in Mr. Partridges [*word illegible*] and grabs him. Ellen Partridge calls to return some books.

7

Same weather. Go to Tenbury market at night for a wonder!

8

Mild, some drizzling rain. Start off to Netley about 10 A.M. to see Mr. Hope concerning the sale of the Parish cottages at Weston the advertisements for so doing being just issued. After waiting for a short time at Netley the old gentleman and his son, Mr. T.H. Hope (this year the high sherriff of the county) make their appearance. After dining with them and Mrs. T.H. Hope we have some conversation respecting the sale. Mr. Hope senr. partly authorizes me to make the purchase provided they are sold within bounds. This is my first visit to Netley and I of course take up my abode with them for the night after being very hospitably entertained.

Novr. 9

Cool wind A.M. with a little rain. Warmer in the afternoon. After taking a walk with Mr. H. round his farm we sit down to breakfast, Mr. Hope Junr. having first read the family prayers. Get some further instructions about purchasing the Houses, and after obtaining leave to break up a part of a pasture field at Nash (the spring [*word illegible*]) for a hopyard, I take my leave and return homewards. Call at the Feathers, Ludlow, for a feed of corn for the mare and come over the Hill and by Nash home, not at all disappointed with my journey but on the contrary very much pleased with my Landlords and with the young and interesting Lady of Mr. Hope (the younger), he having been married to her about 3 or 4 years and they having already 3 in family. The old Lady Mrs. Hope senr. I find died about last June and in consequence at the end of the death year the property at Greet[220] and Nash comes to the eldest son (mine host). The Netley property is already given up to him.

Novr. 10

Hard rain in the morning, mild all day and fair in the afternoon.

11

Fair and very mild day. Being at Tenbury call to see Matt. Trumper who has a very bad pain in his neck. Lies in bed. Stay Tea with them.

12

Fair A.M. – little rain in the afternoon. Go to Nash chapel to hear Mr. Wybrow preach the funeral sermon for the late Rector of Nash & Boraston[221] who died a short time since. Dine at Lodge along with Mr. & Mrs. Trumper, Mr. Reynolds and the family. Mrs. Reynolds and brother Willm. drop in in the afternoon. Mr. Wybrow did full justice to the subject giving us a most excellent and appropriate discourse. A very large congregation.

Novr. 13

Mild – rains all the afternoon.

14th

Rain nearly all day. Go to Park at night to take the acct. of Mr. Mason with my late Father, young Mason calling there to settle it.

15

Very fine clear day. Call at Lodge coming from Nash and agree with Mr. Partridge for his cider [*word illegible*] to go to Nash.

Novr. 16th

Same weather.

17

Sharp frost and very fine day. Call to look at the Weston Cottages which are advertized for sale. See Mr. Reynolds also with regard to them.

18

Another sharp frost – rather cloudy and dull day.

Novr. 19th

Mild. Rains all the afternoon. <u>Sunday</u>.

20th

Small frost. Boisterous storm at noon. Go to Ludow Market. Pay to

45. The front of the former Poor Law Union Workhouse, Teme Street, Tenbury (more recently the local council offices); designed by George Wilkinson, it cost £1,365 to build in 1837.

Mr. Anderson the expenses of the surrender of Deptcroft for Samuel – £27.6s.0d. Dine at Fethers and return home with Mr. Edwards.

21st Novr.
Stormy. Go to Tenbury market and stay the sale of the Parish houses at Weston. Buy them for Mr. Hope at 200£. Mr. G. Dansey the last bidder before myself at 195£. Mr. G. Winton the auctioneer. Sale in the new workhouse at Tenbury[222].

22nd
Slights storms of rain, mild wind.

Novr. 23
Hard rain. Mild. Go to Nash in afternoon and call on Mr. Baker, he now being in the humour to sell the Hay. But no go for me now thank you. Write to Mr. Hope acquainting him of the purchase I made for him of the Weston Cottages.

24th
Small frost. Beautiful day, very mild. Mr. Wm. Russell calls here in the afternoon to ask me whether I meant taking his house now fitting up at

46. The nearest we have to a portrait of the diarist.

Tenbury – which I decline.

25th

Frost. Another most delightful day. Call at Nash Court to ascertain their intention about the House but they decline taking it.

26th

Wind – little rain in the afternoon. Sunday. Mr. Rodmell does the whole Church duty. Dine at Park and spend the evening there. Mr. E. Edwards to Tea here. John Preece from Boraston calls on me this morning to know about the cottage I having promised him one of those at Weston lately bot. Nothing agreed upon he promising to see me again within a fortnight concerning it[223].

Notes

1. Of Tenbury: see Appendix 5 generally for biographical details all those mentioned in the diary, when known.
2. See Appendix 2 for an index of places mentioned in this diary, with their distance and direction from Burford. Peter Davis' great-uncle Peter Reynolds and his wife Ann lived at Burcote. This Peter Reynolds is not to be confused with Peter Davis' grandfather (see below); they were brothers-in-law, Peter Davis' grandparents being first cousins.
3. New House was the home of Peter Davis' grandfather, Peter Reynolds and uncle Joseph Reynolds (and his wife). See also the travel diary entry for 22 June 1835.
4. That is, Dean Park: see Introduction.
5. Of Eardiston – not to be confused with William Mytton of Deepcroft: see Appendix 5.
6. James Rose: see Appendix 5.
7. 'Mr. Edwards' generally means Edmund Edwards, as opposed to his elder brother, 'Mr. B. Edwards'.
8. Castrated male sheep.
9. The Swan Hotel and Posting House, Ludlow Road, Burford – proprietor William Grove.
10. William Trumper, Peter's future brother-in-law.
11. William Partridge, Peter's uncle by marriage.
12. Peter Davis wrote to his brother in Devon.
13. References to the 'Joneses' pure and simple invariably mean the Revd David and his wife Elizabeth Jones.
14. A pasture towards the north extremity of the Dean Park land
15. In Samuel Davis' will, he refers to his Eastham Park estate, Worcestershire 'now in the occupation of Mr. Nott'. This comprised 281 acres.

16. The mountain ash or rowan was also known as the quickbeam (quick meaning alive). Quickset hedging was prevalent throughout the Enclosure period.
17. A young female pig.
18. There are various Lowes referred to in the diary: Peter Davis takes care to distinguish them by reference to their homes. See Appendix 3.
19. Agnes Wilkinson, the eldest of the Revd George Hall's nieces.
20. Held on the first Tuesday of March, one of six such fairs (as opposed to markets – see note 38 below) which were held in Tenbury each year: see also the entries for 22 April and 26 September 1836, and 7 March 1837. Others were on the first Tuesday after Trinity, 18 July and 9 December.
21. Mr Nott (see note 15 above) was entitled to all the income from the Eastham estate, in return for paying his own rent to Samuel Davis.
22. Samuel Davis' will refers to property known as the Dingles, owned by him and occupied by William Mytton – see note 40 below.
23. Trappings (or belongings).
24. Robert Southey wrote the life of his fellow-poet William Cowper (1731–1800) in fifteen volumes, the first published in 1833.
25. The pikelet remains a traditional British (particularly Welsh) teatime treat.
26. To the rectory: see entry for 20 February.
27. William and Eleanor Partridge and family lived at the Lodge, Burford, which is situated a little way south of Nash Court. Maria and Eleanor were sisters. See Introduction and Appendix 5.
28. The Revd George Hall, vicar of Tenbury.
29. The river.
30. March 1836 was one of the wettest on record throughout England and Wales.
31. There were six volumes of this, the standard work on English history. Peter Davis noted where Hume had died on his visit to Edinburgh; see travel diary entry for 14 June 1835.
32. The *Athenaeum* was a literary magazine published in London from 1828 to 1921, with the reputation for publishing the best writers of the age.
33. Just opposite Burford Rectory, the home of the Hon. and Revd George Rushout-Bowles; see Introduction and Appendix 5.
34. George Rushout-Bowles junior was not in fact 'The Honourable' (though his father was).
35. See note 15 above. This was unusual, since rent was traditionally paid in four instalments, due on the Quarter Days: Lady Day (25 March), Midsummer Day, Michaelmas and Christmas Day.
36. Each parish had an overseer or overseers who could levy a rate to raise money for the poor. There could be more than one overseer in a parish, depending upon its population and/or size. The overseer was chosen at a meeting of the parish vestry, the appointment being reviewed annually; the post was unpaid. See further note 88 below.
37. Woodston, Lindridge, some 6 miles east of Burford.
38. Tenbury market has been held every Tuesday since the year 1249.
39. Coney Green; he may have stayed with John Smith; see entry for 12 May 1836.
40. Peter Davis sometimes mentions his father's tenant, William Mytton, as of 'Deptcroft' – as here – but elsewhere as of 'Deepcroft'. Samuel Davis refers in his will to his farm 'Dead Croft', Knighton-on-Teme, an obvious copying error. (It is today known as Deepcroft Cottage, a Listed Building, originally seventeenth-century with mid-nineteenth-century alterations and additions.)
41. Mortimer Buckingham had been at school at Rugby (some 65 miles east of Burford). The coach on which he travelled called at the Swan, Burford, at 9.15 a.m. on its way from Ludlow; on one occasion, 'speed caused one of the wheels of the Red Rover to catch fire. A spare wheel was always carried on the back of the coach, and the change was made in a few minutes.' (Gwilliam)
42. Hill Top Farm, Rochford, the home of William Cooke, his wife Charlotte and their large family, including a Sarah Cooke.
43. With her brother William Reynolds at Nash Court Farm.
44. Hartall (or Harthall) is a mile north of Burford, just to the west of the Clee Hill road.

45. Netherwood, near Stoke Bliss, is 6 or so miles south-east of Burford.
46. Intended as a rival to Smithfield, it was not a success, due to vested interests which ensured that sales never reached viable levels.
47. As mentioned in the Introduction, by 7 June 1841 (the date of the census for that year), Peter Davis was established at The Lodge, Broncroft Farm, Diddlebury, 15 miles north-west of Burford.
48. See travel diary, note 8.
49. Ackhill is some 2 miles north-west of Presteigne.
50. Cob: a close-built, strong, hardy kind of pony.
51. It was in Foregate Street, Worcester. The original eighteenth-century building was demolished in 1900.
52. The bride and groom were first cousins; see Appendix 3. They set up home at Coney Green Farm, Ribbesford.
53. This was an annular eclipse, occurring when the moon is near apogee and its apparent diameter is smaller than that of the sun, so that a ring, or *annulus*, of the sun's disk remains visible at mid-eclipse along the narrow central ground track on the earth.
54. Stanford-on-Teme, 9 miles to the east.
55. Thomas Davis of Orleton died aged seventy-eight in the early spring of 1837, though this death was not recorded in the diary.
56. It was Whitsun.
57. The right of first refusal.
58. V. W. Wheeler.
59. Ann, wife of Peter Davis' great-uncle Peter; see Appendix 3.
60. Edward Mytton and his daughter Mary; see Appendix 3.
61. See note 42 above.
62. Nash Court Farm was the home of Peter Davis' Uncle William Reynolds and his wife.
63. Between Hanley Child and Hanley William – 750 feet above sea level, the highest point between Tenbury and Worcester.
64. Location unknown.
65. Davenport House, dating from 1726; it is now used for weddings, etc.
66. The Revd E. S. Davenport.
67. Coalport, a village in Shropshire, now part of Telford, is located on the River Severn, a mile downstream of Ironbridge, and some 8 miles upstream of Bridgnorth. It was home to an important pottery, founded 1795, producing Coalport China, which became popular worldwide and is now part of the Wedgwood group.
68. Bridgnorth is split into Low Town on the River Severn, and High Town above. Donkeys with panniers plied up and down the 200 pebbled Stoneway Steps.
69. A place to eat where the price is fixed (as opposed to somewhere 'out of the ordinary').
70. Lea Farm is west of Cleobury Mortimer, 23 miles south of Kemberton.
71. Eleanor Nurs, Peter Davis' great-aunt, and Mary Ann Bright, his first cousin once removed; see Appendix 3 – John Reynolds' Descendants.
72. There was one Royal Mail coach each day from London via Worcester (and Abberley) to Ludlow, halting at the Swan, Burford at 12.30.
73. Edward Davis: see entry for 22 May above.
74. William Mytton married his cousin Elizabeth Smith; thus, within two months (see entry dated 7 May above) a brother and a sister had married a sister and a brother. See Appendix 3.
75. The Revd James Buckingham's sixth child (of eleven) was married to Samuel junior at Burrington, North Devon, on 16 June.
76. Upper Woodston lies just to the north-west of Woodston itself, and of Lindridge.
77. As referred to elsewhere, Dr Henry Davis married Isabella Henderson of Edge Hill, Lancashire; this may have been her sister.
78. Oakly Park was at the time the residence of the Hon. Robert Clive, second son of the 1st Earl of Powis, and of his wife Baroness Windsor, sister of the 6th Earl of Plymouth (who died in 1833). Still the home of the Earls of Plymouth, it is situated just outside Bromfield, near to Ludlow racecourse. (As mentioned in the Introduction, Peter Davis was to hold the

tenancy of King's Head Farm, Bromfield, in the 1850s, before moving to Bickmarsh Hall, Warwickshire, which he took from Michaelmas 1860.)

79. See Introduction. Tithes were originally one-tenth of the produce of the land (crops, eggs, cattle, timber, fishing etc.), paid to the rector of the parish as alms and for payment for his services. (Vicarial tithes were payable to a vicar.) By the time of the Tithe Commutation Act, 1836 (which received the Royal Assent on 13 August), there was considerable discontent over payment of tithes, giving rise to disputes in court. The Act substituted a variable monetary payment for any existing tithe in kind.

80. New House is more than 2 miles from The Hundred House, where the coach would have delivered them.

81. The racecourse was about a mile to the south of Tenbury.

82. He rode his own four-year-old, 'Tenbury'.

83. 'Nell Gwynne' was a six-year-old bay mare (by 'Master Henry'), owned by Joseph Fuller. She also won races at Leominster and Swansea, earning Mr Fuller rather more on those occasions. 'Jewstone' was Mr. Dunn's four-year-old brown gelding, a half-brother to 'Tenbury'.

84. Peter Davis' uncle, Joseph Reynolds; see Appendix 3 – John Reynolds' Descendants.

85. Clee Hill; the Queensbury Rules not having been introduced until 1865, the fight would have been subject to the London Prize Ring Rules of 1743. They governed the conduct of prizefighting or bare-knuckle boxing for over 100 years.

86. The Bank Farm, Burford.

87. This is most likely to be Samuel Davis' landlord's two sons, namely Thomas Henry Hope and the Revd Frederick William Hope; see Appendix 5.

88. The Poor Law Commission was a body established to administrate poor relief following the passing of the Poor Law Amendment Act, 1834. That Act changed the relief of the poor from being a local (parish) responsibility to a group one: the group's workhouse became the primary source of relief. One of the Commission's first tasks was to set about dividing the 15,000 or so parishes of England and Wales into new administrative units (Poor Law Unions), each run by a locally-elected Board of Guardians. The Tenbury Poor Law Union consisted of nineteen parishes split into two districts: the first comprised Tenbury, Burford, Boraston, Whitton, Nash, Greet, Brimfield and Little Hereford. The funding of each Union and its workhouse continued to come from the local poor rate; poor rates were usually levied annually, with the income recorded in poor rate books. A team of Assistant Commissioners undertook the creation of the new unions, visiting each area and conducting meetings with local parish officials and landowners.

89. To Samuel and Lucinda Davis.

90. To supply the labour force with its accustomed drink, every farm had its orchard and its cider mill. The mill was generally at the end of a building, but was sometimes in an open shed. It consisted of a circular stone trough – the chase – in the centre of which was a vertical post as an axle for the stone runner, which was pulled in a circle by horsepower, the apples being placed in the trough. When they had been reduced to a paste – must – they were put into a screw press to extract the juice. Cider-making was not entirely popular with many of the farmers, although the labourers were always keen to have it done. A conversation between a farm labourer and a Herefordshire farmer ran thus: Labourer, 'Master, what horse shall I take to drive cider mill?' Farmer, 'Damn the cider and the mill too; you waste one half of your time in making cider and the other half in drinking it. I wish there was not one apple in the county. You all think of cider, no matter what comes of plough.'

91. Thomas and Susanna Lowe.

92. Notable absentees are the bride's father, who disapproved of the match (but see entry for 12 October 1836), and her brother Samuel.

93. With the Cooke family.

94. Sir Christopher Smith was elected chairman and the Revd C. Turner vice-chairman. William Trumper was appointed clerk at a salary of £60 p.a.

95. After a ride of some 10 miles.

96. Hannah Davis, mother to Henry Davis.

97. About a mile south of Orleton village.

98. Their respective salaries were £70, £60 and £45 p.a.

99. The Royal Oak remains open, a handsome, three-storey black and white building in Market Street, Tenbury; in 1808 the Burrel family sold the inn to the Drew family as trustees for Thomas Drew, who was the landlord until 1840.
100. Of Church House, Tenbury.
101. Of Hope Court.
102. His thirty-first.
103. Uncle William.
104. V. W. Wheeler.
105. About 4 miles.
106. The George Hotel, a fifteenth-century inn situated in the centre of Bewdley.
107. From the 1841 Census, it appears that he exercised his right to take the tenancy.
108. A Heart of Oak and a Swan inn are both still in business, on the north side of the city of Hereford. (It must have been a short night, since 'The company separated at a late hour, after an evening of social and most pleasing enjoyment,' according to *The Hereford Journal*'s report of the dinner.)
109. William Reynolds was fifty-eight.
110. See 25 April 1836 entry.
111. Mainstone Farm, Trumpet, is indicated, not Broncroft, which is in the opposite direction.
112. An alternative site at Oldwood Common had also been considered, but in the end Mr Rushout offered a site by way of gift – at the north end of Teme Street, almost bordering upon the river: see entry for 1 March 1837. (Only with some difficulty did Mr Rushout satisfy the Guardians of his title to his site.) The workhouse had room for seventy inmates, though it was seldom much more than half full. In 1937, the building became local council offices and a fire station.
113. The Reform Act, 1832, made the Overseer of the Poor of each parish responsible for the initial voters' list being drawn up. Section 41 further provided that, '... the Lord Chief Justice of the Court of King's Bench ... for Middlesex, and the Senior judge for the Time being in the Commission of Assize for every other County shall ... nominate and appoint for every such County ... or Divisions of such County, a Barrister or Barristers to revise the Lists of Voters in the Election of a Knight or Knights of the Shire; and such Barrister or Barristers ... shall give public Notice ... of the several Times and Places at which he or they will hold Courts for that Purpose, such Times being between the Fifteenth Day of September inclusive and the Twenty-fifth Day of October inclusive in the present and in every succeeding Year, and he or they shall hold open Courts for that Purpose at the Times and Places so to be announced ...' (This is the sole instance of Peter Davis entering a critical note about each of his brothers upon the same day.)
114. Church Stretton; it is not clear why a court was being held there after the statutory deadline date.
115. Withypool Farm; and Curdall or Curdale, which is nearer to Cleobury Mortimer.
116. Philip Ledington.
117. A cask holding 63 gallons.
118. Mr and Mrs Thomas Baylis, Mrs Baylis being a sister-in-law of Eleanor Partridge.
119. About 3 a.m. in order to cover 27 miles.
120. About 4 miles south of Badger.
121. Burcote is 5 miles south of Badger. From Burcote to Milson is 19 miles, and from Milson to Burford a further 4.
122. Between Eardiston and Stockton-on-Teme.
123. Phillips was a farm employee: this was likely to have been a form of saving scheme, with Samuel Davis as banker ('use' indicating that interest would be paid).
124. The 1840 Burford field map (see page 74) shows three fields designated as Adneys – Upper, Middle and Lower – all lie on the north side of the River Teme, just east of the bridge, the Upper Adney being nearest to it.
125. Her fifty-eighth.
126. See note 88.
127. Halesowen – towards Birmingham from Kidderminster.
128. Refreshments while travelling, no doubt needed after 18 miles on the road.

129. Wybrow.
130. From Burford to Milson is 4 miles; from Milson to The Lea is a further 4 miles.
131. In the previous century, Humphrey Bowles of Burford is recorded as selling wheat cheaply to the poor and distributing bread and meat when work was not available.
132. The Hundred House Hotel, Great Witley; Tenbury lay in the hundred of Doddingtree, a place in the parish of Great Witley, probably close to where the Hundred House Hotel still stands.
133. An inn about a mile east of Burford, on the main Worcester road, before Newnham Bridge.
134. The Reindeer Inn, Ombersley.
135. See note 41.
136. There is to this day a Golden Lion in George Street, Kidderminster.
137. About 8 miles east of Burcote.
138. Sir John Wrottesley MP.
139. Richard Eykyn.
140. Worfield – the church 'looks very handsome from a distance', says Pevsner.
141. The birthplace of Peter Davis' mother Elizabeth, née Reynolds, and grandfather, Peter Reynolds. Elizabeth Reynolds' mother was her father's cousin, Mary Reynolds of Kemberton: Peter Reynolds of Burcote was her younger brother. It seems from this entry that at least one member of the Reynolds family may have remained living at Kinlet in 1837. Kinlet to Burford is 12 miles, a long walk along muddy roads – especially on your twenty-fifth birthday, of which the diarist makes no mention.
142. See note 99.
143. Near Patshull, 3 miles or so north-east of Badger.
144. From the 9 February entry, it is apparent that Peter Davis then based himself at the rectory, his father perhaps having moved back to Dean Park: see for instance the entry for 7 March, post.
145. 2 February.
146. A plan was approved in January 1791 for a 46-mile canal from Kington, Herefordshire, through to the River Severn near Stourport. It was never fully completed: by 1800 financial difficulties prevented further development beyond the then-existing run of 18½ miles, which was used for transporting coal from the Mamble pits (Sir Walter Blount's collieries, seven miles north-east of Burford) to Leominster. Later, from 1864 to 1964, the route of the canal was used for the Tenbury & Bewdley Railway ('The Blue Bell Line').
147. Curates in the adjoining Worcester diocese received an average income of £81 a year in 1836.
148. Silvington, five miles north-west of Cleobury Mortimer.
149. This was as a result of a by-election caused by the death of the Tory Sir Charles Cockerell of Sezincote aged eighty-two; he had been an MP for Evesham for 17 years until his death the month before. George Rushout-Bowles (whose first cousin was the late Sir Charles' widow) defeated the Whig candidate, Lord Marcus Hill, by 165 votes to 120.
150. The Crown Inn (proprietor, Richard Deakin) in Teme Street, Tenbury, is not to be confused with the Rose & Crown, which was (and remains) on the main road through Burford, that is on the north side of the River Teme. (The Rose & Crown is referred to later – see entry for 16 May 1837.)
151. Sky.
152. This appearance was called 'Burning Spears' in *A Description of Meteors* by W. F. DD (London, 1654).
153. Possibly 'longland', a celebrated variety of perry pears according to Dr Robert Hogg, writing in his *Fruit Manual* of 1884.
154. See the earlier entry dated 25 October 1836, and note 112.
155. Peter Davis had been impressed by the reading rooms in Liverpool and Edinburgh; see travel diary entries for 9 and 15 June 1835.
156. The Feathers Hotel still exists, in the Bull Ring, Ludlow.
157. Smith was groom at the rectory – see entry for 23 March, below.
158. Throughout the country, it was the coldest spring on record.
159. The Easter Vestry.
160. Peter Davis' arithmetic is hard to follow.
161. See note 40.

162. By 1859, there was in existence a Tenbury Young Men's Reading Room.

163. Christ's Hospital (popularly known as The Bluecoat School), a co-educational independent boarding school, was founded in the sixteenth century following the dissolution of the monasteries. It is unique for a British independent school in that it educates a large proportion of its students free, and most at a reduced rate. Until the late nineteenth century, it was situated at Newgate on the western edge of the City of London.

164. Bleathwood.

165. See entry for 9 January, above.

166. This corresponds with a recital in Samuel Davis' will (see note 187 below): 'Whereas I have lately placed my two sons William and Peter in two Farms formerly occupied by myself and have given up to them all my live and Dead Farming stock, and upon such arrangements taking place the same was valued by competent persons, and which amounted to a considerable sum of money ...' See also the entry for 9 August, below.

167. James Robinson, a Tenbury attorney, who died aged sixty-five and was buried on 30 January 1837.

168. (Sadly)

169. Knacker's Hole Farm, Eastham.

170. Benjamin Giles, of Church House, Tenbury.

171. Hopton Wafers, about two miles east of Cleobury Mortimer.

172. No such feast was, however, referred to in the diary entry for 24 May 1836, the Tuesday after the previous Whitsun.

173. An enema, more particularly one administered by syringe.

174. See entry for 13 January, above.

175. Peter Davis' great-uncle, James; see Appendix 3 – John Reynolds' Descendants.

176. Another Maria.

177. The Grand Junction Railway opened for passenger travel between Birmingham and Liverpool in July 1837.

178. Its architect was Charles Cope Trubshaw; following use as a camp for prisoners of war during the Second World War, all but the stable block was demolished in 1954.

179. Rugeley is seven miles east of Teddesley; five of John and Mary Ann Bright's children were baptised there.

180. Between Cannock, Lichfield, Rugeley and Stafford, it comprises a mixture of natural deciduous woodland, coniferous plantations, open heathland and the remains of early industry, such as coal mining. The Chase was designated as an Area of Outstanding Natural Beauty on 16 September 1958 – the smallest area so designated in mainland Britain, covering 68 km² (26 square miles). Much of the area is also designated as a Site of Special Scientific Interest. Despite being relatively small in area, the Chase provides a home to a range of wildlife, including a herd of around 800 fallow deer and a number of rare and endangered birds, not least migrant nightjars.

181. The drill probably pulled by horses.

182. William and James Lowe of Greenway Head.

183. 'For the love of Christ constraineth us; because we thus judge, that if one died for all, then were all dead' [King James Version]. ('We are ruled by the love of Christ, now that we recognize that one man died for everyone, which means that they all share in his death' [Good News Translation].)

184. See note 18.

185. (An isolated instance of a practical joke.)

186. The Revd Rodmell was the third of four brothers; there were also three sisters.

187. He also went to the office of his solicitor, Mr Anderson of Ludlow, to sign his will; only three days later, there began his final illness.

188. See note 79.

189. Such a late frost must have been extremely unusual.

190. The King died aged seventy-one after an illness lasting a month or so, 'leaving behind him the memory of a genial, frank, warm-hearted man, but a blundering, though well-intentioned prince'. (*Encyc. Brit.*) The new Queen, his niece, was aged eighteen.

191. Emma Reynolds, illegitimate daughter of Eleanor Partridge; see Appendix 3 – John Reynolds' Descendants

192. The Angel Inn, Broad Street, Ludlow – now not so used.

193. And see entry for 27 July, below.

194. Possibly 'blistered'.

195. Joseph Bailey of Glanusk.

196. Colonel Thomas Henry Hastings Davies of Elmley Park.

197. George Richard Robinson.

198. Richard Godson QC.

199. Peter Borthwick's election was subsequently declared void; see Appendix 5.

200. The election overall saw an increase in the number of Tories elected, even though the Whig Government remained in power; however, at Ludlow, while Viscount Clive was re-elected, the Whig Henry Salwey was elected in place of the Tory Edmund Lechmere Charlton.

201. Samuel will no doubt have reported to his father the birth of his first child, a boy, on 21 July.

202. Burford to Worcester via Clifton-on-Teme and Wichenford is all of 22 miles; assuming Peter Davis rides back on the direct route, this makes a round trip of 42 miles.

203. The Bell was an inn from at least 1820 to 1910: it was in Market Street, Tenbury, at what is now number 19. The yard at the rear is known as Bell Yard.

204. As anticipated on 20 April last.

205. Tenbury was in the West Worcestershire constituency.

206. See note 10.

207. Court of Hill – in a magnificent position, 650 feet above sea level – is described by Pevsner as a 'fine sturdy brick house dated 1683'. The Hill family had owned the estate since the fourteenth century: see Appendix 5 – Baker and Salwey.

208. The Revd David Jones.

209. Burford to Monmouth is 40 miles: Monmouth to Dawlish, some 120 miles further.

210. This sentence is crossed out.

211. See entry for 6 August 1837.

212. That is, to Tenbury.

213. In medieval England the lord of the manor claimed certain jurisdictional rights concerning the administration of his estate over his tenants and bondsmen, and exercised those rights through his court baron. Although this court had no power to deal with crimes, criminal jurisdiction could be granted to a trusted lord by the Crown by means of an additional franchise. Some time in the later Middle Ages the lord, when exercising these powers, gained the name of leet, which was a jurisdiction of a part of a county: hence the franchise was of court leet. Although there was originally a sharp distinction between the court baron, exercising strictly manorial rights, and the court leet, depending for its jurisdiction upon royal franchise, in many areas it became customary for the two courts to meet together. The court leet was a court of record, and its duty was not only to view the pledges (the freemen's oath of peacekeeping and good practice in trade), but also to try by jury and punish all crimes committed within the jurisdiction (although more serious crimes were committed to the Queen's Justices). It also developed as a means of proactively ensuring that standards in such matters as food and drink, and agriculture, were adhered to. The court generally sat only a few times each year – sometimes just annually. Mr Rushout was said to hold a court leet and a court baron 'occasionally'. The jury's role included electing the officers, other than the Steward – Mr Godson in this case – who was appointed by the lord for bringing matters to the attention of the court and deciding on them. Courts leet survived for formal purposes until the 1970s, and indeed some even survive to this day (though not Burford's).

214. This was in fact an anniversary celebration: the marriage of William Lowe (of Sutton) and Sarah Giles (of Church House, Tenbury) took place a year and a day earlier, on 24 October 1836.

215. Mary Christiana Jones, eldest daughter of the Burford curate and his wife, then barely sixteen; the eldest Cooke child was five.

216. Woofferton, five miles to the west of Burford.
217. Extended thanks were being given to God for delivering the country from the scheming of the Gunpowder Plotters of 1605.
218. Matthias Trumper.
219. Presumably a dog.
220. The Greet or Greete estate land was thought to be the most productive in the Teme Valley.
221. The Revd Alexander Stewart.
222. The tender for building the workhouse had been accepted on 4 April 1837; its construction was a slow process, and it was only insured from 2 January 1838, so the auction may have taken place in a partly-built workhouse.
223. Preece and family were still living at Boraston Dale at the date of the 1841 Census.

APPENDIX 1

The Travel Diary: Distances and Modes of Travel

June 1835	From	To	Means of Transport	Miles	Total
8th	Dean Park	Ludlow	Horseback	8	
	Ludlow	Shrewsbury	Coach	30	
	Shrewsbury	Birkenhead	Coach	60	
	Birkenhead	Liverpool	Steam packet	1	99
9th	In Liverpool				
10th	Liverpool	Manchester	Steam train	31	
	Manchester	Lancaster	Coach	54	85
11th	Lancaster	Bowness	Walking	30	30
12th	Bowness	Ambleside	Rowing	5	
	Ambleside	Glenridding	Pony	10	
	Glenridding	Pooley Bridge	Rowing	8	
	Pooley Bridge	Penrith	Walking	6	
	Penrith	Carlisle	Coach	18	47
13th	Carlisle	Edinburgh	Coach	90	90
14th/15th	In Edinburgh				
16th	Edinburgh	Leith	Walking	2	
	Leith	Edinburgh	Walking	2	
	Edinburgh	Tranent	Walking	10	
	Tranent	Berwick	Coach	47	61

17th	Berwick	Newcastle	Coach	61	61
18th	Newcastle	York	Coach	82	
	York	Tadcaster	Walking	11	93
19th	Tadcaster	Ferrybridge	Walking	13	
	Ferrybridge	Doncaster	Coach	17	
	Doncaster	Tickhill	Walking	7	
	Tickhill	Nottingham	Coach	36	73
20th	Nottingham	Leicester	Coach	26	
	Leicester	Northampton	Coach	31	
	Northampton	Towcester	Walking	8	
	Towcester	Brackley	Covered Cart	12	77
21st	Brackley	Banbury	Walking	10	
	Banbury	Chipping Norton	Pony	13	
	Chipping Norton	Pershore	Coach	28	51
22nd	Pershore	Worcester	Walking	9	
	Worcester	Tenbury	Coach	24	33

Total Miles Covered:	800
Coach/Covered Cart	616
Walking	108
Steam Train	31
Pony/Horse	31
Steam Packet/Rowing Boat	14

Local Places Mentioned, Together with their Distance and Direction from Burford

Abberley, 11 miles east
Ackhill, 26 miles north-west
Acton Beauchamp, 16 miles south-east
Albrighton, 31 miles north-east
Aston/Aston Bank, 2½ miles east
Badger, 27 miles north-east
Berrington, 3 miles south-west
Bewdley, 14 miles north-east
Birmingham, 35 miles north-east
Bleathwood, 3 miles west
Bockleton, 5 miles south
Boraston, 2 miles north-east
Brampton Bryan, 17 miles west
Bridgnorth, 21 miles north-east
Brockmanton, 8 miles south-west
Bromyard, 12 miles south-east
Bromyard Downs, 13 miles south-east
Burcote, near Worfield, 24 miles north-east
Burnall Green, near Patshull, 28 miles north-east
Cannock Chase, 45 miles north-east
Church Stretton, 20 miles north
Clater Park, near Bromyard, 14 miles south-east
Clee Hill, 5 miles north
Cleobury Mortimer, 8 miles north-east
Coalport, 28 miles north-east
Coney Green, 14 miles north-east
Coreley, 4 miles north-east
Court of Hill, 3 miles north
Davenport House, 25 miles north-east
Deepcroft, Knighton-on-Teme, 3.5 miles east
Diddlebury, 15 miles north-west
Drayton, Worcs., 24 miles north-east
Droitwich, 22 miles east
Eardiston, 7 miles east
Eastham, 5 miles east
Evesham, 36 miles south-east
Garnons, 25 miles south-west
Greenway Head Farm, 1 miles north
Greete (or Greet), 1½ miles north-west

Halesowen, 25 miles north-east
Hanley, 6 miles south-east
Hartall (or Harthall), 1 mile north
Hereford, 22 miles south
Hill Top Farm, Rochford, 4½ miles south-east
Hilton, 25 miles north-east
Hope Bagot, 4 miles north
Hopton Wafers, 7 miles north-east
Hundred House Hotel, Great Witley, 12 miles east
Kemberton, 30 miles north-east
Kidderminster, 18 miles north-east
Kingsland, 12 miles south-west
Kinlet, 12 miles north-east
Knacker's Hole Farm, 4 miles east
Knighton Common, 4 miles north-east
Kyrewood, 1½ miles south-east
Lambswick, near Lindridge, 5 miles east
Lea Farm, near Cleobury Mortimer, 8 miles north-east
Ledbury, 24 miles south-east
Leominster, 10 miles south-west
Lindridge, 6 miles east
Lodge (the), 1½ miles north
Ludlow, 8 miles north-west
Mainstone Farm, near Ledbury, 23 miles south
Milson, 4 miles north-east
Nash, 2 miles north
Netherwood, near Stoke Bliss, 6 miles south-east
Netley, near Dorrington, 29 miles north
New House, Heightington, 13 miles east
Oldwood, 2 miles south
Orleton, Herefordshire, 7 miles west
Orleton, Worcestershire, 7 miles east
Pattingham, 29 miles north-east
Penkridge, 42 miles north-east
Pershore, 29 miles south-east
Presteigne, 24 miles west
Rochford, 3 miles east
Rugeley, 49 miles north-east
Shifnal, 32 miles north-east
Silvington, 10 miles north
Stanford-on-Teme, 9 miles east
Stoke, 1½ miles north-west
Stoke Bliss, 7 miles south-east
Stourbridge, 24 miles north-east
Stourport-on-Severn, 17 miles east
Suckley, 17 miles south-east
Sutton/Sutton Park, 1½ miles south
Sutton, near Kidderminster, 17 miles north-east
Teddesley, 42 miles north-east
Tennall, Harborne, 33 miles north-east
Trysull, 29 miles north-east
Weobley, 19 miles south-west

Weston Township, 1 mile north
White house (the), 1 mile north
Whitton, 3½ miles north-west
Wichenford, 16 miles south-east
Withypool Farm, near Cleobury Mortimer, 8 miles north-east
Wolverhampton, 33 miles north-east
Wolverley, 18 miles north-east
Woodston, 6½ miles east
Woofferton, 5 miles west
Worcester, 20 miles south-east
Wrottesley, 33 miles north-east

APPENDIX 3

Genealogies

Samuel Davis' children and grandchildren

Samuel Davis Sr, b. 1768, d. 1837 +Elizabeth Reynolds, bap. 1782, m. 1804, d. 1813
——William Davis Sr, b. 1805, d. 1888 +Martha Child, b. 1819, m. 1844, d. 1902
————William Samuel Davis, bap. 1847, d. 1928 +Elizabeth Cranstoun, b. 1850, m. 1891, d. 1915
————Beatrice Mary Davis, bap. 1849, d. 1926 +The Rev. William Humphrey Child, b. 1845
————Peter Davis, bap. 1850, d. 1920 +Fanny Child, b. 1855, m. 1880, d. 1941
——————Edward William Davis, b. 1881, d. 1955
——————Roger Child Davis, b. 1883, d. 1883
——————Humphrey Peter Davis, b. 1885
——————John Clement Davis, b. 1886, d. 1886
——————Commander (Charles) Jancey Davis RN, b. 1888, d. 1976
——————(Frances Eliza) Helen Davis, b. 1890, d. 1969
——————The Rev. Ralph Leigh Davis, b. 1893, d. 1968
————Edward Prosser Davis, bap. 1852, d. 1927 +Mary Gent, b. 1864, m. 1883
——————Frank Davis, b. circa 1873, d. 1968
——————Phyllis Davis, b. circa 1874, d. circa 1940
——————Eric Davis, b. circa 1874, d. circa 1940
——Caroline Davis, bap. 1807, d. 1815
——The Rev. Samuel Davis, bap. 1810, d. 1883
+Lucinda Buckingham, b. 1810, m. 1836, d. 1855
————The Rev. (Samuel) Clement Davis, b. 1837, d. 1894 +Arthurina Pridham, b. 1840, m. 1872, d. 1890
+Jane Elizabeth Blackmore, b. 1833, m. 1857, d. 1866
————Alice Jane Davis, b. 1858, d. after 1929 +The Rev. Charles Millar, m. 1886
————John Samuel Champion Davis CBE, DL, JP, VD, b. 1859, d. 1926 +Minnie S. Butt, b. 1861, m. 1880
——————Hilda Davis
——————Dora Davis, b. 1882, d. 1905
————Arthur William Davis, b. 1861, d. 1913
————Alexander ("Alec") Platt Davis, b. 1863
————Alfred Herbert ("Bertie") Davis, b. 1864, d. 1934 +Ethel Harriet Gedge, b. 1875, m. 1897, d. 1963
——————Lorna Mary Davis, b. 1899
——————William ("Bill") Herbert Victor Davis, b. 1902
——————Francis ("Frank") Clement Davis, b. 1904
——————Ruth Davis, b. 1911
+Ellen Elizabeth Walker, b. 1833, m. 1870
——Peter Davis, b. 1812, d. 1873 +Jane Jeffries, b. 1825, m. 1845, d. 1891
  ten children and 35 grandchildren – see separate list
——Eliza Davis, b. 1813, d. 1901
+William Trumper, bap. 1801, m. 1836, d. 1838
+John Corser, bap. 1804, m. 1842, d. 1871
————Mary Corser, b. 1842, d. 1932
————Ann ("Annie") Corser, b. 1846, d. 1922
————Caroline Corser, b. 1847, d. 1916
————William Reynolds Corser, b. 1851, d. 1894 +Elizabeth Taylor, b. 1847, m. 1875, d. 1923
——————(William) Hombersley Corser, b. 1876, d. 1880
——————(John) Sidney Corser, b. 1878, d. 1942
——————Elizabeth ("Bessie") Caroline Corser, b. 1879, d. 1970
——————Annie Corser, b. 1881, d. 1881
——————(Jane) Margery Corser, b. 1885, d. 1918

Peter Davis' children and grandchildren

Peter Davis, b. 1812, d. 1873 +Jane Jeffries, b. 1825, m. 1845, d. 1891
——John Jeffries Davis, b. 1845, d. 1896 +Catherine ("Kate") Freer, b. 1846, m. 1874, d. 1906
————Eliza J. Davis, b. 1875, d. 1943
————Katherine ("Kay") Jeffries Davis, b. 1876, d. 1953
————Anne Jeffries Davis, b. 1878, d. after 1898
————Captain Henry J. ("Harry") Jeffries Davis, b. 1879, d. 1963
————Joyce Jeffries Davis, b. 1881, d. 1933
————Mary Jeffries Davis, b. 1883, d. 1961
————Edith Jeffries Davis, b. 1885, d. 1980
————Hilda Jeffries Davis, b. 1889, d. 1964
——Gertrude Louisa Davis, b. 1847, d. 1932 +M. Howard Freer, b. 1847, m. 1872, d. 1892
————Mary Gertrude Freer, b. 1874, d. 1882
————Kate Freer, b. 1877, d. 1882
————(Howard) Dudley Freer, b. 1879, d. 1960
————Edith Howard Dudley Freer, b. 1882, d. after 1949
————(William) Leacroft ("Lea") Howard Freer, b. 1884, d. 1915
————Lena Howard Freer, b. 1886, d. before 1972
——Laura Jane Meredith Davis, b. 1850, d. 1913 +Dr. M. Alfred Lutwyche, b. 1851, m. 1874, d. 1878
——Arthur Henry Davis, b. 1852, d. 1903 +Emily Child, b. 1856, m. 1881, d. 1906
————Harry William Davis, b. 1882, d. 1954
————Arthur Bertram Davis, b. 1885, d. 1957
——Agnes Elizabeth ("Lily") Davis, b. 1854, d. 1929 +Henry Freer, b. 1835, m. 1881, d. 1930
————Harold Henry Freer, b. 1884, d. 1904
——Georgina ("Ina") Reynolds Davis, b. 1856, d. 1940 +Dr. Henry Flamank Marshall, b. 1845, d. 1901
————Mary Flamank ("Madge") Marshall, b. 1869, d. 1962
————Flamank George Marshall, b. circa 1876, d. 1917
————Howard Marshall, b. circa 1886
——Eliza Augusta Davis, b. 1858, d. 1954
——Constance Alathea Davis, b. 1860, d. circa 1946 +Dr. Trevor Webster, b. 1862, m. 1885, d. circa 1904
————Cecil Trevor Webster, b. 1886, d. circa 1946
————Gladys Trevor Webster, b. 1889, d. 1923
————(Constance) Hilda Trevor ("Yeo") Webster, b. 1890, d. 1978
————Douglas Trevor Webster, b. 1891, d. circa 1970
————John Theodore Trevor Webster, b. 1894, d. 1979
————Patrick ("Pat") Trevor Webster, b. 1897, d. 1960
————Mary Trevor Webster, b. 1898, d. 1977
——Flora May ("Floo") Davis, b. 1862, d. 1957 +Herbert William Marshall, b. 1855, m. 1888, d. 1921
————Harold Ernest Marshall, b. 1889, d. 1969
————Cedric Herbert Marshall, b. 1890, d. 1956
————Ina May Marshall, b. 1892, d. 1975
————(Gertrude) Helen Marshall, b. 1895, d. 1961
————Peter George Marshall, b. 1897, d. 1952
————Phyllis Mary Marshall, b. 1900, d. 1981
————Eadith Flora Marshall, b. 1903, d. 1996
————Norman Jeffries Marshall, b. 1904, d. 1960
——Alice Marian Davis, b. 1867, d. 1922

Three marriages took place between children of Peter and Jane Davis, and children of Leacroft Freer of Kingswinford (1797-1887). Two marriages took place between Davises and Marshalls – both sons of Dr. George Henry Marshall of Kington (1813-84) and his wife Elizabeth née Mitchell, first cousin of Jane Davis.

John Reynolds' descendants

John Reynolds of Meole Bruce, b. circa 1698 +Elizabeth Boothby, b. circa 1702, m. 1723
—John Reynolds of Kemberton, bap. 1726, d. after 1772 +Mary Foxall, m. 1753, d. after 1772
  —Sarah Reynolds, bap. 1753
  —Anna Mia Reynolds, bap. 1755
  —Mary Reynolds, bap. 1757, d. 1830 + (her cousin) Peter Reynolds, bap. 1757, m. 1777, d. 1838
    —WILLIAM REYNOLDS of Nash, b. 1778, d. 1866 +RACHEL MYTTON, b. 1778, d. 1858
    —John Reynolds, bap. 1780, d. 1780
        —Elizabeth Reynolds, bap. 1782, d. 1813 +SAMUEL DAVIS Sr, b. c. 1768, m. 1804, d. 1837
          —WILLIAM DAVIS   )
          —Caroline Davis   )
          —THE REV. SAMUEL DAVIS) (see Samuel & Peter Davis's descendants' lists)
          —PETER DAVIS   )
          —ELIZA DAVIS   )
    —Mary Reynolds, b. 1783 +(--?--) Nurse,
      —William Nurse
    —ELEANOR REYNOLDS, b. circa 1785, d. 1843
      —EMMA REYNOLDS of Pershore, b. c. 1808, d. 1880 +Henry Bullock b. c. 1803, m. 1845, d. 1852
      +WILLIAM PARTRIDGE, bap. 1788, m. 1815, d. 1859
        —ELLEN PARTRIDGE, bap. 1817, d. 1870
        —Jane Partridge, bap. 1820, d. 1825
        —MARY PARTRIDGE, b. circa 1821
    —PETER REYNOLDS of Kemberton, b. circa 1790, d. 1865 +Sarah, b. 1805, d. 1878
      —Peter Reynolds, bap. 1832
      —William Reynolds, b. 1837
      —Mary Ann Reynolds, b. 1840
    —JOSEPH REYNOLDS of New House, b. c. 1791, d. 1868 +Mary Ann Seager, b. c. 1808, m.
      1831, d. 1881
    —MARIA REYNOLDS of Dean Park, bap. 1792, d. 1877 +William Harper, bap. 1795, m. 1852, d. 1871
  —John Reynolds, bap. 1759
  —Thomas Reynolds, bap. 1760
  —William Reynolds, b. 1762, d. 1841 +Elizabeth Bolton, m. 1792
    —William Reynolds, bap. 1793
    —John Reynolds, bap. 1795
    —Maria Reynolds, bap. 1797
    —Elizabeth Reynolds, bap. 1799
    —James Reynolds, b. 1802, d. 1882
    +(1)Susannah, b. circa 1802 (five children)
    +(2)Minella Mullard, bap. 1808, m. 1850, d. 1887 (one daughter)
  —ELEANOR REYNOLDS, bap. 1764, d. 1848 +John Nurs of Shifnal, b. circa 1757, m. 1785, d. 1824
  —PETER REYNOLDS of Burcote, bap. 1766, d. 1843 +ANN DAVIS HARPER, b. 1766, m. 1800, d. 1849
  —Margaret Reynolds, bap. 1768 +George Bradborne, m. 1792 (two sons)
  —Elizabeth Reynolds, bap. 1768 +Robert Robinson (his 2nd wife), bap. 1755
  —Joseph Reynolds, bap. 1770, d. 1840
  —James Reynolds, bap. 1772, d. 1841 +Charlotte Pearce, b. circa 1791, m. 1800, d. 1857
    —MARY ANN REYNOLDS, b. 1802 +JOHN BRIGHT, b. circa 1801, m. 1824 (six children)
    —MARIA REYNOLDS of Shifnal, bap. 1803
    —(five other children)
—Peter Reynolds of Meole Bruce, bap. 1728, d. 1770 +Jane, m. 1756
  —Peter Reynolds, bap. 1757, d. 1838 + (his cousin) Mary Reynolds, bap. 1757, m. 1777, d. 1830 (8
    children – see above)
  —Elizabeth Reynolds, b. 1758, d. 1809
    +(1)George Webb, m. 1777
    +(2)Robert Robinson (his 1st wife), bap. 1755, m. 1782

(Those in capitals are mentioned in the diary.)

Thomas Partridge's descendants

Thomas Partridge, bap. 1757 +Mary Lamb, bap. 1762, m. 1784, d. 1840
——John Partridge, bap. 1785
——Thomas Partridge, bap. 1786
——WILLIAM PARTRIDGE, bap. 1788, d. 1859 +ELEANOR REYNOLDS, b. circa 1785, d. 1843
————ELLEN PARTRIDGE, bap. 1817, d. 1870   )
————Jane Partridge, bap. 1820, d. 1825   ) (see John Reynolds' descendants)
————MARY PARTRIDGE, b. circa 1821   )
——Samuel Partridge, bap. 1789
——MARY SMITH PARTRIDGE, bap. 1791 +THOMAS BAYLIS, b. circa 1773, m. 1831
——JAMES PARTRIDGE, bap. 1793 +CATHERINE PURCHASE DEE, bap. 1804, d. 1844
————John Partridge, b. circa 1828
————Mary Ann Dee Partridge, b. circa 1831
————Catherine Partridge, b. circa 1831
————Charles James Partridge, b. circa 1832, d. 1889
——————+(1)Elizabeth Edwards, bap. 1834, m. 1857
————————James Adams Partridge, b. 1858
————————Charles George Partridge, b. 1860
————————Elizabeth M. C. Partridge, b. 1861
————————Ellen Kate Partridge, b. 1863 +Thomas Edward Baker, m. 1885
——————————Thomas James Baker, b. 1877
————————Harry Partridge, b. 1865
————————Arthur Frederick Partridge, b. 1866
————————Gertrude Partridge, b. 1868
——————+(2)Margaret Ann Philpots (see below)
————————Margaret E. Partridge, b. 1872
————————George A. Partridge, b. 1873
————————John H. Partridge, b. 1874
————————Florence M. Partridge, b. 1877
————Frederic Partridge, b. circa 1834
————Elizabeth Partridge, b. circa 1838
————Ellen Partridge, b. 1839
————Fanny Partridge, b. 1841
——Margaret Lidia Partridge, bap. 1795
——Edward Partridge, b. circa 1797
——MARGARET ANN PARTRIDGE, bap. 1800 +JOHN HARVEY, b. 1807, m. 1835
————Ellen M. Harvey, b. 1837
————Eliza M. Harvey, b. 1839
————Lucy Harvey, b. 1841
——Maria Jane Partridge, b. circa 1802, d. 1892 +George Adams Philpots, b. circa 1802, m. 1829, d. 1852
————Margaret Ann Philpots, bap. 1836 +Charles James Partridge (see above)
——————Margaret E. Partridge (see above)
——————George A. Partridge (see above)
——————John H. Partridge (see above)
——————Florence M. Partridge (see above)
————Elizabeth Mary Philpots, b. 1841
——ELIZABETH PARTRIDGE, bap. 1804

(Those in capitals are mentioned in the diary.)

Edward Mytton's children and grandchildren

EDWARD MYTTON of Boraston, bap. 1748, d. 1839
+Elizabeth Morris, b. 1746, m. 1776, d. 1819
——MARY MYTTON, b. 1777, d. 1868
　+John Smith of Ribbesford & Kimbolton, m. 1804, d. before 1836
　——EDWARD SMITH, b. 1805
　——JOHN SMITH of Coney Green, Ribbesford, b. 1810, d. 1871
　　+ELIZABETH MYTTON, m. 1836 Lindridge, see below
　——Letitia Smith, b. 1811
　——CATHERINE SMITH, b. 1811
　　+GEORGE WINTON of The Vine, Sutton, b. 1806, d. 1868
　——ELIZABETH SMITH, bap. 1815, d. 1876
　　+WILLIAM MYTTON of Vicarage Farm, Lindridge, m. 1836, see below
——RACHEL MYTTON, b. 1778, d. 1858
　+WILLIAM REYNOLDS of Nash Court Farm, see John Reynolds' descendants – no issue
——William Mytton, b. 1780, d. 1818
　+Catherine Jones of Knighton-on-Teme, m. 1804
　——WILLIAM MYTTON of Vicarage Farm, Lindridge, b. 1809, d. 1871
　　+ELIZABETH SMITH, see above
　——EDWARD MYTTON, b. 1814, d. 1899 Nelson, New Zealand
　　+Martha Nottingham of Brimfield, m. 1837
　——ELIZABETH MYTTON, b. 1816, d. 1864
　　+JOHN SMITH of Coney Green, see above

(Those in capitals are mentioned in the diary.)

Lowes of Trysull and Sutton, and the Giles family connection

Lowe families mentioned in the Diary

Lowes of Trysull and Sutton, and the Giles family connection

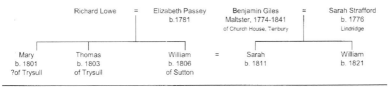

	Richard Lowe	=	Elizabeth Passey b.1781		Benjamin Giles Maltster, 1774-1841 of Church House, Tenbury	=	Sarah Strafford b. 1776 Lindridge

| Mary b. 1801 ?of Trysull | Thomas b. 1803 of Trysull | William b. 1806 of Sutton | = | Sarah b. 1811 | William b. 1821 |

Lowes of Milson and of The Lea

Thomas Lowe = Susanna
of Church House, Milson

William Henry
bp. 1809
of The Lea, near Cleobury Mortimer

Lowes of Greenway Head

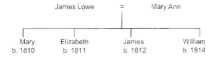

James Lowe = Mary Ann

| Mary b. 1810 | Elizabeth b. 1811 | James b. 1812 | William b. 1814 |

Reference is also made to a seemingly different William Lowe and Miss Lowe of Weston, a hamlet some little distance to the North of Greenway Head.

The Preservation and Discovery of Peter Davis' Original Diaries

On the first page of the diary is the following inscription:

Gertrude Louisa Freer
Her "Father's Diary"
With much love
from her Mother
Jane Davis
Dowles Rectory, Bewdley
Feb 14th 1884

Gertrude Freer was the second child and eldest daughter of Peter and Jane Davis. As a widow then in her sixtieth year, she moved in 1906 from England to the west coast of Canada with her two daughters. There she occupied a house which had been built for her the previous year by her two sons in what is now Maple Ridge, British Columbia (BC). Freer House was in 2000 awarded the Residential Heritage Award by the city of Maple Ridge.

In the spring of 2009, my wife, Genie, and I made a trip from New Brunswick (NB) to BC and made a point of going to see Freer House. There we discovered that the last known descendant of Gertrude had died about three years earlier, at the age of ninety. After returning to NB a few weeks later, we had a call from Maple Ridge reporting that some old diaries had been discovered in a desk given to a friend by the last surviving member of the family. Since there were no immediate descendants, members of the community had planned to destroy the diaries, but arrangements were made to have them sent instead to NB. Being a great-great-grandson of Peter Davis and also being related to the Maple Ridge family through my great-grandmother, who was a Freer, I felt certain that the diaries would be of interest.

When the diaries arrived in NB in the late autumn of 2009, it was discovered that the 26 January 1836 to 26 November 1837 diary of Peter Davis and also his original 1835 travel diary were included in the package. Both volumes were in exceedingly good condition, indicating that they had been treasured and safely guarded by at least three generations of Davis descendants.

It was only by a stroke of fate, good luck and good timing that the diaries were discovered and saved from destruction.

Bruce Coates

Biographies

Adams, Messrs. James & George
The brothers Adams lived in Lindridge Parish: the younger, George (1804–1843), lived with two of his five sisters at Eardiston, where he farmed as tenant of his older brother. James (1800–1884) inherited the Woodson estate (3,500 acres in total), part of which he farmed likewise. James never married, but had a daughter, Elizabeth (born 1834), by Sarah Edwards of Thornbury, Herefordshire. (Subsequently, Elizabeth married Charles Partridge, a son of James and Catherine Partridge – see Appendix 3. They had seven children, the eldest, James Adams Partridge, inheriting Woodson in 1892: he employed 1,200 hop pickers there during the season.)

Alcock, Thomas (1801–1866)
He was the Whig MP for the rotten borough of Newton, 1826–1830. By 1831 it was estimated that the electorate had fallen to fifty-two: each elector had as many votes as there were seats to be filled – two in this case – and votes had to be cast by a spoken declaration in public. Alcock contested Ludlow in the 1837 election, without success. Two years later, however, one of the victorious candidates, Viscount Clive, succeeded to his father's title, causing a by-election; Alcock stood again, and eventually became the MP after the election of his opponent Henry Clive was set aside for bribery. He lost his seat in 1840, but was MP for East Surrey from 1847 until the year before his death. In 1837 he was High Sheriff of Surrey.

Anderson solicitors of Ludlow
George Anderson (born 1780), Rodney Anderson (born 1810) and Francis Anderson were all in practice together; they were the witnesses to Samuel Davis' will. Rodney Anderson was subsequently secretary to the committee which worked unsuccessfully for the election of Thomas Alcock as MP for Ludlow in 1839, giving evidence to the select committee on the petition which was submitted following that election; the result was set aside for bribery and Mr Alcock deemed elected in place of the corrupt Henry Clive.

Aunt Maria – See Reynolds, Maria

Aunt Partridge – See Partridge, Eleanor

Bailey, Joseph (1783–1858)
An ironmaster in Glanusk, south Wales, he was High Sheriff of Monmouthshire in 1826, and one of the two MPs for Worcester (a Tory) from 1835 to 1847. He was elected for Breconshire in 1847, and represented that constituency until his death.

In 1852, he was created a baronet. He married twice, with nine children in all. His grandson, the 2nd baronet, was later created 1st Baron Glenusk.

Baker, the Revd (born 1803)
John Durand Baker was the son-in-law of Mrs Lucy Fowler, née Hill, coheiress of Court of Hill; he became vicar of Bishop's Tawton, Devon. With his wife Sarah, he had seven children.

Bangham, Mr
This could be either of two who lived at Mount Pleasant, Burford, namely Edward (1787–1847), a maltster of Teme Street, Tenbury, or William (1786–1861).

Baylis, Thomas (born c. 1773)
He married William Partridge's sister, Mary Smith Partridge (born 1791), in 1831.

Baylis, William (born 1806)
He lived at Canal Cottage, Burford.

Beddoe family
Charles Beddoe, a farmer (born 1771), lived at Curdall, west of Cleobury Mortimer, together with his son Thomas, a maltster (born 1806).

Benbow, John (born c. 1800)
A farmer living just outside Tenbury, he later moved with his wife Ann to Staffordshire and became a shopkeeper in Penn.

Bishop, Mr
It is possible that this is the John Bishop who went bankrupt, and from whose administrators Samuel Davis bought land at Eastham, let to John Nott.

Blakeway, Thomas (1770–1852)
A mercer, born in Tenbury, he was unmarried and lived in Teme Street. He was also a keen gardener, 'whose zeal in the encouragement of horticultural pursuits is equalled only by his benevolence and generosity'. [Maund]

Blashill, Thomas (1793–1871)
A Yorkshireman, he married a Hereford girl, Ann Preece, and worked as a land agent.

Boraston, John
A farmer who, with his family, is listed in the 1841 Census as residing at Sutton Farm, Kidderminster.

Borthwick, Peter (1804–1852)
A Scot, he went from Edinburgh University up to Cambridge, and became known as a speaker against the abolition of slavery. 'With all his self-conceit, he had a plausible and insinuating address,' in the words of a contemporary. He stood unsuccessfully for Parliament in Evesham in 1832, but won a seat there three years later. He was re-elected alongside George Rushout-Bowles in 1837; on petition, though, he was found guilty of bribery in giving a silver snuff-box to a voter, and Lord Marcus Hill (a Whig) declared elected in his place. 'The Conservative ladies of Evesham, however, were much attached to the clever, attractive, and fluent Peter, and at a

dinner presented him with a huge silver salver, on which occasion he commented on Mr. Rushout having abandoned him, and used such terms as led to a duel. Nothing resulted, and Borthwick withdrew the offensive remarks. Rushout was rejected at the next election, in 1841, in consequence of the sympathy generally felt for the ladies' favourite.' [Noake] George Rushout-Bowles fought the duel with Borthwick on 8 May 1838 (one of the last in England). Borthwick remained a member for Evesham until 1847, Carlyle describing him in Parliament as 'tossed from side to side like a dead cat'. He was nevertheless responsible for an important provision in the new Poor Law, 'the Borthwick Clause', ensuring married couples were not compelled to separate when entering the Workouse. Four years before his death, Borthwick was made editor of the *Morning Post*. He was married to Margaret, née Colville; they had four children, one of their sons becoming the 1st Baron Glanesk.

Brancker, James
The name of the architect who designed a strange Gothic fantasy mansion at the head of Windermere was Webster of Kendal. The Croft was built for wealthy Liverpool 'sugar king' James Brancker in around 1830, and his stately Clappersgate residence boasted elegant ironwork and clusters of castellated chimneys. Father and son firm Francis & George Webster, and their draughtsman Miles Thompson, designed fine country houses, banks, churches and smaller dwellings in Kendal and further afield. Classical touches were worked into The Croft, such as fluted Doric columns. Now flats, the Clappersgate house is lucky to be standing at all. Cleveland County Council wanted to demolish it and put an outdoor pursuits centre in its place. There was an outcry, the Victorian Society being one of many voices calling for the 'strange gothic fantasy' to be preserved. In its glory days, it had been home to high society. Describing Brancker's mansion, Hartley Coleridge – son of the poet – wrote that it offered 'good dinners, enough and not too much good wine and excellent bad puns'.

Bright, John (*c.* 1801 – after 1871)
Married to Mary Ann, see below. Originally from New Radnor, he was land agent to the 1st Baron Hatherton.

Bright, Mary Ann (born *c.* 1802)
Née Reynolds, she was Peter Davis' first cousin once removed. She married John Bright in Shifnal in 1824, and they had at least six children – a son and five daughters.

Broadbent, the Revd C. F. (1810–1872)
Born in East India, he was educated at Eton and St Mary Hall, Oxford, and married Barbara Anne, one of the five daughters of the patron of the living of Worfield, the Revd E. S. Davenport, whom he succeeded as vicar; later, he became rural dean of Trysull. He and his wife had one son and one daughter.

Brougham, Henry Peter, 1st Baron Brougham and Vaux (1778–1868)
By 1835, the reformer Brougham, who had been Lord Chancellor in Lord Grey's Whig administration, was out of office; he never again served in government. See also the Revd George Hall (who would have spoken of Lord Brougham to Peter Davis).

Buckingham, Richard Snow Mortimor (born 1817)
The Revd Samuel Davis' wife's younger brother.

Buckingham, the Revd James (born 1770)
Vicar of Burrington, near Chulmleigh, Devon, and rector of Doddiscombleigh, he
was also patron of the living of Burrington, to which his son-in-law, Samuel Davis,
succeeded in 1852; his wife Lucinda was one of eleven children.

Byron, Lord (1788–1824)
The poet used the great hall and dining room of his Nottinghamshire home to
practice fencing, boxing and pistol shooting with friends, and kept a bear, among
other pets.

Chambers, Lydia (born 1801)
The Burford schoolmistress. To the west of Dean Park, and part of the Davis farm,
was 'Chambers Orchard' as marked on the 1840 Burford field map; this may,
however, be a red herring.

Charles II, King (1630–85)
Charles II was crowned King of Scots at Scone in 1651, nine years before he became
King of England.

Charlton, Edmund Lechmere (1789–1845)
He was one of the two MPs for Ludlow from 1835–37 – a Tory. He owned Ludford
Park, Herefordshire; Whitton Court, Shropshire; and Hanley Castle, Worcestershire.
A barrister, he died unmarried.

Clive, Viscount (1785–1848)
Son of the 1st Earl of Powis, he was a staunch Tory, one of the two MPs for Ludlow
from 1806 to 1839, when he succeeded his father as 2nd Earl. One of the conditions
of his inheriting the Powis Castle estates was that he settled an uncle's massive
gambling debts. As Lord Lieutenant of Montgomeryshire, he played a major part
in suppressing the Chartist Riots of 1839. By his wife, a daughter of the 3rd Duke
of Montrose, he had two daughters and five sons, one of whom (out shooting
pheasants on the Powis Estate) accidentally shot his father in the leg: he died as a
result.

Cockburn Lord (1779–1854)
Henry Lord Cockburn – besides being a judge of the Court of Session – wrote the
Life of Lord Jeffrey, with a Selection from his Correspondence, which appeared in
1852; both of them had earlier been prominent Whig politicians.

Collins, Samuel (born 1795)
Burford registrar, subsequently appointed relieving officer of the Tenbury Poor Law
Union, first district. Samuel and his wife Ann had a daughter, also Ann (born 1826).

Collis, George (1783–1838)
He was married to Mary, née Muscott: they had one daughter. A memorial to
him is to be found in Titley church, Herefordshire, his wife's family home being
nearby.

Collis, Mrs Ann
Of Greenfield House, Stourbridge; her late husband was related to George Collis
(above).

Cooke family of Hill Top
William Cooke (born 1801) farmed 700 acres at Hill Top, Rochford, where he lived with his aunt Sarah, wife Charlotte (born 1800) and five children.

Cooke, Joseph (born 1806)
Surgeon, of The Cross, Tenbury.

Corehouse, Lord
A grandson of the 5th Lord Cranstoun, the Hon. George Cranstoun, Lord Corehouse, was, besides being a member of the Court of Session, a Greek scholar and lifelong friend of Sir Walter Scott.

Cotterell – see Geers-Cotterell, Sir John.

Coucher, Martin (1802–1836)
His home, Clater Park, lies to the east of Bromyard. He was buried on 12 May 1836 at Alfrick, Worcestershire, survived by his wife Winifred and a number of children.

Courtney, Thomas (born 1801)
He occupied Harp Cottage, near Newnham Turnpike, as tenant of Samuel Davis. (Eliza Trumper inherited this property subsequent to her father's death.) Born in Burford and married to a Knighton girl, with one daughter, he was listed as a tailor with three employees at the time of the 1841 Census.

Cowdell, George
Lived in Burford parish with his wife Anne and five children (born between 1801 and 1809 – all baptised on the same day).

Curwen, John Christian (1756–1828)
The Whig MP bought Belle Isle House (built in 1774 and circular in plan) in 1781 as a wedding present for his wife, Isabella: he named the island in her honour. Their descendants lived on the island until 1993.

Dansey, George Henry (1796–1853)
Attorney, of Broad Street, Ludlow, he acted for Mr Edward Salwey. He also acted as one of the election agents for Henry Clive in the 1839 Ludlow by-election, the result of which was set aside for bribery. He and his wife Margaret had two daughters. He owned a rare stuffed Squacco heron. The Dansey family at one time owned 7,500 acres locally including the Bleathwood estate in Herefordshire, just over the border from Burford.

Davenport, the Revd Edmund Sharington (1778–1842)
He married the heiress Elizabeth Tongue and had been vicar of Worfield for thirty years. His wife bore five sons and five daughters, one of the daughters marrying the Revd Cornelius Broadbent, vicar of Worfield in 1837.

Davies, Thomas Henry Hastings (1789–1846)
Of Elmley Park, he was a Lt-Col. in the Army and one of the two MPs for Worcester from 1818 to 1835 (opposing the Reform Bill and supporting protective trade measures), and again from 1837 to 1841. He married Augusta Anne, née Crespigny, but died without issue.

Davis, Edward
Peter Davis' uncle, eleven years older than his brother Samuel. Apart from what is in
the diary, the only thing known about Edward Davis is that he died aged seventy-eight.

Davis, Eliza (1813–1901)
Peter Davis' younger sister – see Introduction.

Davis, Francis
One of those landowners in Tenbury who were involved in the tithe litigation with
the Revd George Hall.

Davis, Henry of Orleton (born 1808)
Christened Thomas Henry, he was a land agent and surveyor, living with his parents,
Thomas and Hannah Davis at Middle House, Orleton, in the parish of Eastham.

Davis, Henry of Tenbury (born 1810)
Henry Davis MD, FRCS lived with his wife Isabella, née Henderson, in Cross Street,
Tenbury. Were Peter Davis and Henry Davis related or just neighbours? The diary
nowhere seems to suggest a relationship.

Davis, Lucinda (1810–1855)
Wife of the Revd Samuel Davis. She was the sixth of eleven children of the Revd
James Buckingham – at least three of whom married clergymen.

Davis, Peter (17 January 1812 – 3 October 1873)
Generally, see Introduction. The third son of Samuel and Elizabeth Davis, he no
doubt learnt his farming from his father and eldest brother William. By the age
of twenty-three, when he embarked on his travels north, he was well-versed in
agricultural practices, and eager for knowledge of modern methods. It is clear from
his diary that, besides farming, he also possessed a wide range of general interests.

Davis, Samuel senior (*c.* 1768–1837)
Peter Davis' father – see Introduction.

Davis, the Revd Samuel (1810–1883)
Peter Davis' older brother – see Introduction.

Davis, Thomas of Orleton (born 1759)
The husband of Hannah and father of Thomas Henry Davis, he lived at Middle
House, Orleton, in the parish of Eastham. Formerly an auctioneer, he died in the
early spring of 1837, though his death was not recorded in the diary.

Davis, the Revd Thomas (born 1804)
A graduate of Queen's College, Oxford, he was curate of All Saints, Worcester,
before becoming perpetual curate of St John's Roundhay, Yorkshire. As well as a
volume of devotional verse, he published, in 1864, *Hymns Old and New*. With his
wife Christiana Maria, née Hobbes, he had six children.

Davis, William (1805–1888)
Peter Davis' eldest brother, a farmer, was a tenant of Mr Rushout at Dean Park,
Burford. His father had held the tenancy previously, and his son Peter took it on
subsequently. See Introduction.

Dickins, John (*c.* 1776–1851)
A retired army captain, subsequently a farmer, he had (successively) two wives, each called Ann, and some nine children.

Edwards, Benjamin (born 1793)
Farmer of The Cliffords, Nash, which he rented from Mr V. W. Wheeler (see below). His younger brother was Edmund (below), and he was married with four sons and a daughter.

Edwards, Edmund (born 1796)
Farmer and miller, he lived at Mill Farm, Burford, with his wife Eliza (born 1803), a daughter Mary (born 1829) and two sons (William, 1830, and John, 1832 – two more sons were born subsequent to 1837), and his widowed mother, Mary. As well as farming some 360 acres (mostly rented from Mr Rushout), Mr Edwards also supplied bread to the Tenbury Workhouse from September 1837, having successfully tendered '7d ¼ per 4lb. Loaf'. He was a churchwarden.

Edwards, the Revd Joseph (born *c.* 1812)
Rector of Croft, married with six children.

Edwards, Mary (1755–1836)
Mother of Benjamin, and of Edmund with whom she lived at Mill Farm, Burford.

Eliza – See Davis, Eliza

Eykyn, Richard (*c.* 1786–1850)
Married to Susanna, née Starr, with at least eight children (one becoming an MP), he was a London stockbroker with a country estate at Ackleton, just south of Badger.

Father – see Davis, Samuel senior

France, Thomas
Solicitor of 22 Foregate Street, Worcester, who was also a Master Extraordinary in Chancery: all his windows were broken in 1831 in the Worcester Reform Bill riots – he was known to belong to 'the unpopular party' opposing the Bill.

Fuller, Joseph Bury (born 1801)
Attorney of Cross Street, Tenbury, married to Mary, with five children.

Geers-Cotterell, Sir John (1757–1845)
1st Bart, of Garnons, eight miles west of Hereford; MP for Herefordshire for many years until 1831.

Gent, James (1784–1868)
Boot and shoemaker, and retailer of beer, of Teme Street, Tenbury and subsequently the Town Crier; his son, also called James, followed in his footsteps.

Giles family of Hope
John Giles lived at Hope Court, Hope Bagot with his wife Hester and eight children (born between 1809 and 1818), including Benjamin (1813) and Mary (1816).

Giles family of Tenbury
Benjamin Giles (1774–1841), corn merchant, maltster and hop dealer lived at
Church House, Tenbury – referred to by Tunstall Evans in 1840 as 'now the romantic
residence of Mr. Giles senior.' He and his wife Sarah, née Strafford (of Lindridge),
had daughters Sarah and Anne (born 1811) and sons Thomas and William. Sarah
married William Lowe of Sutton on 24 October 1836. See Appendix 3.

Godson, Richard QC (1797–1849)
Mr Godson was the brother of Septimus Godson of Tenbury (see below). A graduate
of Caius College, Cambridge, he was first called to the bar before entering politics as
MP for St Albans, 1831–2. He was then elected for Kidderminster in 1832, when the
town was enfranchised following the passing of the Reform Bill, '… a remarkably
small constituency – something under 500. Mr. Godson, a barrister on the Oxford
Circuit, who was highly popular with the weavers for having defended some of them
at Worcester Assizes in a case of riot, was the first Member chosen… Mr. Phillips, a
gentleman from Warwickshire, opposed him, but lost the election. In 1835, however,
Mr. Phillips persevered and ousted his opponent, but retired in 1837, when Mr.
Godson returned to his *old love*, beating a Mr. Bagshaw' (Noake). From 1837, he
served Kidderminster in Parliament until his death. He voted against slavery, and
described himself as 'A Reformer pledged to uphold the Established Church.' He
married Mary, née Hargreaves, from Lancashire: they had at least two children.

Godson, Septimus Holmes
Mr Godson of The Court, Tenbury, was an attorney with an office in Teme Street
and a local landowner; he was the first to discover the benefits of Tenbury spring
water, in 1839, which gave rise to the town changing its name to Tenbury Wells. He
and his wife Susannah endowed Tenbury church with its organ gallery and organ (in
1843). Mr Godson was the brother of Richard Godson MP – see above.

Gordon, Dr Robert (1786–1853)
A highly popular preacher in Edinburgh, he was described in his obituary in the
Free Church Magazine as 'one of the great instruments of the Evangelical Revival in
Edinburgh and Scotland'. Having been Moderator of the General Assembly in 1841,
he was one of the many ministers of the established church who broke away to form
the Free Church of Scotland two years later. 'A quiet, capable man,' he was also a
scientist; with his wife Isabella, he had twelve children.

Graham, Sir James MP (1792–1861)
The Graham family owned the Netherby Park estate from the 1600s. Dr Robert
Graham (1711–1782) was a leading agriculturalist of his day. 'By his improvements
the rent was more than quadrupled, and the wealth of the tenants increased in a much
greater proportion; and, what was still better, he saw them, as it were, metamorphosed,
from an ignorant, quarrelsome, and disorderly rabble, into an intelligent, peaceable,
regular, and respectable class of men' (Mannix and Whellan). Sir James Robert George
Graham MP, his grandson, inherited the estate in 1824 on the death of his father,
the first baronet. Though much of his life was taken up with politics, he had the
reputation of a good landlord, rebuilding cottages and farm buildings, introducing tile
drains to reclaim marshland, and improving the breed of stock on his estate.

Grove, William (born 1796)
The proprietor of the Swan Hotel, the Burford coaching inn, he lived there with his
wife Margaret (born 1793). The artist Sir Thomas Lawrence (1769–1830), whose

uncle was the Revd Francis William Read, vicar of Tenbury, is said when a young man to have portrayed William Grove's mother.

Hall, the Revd George (1783–1845)
Formerly curate of Chesterfield, he became vicar of Tenbury and rector of Rochford from 1827 till his death. He was also Domestic Chaplain to Lord Brougham and Vaux, Lord Chancellor, 1830–1834: they were both Whigs from Westmorland. Mr Hall was the compiler of *The Dictate Book; being Lessons on Life, Men and Manners*, published in London in 1831: an advertisement reads, 'Here the path to Riches, Reputation and Happiness is marked out, and directions for forming the Mind, the Morals, and Manners set forth.' *The British Critic*, a quarterly theological review, reported on a sermon he gave in Tenbury in 1832, subsequently published in London: 'The first fourteen pages present us with a powerful description of death by cholera ... The next portion informs us that the plague has been sent upon our land on account of the violent opposition that has been made to the Reform Bill ... Mr. Hall proceeds to vindicate the right of the Church to the property with which it is endowed, and to denounce the newspapers and periodicals ... There is no mention of Christianity in this discourse.' It is interesting that Peter Davis, a Conservative, should have enjoyed what seems like a warm friendship with Mr Hall. See Introduction.

Hand, William
Maltster of Corve Street, Ludlow.

Harding, Henry (1784–1876)
Maltster of 105 Corve Street, Ludlow.

Hardwick, Mrs & Miss
Sarah Hardwick (born *c.* 1786) was the wife of John Bell Hardwick of Worfield. They lived with their son, John, a farmer, and their unmarried daughter Mary (born 1805).

Harvey, John
A tobacco manufacturer, he married Margaret Ann Partridge on 11 May 1835, at Ombersley, Worcestershire: she was sister-in-law to Peter Davis' aunt Eleanor. See Appendix 3: Thomas Partridge's Descendants. They lived in Leazes Terrace, to the west (and north) of the old centre of Newcastle. Leazes Terrace was designed by Thomas Oliver and built by Richard Grainger between 1829 and 1834. (By 1841 the Harveys had acquired three daughters and four servants.)

Hastings, Dr Charles (1794–1866)
Born in Ludlow, the 'zealous and enlightened' Dr Hastings was thought to be the best-known physician in the West Midlands. In 1832, he was one of the founders of what was to become the British Medical Association, and was eventually knighted in 1850. He was also an Alderman for the City of Worcester, a founder of the Worcester Natural History Society and a lifelong philanthropist. Married to Hannah, née Woodyat, they had three children.

Hatherton, 1st Baron (1791–1863)
Formerly Edward Littleton MP, he lived at Teddesley Park, Penkridge, where he 'undertook an extensive development of his lands. By 1850, despite the gravelly nature of the soil and the neglected state of the land before he began his draining

and irrigation, he was farming 1,700 acres with great success, producing good crops of wheat and barley and supporting 200 head of cattle, including a herd of Herefords, and 2,000 head of Southdown sheep. There were 700 acres in regular cultivation, mainly on four-course rotation, and the rest was parkland, irrigated meadow, and some less developed high ground adjoining Cannock Chase. Lord Hatherton also gave much encouragement to the tenant farmers of the district and by 1860 had established a free agricultural college at Teddesley Hay, where 30 boys were educated, spending most of the day on his farm and the rest in "educational pursuits".' (*Victoria County History*)

Head, Sir Edmund Walker Bart (1805–1868)
An Assistant Poor Law Commissioner from 1836–1841.

Hemming, Richard
Cattle breeder and magistrate, originally from Silvington, Worcestershire.

Holland, the Revd Thomas Edward Mytton (born 1793)
Educated at Charterhouse, he was vicar of Stoke Bliss.

Home, Thomas (born 1776)
Schoolmaster, he and his wife Mary lived in Teme Street, Tenbury, with their sons, Benjamin (born 1793) and William (born 1801), printers, and daughter Sarah Home (born 1804); William Davis recalled witnessing (aged nine) the Proclamation of Peace after the Battle of Waterloo in the Market Square, Tenbury, read by Mr Home seated on a white horse.

Hope family
John Thomas Hope (*c.* 1769–1854) of Netley Hall, Dorrington, Shropshire, and 37 Upper Seymour Street, London, 'that benevolent Christian', in the words of Charles Hulbert, put together an important collection of newspapers, now in the Bodleian Library. He married Ellen Esther Mary Edwardes, daughter and heiress of Sir Thomas Edwardes Bart, of Greete, Shropshire, who died on 4 June 1837. Samuel Davis was tenant of property formerly owned by Sir Thomas. The Hopes had a daughter and two sons. The daughter, Louisa Mary Anne, married her cousin Sir Henry Edwardes Bart. The elder son, Thomas Henry (born 1794), was High Sheriff of Shropshire in 1837; he married (in 1833) Louisa Charlotte, née Leighton (born 1808), the daughter of a former mayor of Shrewsbury (their three eldest children being Henry, William and Ellen). The younger son, the Revd Frederick William Hope MA, DCL (1797–1862) founded the Hope Department of Entomology at the University of Oxford.

Hotchkiss family
Thomas Hotchkiss (born *c.* 1786), saddler, of King Street, Ludlow, lived there with his wife Elizabeth and three daughters, Maria, Elizabeth and Caroline.

Hume, David (1711–1776)
The celebrated philosopher and author of a popular *History of England* possessed a 'famously but also genuinely equable, sociable, and cheerful character'. Married three times, he had six children and seven step-children.

James I, King (1566–1625)
James I of England, from 1603, and VI of Scotland (from 1567).

Jameson, Robert (1774–1854)
A Scottish naturalist and mineralogist, he held the post of Regius Professor of
Natural History at the University of Edinburgh for fifty years. Charles Darwin, aged
sixteen when a pupil at the University, had (also) found his lectures boring.

Jeffrey, Lord (1773–1850)
Francis Lord Jeffrey was – besides being a judge of the Court of Session – the first
salaried editor of the *Edinburgh Review*. His colleague Lord Cockburn wrote the
Life of Lord Jeffrey, with a Selection from his Correspondence, which appeared in
1852. Both had earlier been prominent Whig politicians.

Jeffreys-Winnington, Captain Henry (1794–1873)
Of Stanford Court, Stanford-on-Teme, the fifth and youngest son of Sir Edward
Winnington, 2nd Bart, he was a captain in the 39th Foot and served as MP for West
Worcestershire between 1833 and 1841.

Johnstone family
Captain John Johnstone JP (born 1784), a former High Sheriff of Herefordshire,
lived at Mainstone Court, Trumpet, near Ledbury, and owned more than 700
acres at Broncroft, north of Ludlow. His second son, George Henry Johnstone
(1818–1897), a graduate of Trinity College, Cambridge, was ordained and later
became rector of Sutton St Nicholas, near Hereford. His sister's father-in-law was
Theophilus Salwey (see below).

Jones, the Revd David (born 1789)
From Breconshire, he was the curate of Burford (second portion). He lived with
his wife Joan Elizabeth, née Price (born 1794), in one of the rectories at Burford,
together with a large family: Mary Christiana (born Burford, 1821), Joan Elisabeth
(1824), Susan Jane (1826), Margaret Wall (1828), Samuel Wall (1829), Sarah
Decima (1830), Charlotte Lydia (1832) and Harriet Helen Burford (1834). ('Miss
Jones' was engaged as governess for the Cooke children at Hill Top on 30th October
1837.) Mr Jones subsequently became rector of Hope Bagot.

Jones, George (born 1799)
He farmed 87 acres at Bank Farm, Burford, rented from Mr Rushout, having
married Caroline, née Webb (born *c.* 1811), on 7 April 1836: they had two children.
By 1837, he was a churchwarden.

Jones, James
Veterinary surgeon of Corve Street, Ludlow.

Jones, William (born *c.* 1795)
A blacksmith of Cross Street, Tenbury, he became the Burford Vestry Clerk
– married with two children.

Jones, William of Bridgnorth
Of The Vaults, Underhill Street, Bridgnorth.

Kinnersley, Francis (1759–1837)
He lived in Burford all his life.

Lambert, William
Father of Susanna Jane, he was one of the executors of the will of her husband
George Nicholls following his premature death.

Lavender, John (1808–1842)
Married with four children; a Court Baron and Court Leet used to be held at Bury
Hall Farm, Wolverly, which he owned.

Lawley, John (born *c.* 1801)
Farmer of Cleobury Lodge Farm, Neen Savage, he was married to Elizabeth, with a
son, John.

Lawson, Mrs Barbara (died 1838)
Née Henderson, she was the widow of the Revd Marmaduke Lawson, rector of
Sproatley, Yorkshire, and mother-in-law of the Revd Alexander Stewart.

Lawson, the Revd James
Vicar of Buckminster, Leicestershire, he was the brother-in-law of the Revd
Alexander Stewart.

Ledington, Philip
Married to Elizabeth, with a daughter, Anne (born 1817)

Lewis, David the Revd
He ran a day school at Cross Street, Tenbury.

Lloyd, Dr Thomas (born *c.* 1806)
Physician to the Ludlow Dispensary, he lived in Broad Street and was married to
Lydia, née Tench; they had no children.

Lloyd, Theodore (1806–1880)
He was a carpet manufacturer, 'with his sensitive, interesting face.' Married to
a young widow, Anna Ash, he moved to London in 1840, where he set up the
stockbroking firm of Lloyd & Ward. He was a member of the Stock Exchange for
more than thirty years. He and his wife left the Friends and turned to the Church of
England in the 1840s.

Lowe of Greenway Head
James and Mary Ann Lowe of Greenway Head Farm (he was a tenant of Mr
Rushout) had sons, amongst them James (born 1812) and William (born 1814), and
daughters Mary and Elizabeth. See Appendix 3.

Lowe of Milson
Thomas and Susanna Lowe were the parents of William Lowe of The Lea. See
Appendix 3.

Lowe of The Lea
Lea Farm, West of Cleobury Mortimer, was the home of William Lowe (a farmer)
and Mary Lowe. William's parents were Thomas and Susanna Lowe of Milson. See
Appendix 3.

Lowe, Thomas of Trysull (born 1803)
The son of Richard and Elizabeth Lowe of Aston Botterell, he was the elder brother of William Lowe of Sutton. See Appendix 3.

Lowe, William of Sutton (born 1806)
The son of Richard and Elizabeth Lowe of Aston Botterell, he was the younger brother of Thomas Lowe of Trysull, and the husband (from 24 October 1836) of Sarah Giles, daughter of Mr & Mrs Benjamin Giles of Church House, Tenbury. See Appendix 3.

Manvers, Earl (1778–1860)
After leaving the Navy, where he served with Nelson, he sat in Parliament for fifteen years as a non-partisan Member for Nottinghamshire before succeeding as 2nd Earl in 1816. He married Mary, née Eyre, and they had four children. Thoresby has been in the Pierrepont family for more than 400 years: the eighteenth-century house burnt down in 1845, and was rebuilt by the 3rd Earl.

Maria – See Reynolds, Maria

Marshall, William (1796–1872)
From Leeds originally, he was MP for Carlisle from 1835–47 and for East Cumberland 1847–65. In 1824 he bought the Patterdale Hall Estate, for many years in the ownership of the Mounsey family (John Mounsey being the last 'King of Patterdale'). The old building was then taken down entirely, and the present Patterdale Hall erected – now a residential outdoor pursuits centre managed by Bolton School.

Mary, Queen of Scots (1542–1587)
Queen from the first year of her life until her forced abdication in 1567, she then spent most of her remaining nineteen years imprisoned by her cousin Queen Elizabeth I, who finally ordered her execution for treason.

Mason, Edward (born *c.* 1811)
He lived at Bleathwood in the parish of Little Hereford with his wife and a large, young family.

Muir, Dr William (1787–1869)
He was the first minister of St Stephen's and (in 1838) Moderator of the General Assembly of the Church of Scotland. His younger contemporary, Dr A. K. H. Boyd, described him as 'the finest-looking human being I ever saw. It was the great Duke of Wellington's face, a thousand times more beautiful. No Archbishop, Cardinal or Pope ever looked the High Churchman better than Dr. Muir.'

Mytton, Edward of Eardiston (born 1814)
Also known as 'Ned', he was the younger son of the late William Mytton of Eardiston and his wife Catharine (née Jones – of Knighton-on-Teme). He married, and – with his wife and family – later emigrated to New Zealand.

Mytton, Edward senior (1748–1839)
A farmer, he built his home, Boraston House, about 1800. He was the father of Mary Smith (who lived with him) and of Rachel Reynolds, wife of Peter Davis' uncle William. See Appendix 3.

Mytton, Elizabeth (born 1816)
Daughter of the late William Mytton of Eardiston and his wife Catharine (née Jones – of Knighton-on-Teme). See Smith, John junior below.

Mytton, William of Eardiston (born 1809)
Eldest child of the late William Mytton of Eardiston and his wife Catharine (née Jones – of Knighton-on-Teme); he married, on 23 June 1836, his cousin Elizabeth Smith, daughter of John Smith of Kimbolton, and Mary, née Mytton. Subsequently (1855) he loaned £600 towards the Baptist chapel in Tenbury, and the following year a further £100 for establishing a Baptist school in the former National School building.

Mytton, William of Deepcroft (born 1796)
Tenant of Samuel Davis, he was married with two daughters.

Newcastle, Duke of (1785–1851)
The unpopular, ultra-Tory Henry Pelham-Clinton, 4th Duke of Newcastle-under-Lyne, inherited his dukedom aged ten. A colourful character, he fought strenuously against political change, claiming that the passing of the Reform Bill cost him £200,000. His wife Georgiana, née Miller Mundy, died giving birth to their twelfth child.

Nicholls family
George Nicholls (born 1771) was a farmer, the tenant of Kyrewood where he lived with his wife Elizabeth. They had three children: a son and two daughters. George junior was farm tenant of Mr. V. W. Wheeler's 182-acre farm, Lambswick, Lindridge; he married (in 1834) Susanna Jane, née Lambert, daughter of William Lambert, but died in May 1836 aged only twenty-four, leaving an infant son. The two Nicholls daughters were Mary (born 1816), who married William Wheeler, farmer of Eardiston; and Elizabeth (subsequently Mrs Edwin Farmer of Kyrewood). In 1832, Mr Nicholls had halted the royal procession of Princess Victoria through Tenbury in order to present her with a basket of Standardine apples; by Royal Command they were thenceforth known as Princess Pippin.

Northumberland, Duke of (1785–1847)
The 3rd Duke served as Ambassador Extraordinary at the coronation of King Charles X of France in 1825, paying his own expenses: he is said to have 'astonished the continental nobility by the magnitude of his retinue, the gorgeousness of his equipage, and the profuseness of his liberality.' Alnwick Castle is the second-largest inhabited castle in England: the Percy family have lived there since 1309.

Nott family of Hartall and Eastham
John Nott (born 1781), farmer of Upper Hartall, just to the north-west of Dean Park, and, like Samuel Davis, a tenant of Mr Hope, was related to James Nott of Eastham (died 1837), father of John (born 1798). The latter was the tenant of Samuel Davis' Eastham Park Estate, where he lived with his wife Amelia and elder unmarried sister Mary. Further towards Worcestershire, John Nott farmed respectively at Lindridge and (see below) at Hallow. (Peter Davis differentiates the John Notts 'of Eastham' and 'of Hallow', with the implication that John Nott of nearby Hartall is otherwise referred to.)

Nott, John of Hallow (born 1801)
Lived at and farmed Park Farm, Hallow, near Worcester.

Nurs, Eleanor (1764–1848)
She was Peter Davis' great-aunt, sister to his late grandmother, to Peter Reynolds of Burcote and to James Reynolds of Shifnal, where she herself lived: she was the widow of John Nurs (who had died in 1824) – they had no children. See Appendix 3.

Parker, John
Though described in one quarter as a 'gallant Master' of foxhounds, in another it was said that 'the sinews of war' with him were weak. On 3 March 1827, however, he fought a duel on Kempsey Ham with John Somerset Russell (later Lord Hampton) over some matter connected with the Hunt. 'They fired at each other, but neither of the balls took effect.' An officer arrived with an arrest warrant, but 'too late'. His favourite horse was 'Coroner'. Long after his retirement as Master, he managed a pack of Worcestershire harriers.

Partridge, Eleanor (1785–1843)
'Aunt Partridge' was a younger sister of Peter Davis' late mother, Elizabeth. She had an illegitimate daughter, Emma (see Reynolds, Emma, below), and subsequently married William Partridge, a farmer, by whom she had three further daughters, one of whom died whilst a child. The Partridges lived at The Lodge (Dean Lodge Farm), just over the fields from Nash Chapel. See Appendix 3.

Partridge, Elizabeth (born 1804)
Peter Davis' aunt Eleanor's sister-in-law, she was the sister to William and James. See Appendix 3.

Partridge, Ellen (1817–1870)
Peter Davis' first cousin, she was the second daughter of his mother's younger sister Eleanor and her husband William Partridge. She never married.

Partridge, James (born 1793)
A farmer, he was Aunt Partridge's brother-in-law, married to Catherine Purchase, née Dee (from South Molton). They had eight children, their second son Charles marrying twice. His first wife was the natural daughter of James Adams of Woodson: his second was his cousin, Margaret Ann Philpots. See Appendix 3.

Partridge, Mary (born 1821)
Peter Davis' first cousin, youngest daughter of Peter Davis' mother's younger sister Eleanor and her husband William Partridge.

Partridge, William (1788–1859)
Farmer, he was the husband of Peter Davis' Aunt Eleanor: they lived at Dean Lodge Farm, Nash, 132 acres, which was rented from Mr Rushout. See Appendix 3.

Patrick, Samuel (born *c.* 1819)
Son of John Patrick, a farmer of Kyre Green, and his wife Margaret.

Peade, Thomas
Husband of Ann, with one son, Benjamin (born 1816), and a daughter, Louisa (born 1817).

Pearman, James (born 1815, in Bridgnorth)
He lived at Tennall Hall, Harborne, Staffordshire, with his nonconformist father, Joseph, brother Francis (born c. 1821), and two sisters.

Perkins, John
He lived at Pendell Court, Bletchingley, Surrey.

Pheysey, John (1806–1845)
He lived at Rochford with his wife Eliza, née Davis (no known relation of Peter Davis).

Pigot, Sir George (1766–1841)
3rd Bart of Patshull, Staffordshire.

Pinhorn, the Revd George MA (1800–1879)
Having graduated from St Edmund Hall, Oxford, he was instituted as rector of Brimfield, Herefordshire in 1832.

Pomfret, Earl of (1824–1867)
George Fermor, 5th and last Earl, lived at Easton Neston, a late seventeenth-century house, built mostly by Hawksmoor.

Portland, Duke of (1768–1854)
The 4th Duke, formerly an MP, inherited a debt-ridden Welbeck in 1809 from his father, who had been Prime Minister. He earned a reputation as an agricultural improver. With his wife Henrietta, née Scott, he had nine children: it was their eccentric son (the 5th Duke) who was responsible for the alterations that mostly give the Abbey its present appearance. (The estate now houses the Welbeck Defence Sixth Form College.)

Potts, Thomas (1787–1873)
Born on Clee Hill, he and his wife Ann had seven children; he farmed in a small way at Oldwood, just south of Tenbury.

Powell, the Revd Frederick
Curate of Pensax; the vicar of Lindridge (four miles to the west) was patron of the living (which perhaps explains why he may have been able to call upon his services).

Preece, John
An agricultural labourer, he lived with his family at Boraston Dale.

Rawlings family
They were farmers (with four children) who lived at Stoke House, Stoke Township, Burford.

Revis, John Brook
After he had been gaoled for debt (nearly £2,000) in Shrewsbury in 1834 or thereabouts, he moved to Ludlow, where he kept a library. He then subsequently (1838) set up a county club in Shrewsbury: this was unsuccessful, and he was again gaoled for bankruptcy. He worked for Henry Clive's election to Parliament in June 1839, but subsequently gave evidence of having bribed voters, due to 'the base way I have been treated by the Tory aristocracy of Shropshire', as

he stated to the Select Committee on the Ludlow Election Petition in 1840.
In Revis' defence, a letter to him from Henry Whittall, Ludlow director of the
Commercial Bank of England, was read out in the House of Commons: 'You have
… left behind such works as can never be forgotten whilst the fame of Revis'
Rooms can be lisped out by the youngest Conservative, or gazed at with envy
by the levelling Radicals. My pen will not do justice to such a willing, able, and
powerful advocate for the good cause of Conservatism; but to that I would wish
to say, honour and integrity in no small degree have ever marked your progress
at Ludlow. These sentiments in a short time will be responded to by a present
of plate now being subscribed for by the intelligent and influential part of our
little borough.' Later, he formed a Librarian Association in London, eventually
returning to Ludlow, where he died in 1847. Though married, he lived apart from
his wife, with a mistress.

Reynolds of Burcote
Peter (1766–1843), Peter Davis' great-uncle, was a farmer, formerly of Kemberton,
the husband of Ann Davis Reynolds (née Harper) (1766–1849). They had no
children. See Appendix 3.

Reynolds, Emma (1809–1880)
The natural daughter of Peter Davis' aunt Eleanor Partridge, she ran a ladies'
boarding school in Pershore. After marriage to a farmer, Henry Bullock of Hill and
Moor near Pershore, in 1845, they had one daughter, Jane (who was to become a
close friend of Peter Davis' eldest daughter, Gertrude Louisa). See Appendix 3.

Reynolds, James (1772–1841)
Peter Davis' great-uncle, brother of Peter Reynolds of Burcote and of Eleanor Nurs,
he was a cabinet maker, who lived in Shifnal. He and his wife Charlotte, née Pearce,
were the parents of at least seven children, the eldest of whom was Mary Ann
Bright. See Appendix 3.

Reynolds, Joseph (c. 1791–1868)
Farmer of New House, Heightington, he was Peter Davis' uncle, and married to
Mary Ann, née Seager (born c. 1808): they had no children. Joseph's father Peter
Reynolds (c. 1757–1838) lived with him, but despite being Peter Davis' grandfather,
he is not specifically mentioned in the diary: Joseph himself is only mentioned once
and by Christian name, although his residence is often referred to. He farmed a total
of 190 acres of rented land in Rock and Abberley parishes. (A mile to the south of
New House is Reynolds Lane, in which is situated Reynolds Farm, some 100 acres
at the time the Tithe Map was drawn up in 1843. The farmhouse looks to be at
least of eighteenth-century origin, which may conceivably indicate that Reynoldses
were established in the area for some while, and that New House was built by a
Reynolds who moved there from Reynolds Farm.) See Appendix 3.

Reynolds, Maria (1792–1877)
The unmarried youngest sister of Peter Davis' late mother. She may have come to
live with the family in 1813 following Elizabeth Davis' death in childbirth, the
children all being very young. She continued to live with Peter Davis' eldest brother
William at Dean Park until at least 1851. The following year, aged sixty, she married
a builder, William Harper, and moved to live with him in Kemberton, where she
later died aged eighty-five. See Appendix 3.

Reynolds, Peter of Kemberton (1790–1865)
Peter Davis' 'Uncle Peter' was a farmer, born in Burford in 1790. He married Sarah, and had three, possibly four children by her between about 1830 and 1840 – Peter, William and Mary Ann for certain, all born in Kemberton, as was their mother. Peter farmed 185 acres there in 1851, and is also listed there as a farmer ten years earlier. Later (1861) he was farming a slightly smaller unit about four miles south-east of Kemberton, at Beckbury. His son Peter became a farmer at Beckbury in his turn. William was a butcher in Kemberton by 1851, possibly working alongside a James Reynolds, also a butcher in Kemberton. See Appendix 3.

Reynolds, William (1778–1866)
Peter Davis' oldest uncle was a farmer, the tenant of Nash Court Farm, Burford. He married Rachel Mytton, daughter of Edward Mytton of Boraston House. They had no children. His father-in-law owned Boraston Farm, which William Reynolds took on as tenant after his death. See Appendix 3.

Rizzio, David (*c.* 1533–1566)
An Italian courtier, he rose to become the private secretary of Mary, Queen of Scots. Mary's husband, Lord Darnley, is said to have been jealous of their friendship, and joined in a conspiracy of Protestant nobles to murder him.

Robinson, George Richard (1781–1850)
Liberal Conservative MP for Worcester, 1826–37 (he opposed the Reform Bill), and for Poole, from 1847 until his death. He was governor of the British American Land Company and, from 1834, chairman of Lloyd's.

Robinson, James dec'd (1772–1837)
He was a solicitor of long standing, who lived in Teme Street, Tenbury until his death.

Rodmell, the Revd (born 1802)
John Rodmell was born in Yorkshire, he graduated from Trinity College, Cambridge, and was curate of Burford third portion from 1837 until at least 1843: he was 'well-known to members of the Camden Society [a Cambridge society, to promote the study of Gothic architecture] as the writer of some very valuable papers in The Ecclesiologist'. In September 1850, he was received into the Roman Catholic Church.

Rose, James (born 1791)
Farmer, of Harp Fields, Burford, 183 acres rented from Mr Rushout, where he lived with his wife Anne: they had three daughters and a son.

Rushout-Bowles, George MP (1811–1887)
Son of 'Mr. Rushout' (see below): educated at Harrow and Christ Church, he was the Conservative MP for Evesham, 1837–41 and for East Worcestershire, 1847–1859, when he succeeded his uncle, becoming the 3rd Baron Northwick and 7th Baron Rushout. The 2nd Baron had been a celebrated collector and art connoisseur; after his death, an eighteen-day sale took place of that part of the collection which was in Thirlestane House, Cheltenham, his nephew purchasing a substantial portion, and removing it to Northwick Park. The 3rd Baron married late in life, and died without any surviving issue. See also Borthwick, Peter above.

Rushout-Bowles, the Hon. and Revd George (1772–1842)
Known in the diary as 'Mr. Rushout', he was the younger brother of the 2nd Lord
Northwick. He lived at Burford House, adjacent to St Mary's church. Formerly
a Fellow of All Souls' College, Oxford, he was 'for a long period an active and
intelligent magistrate for Worcester and Salop' [C. R. Dodd]. He was also lord of
the manor of Tenbury. William Bowles, who had purchased the Burford estate,
died in 1748, succeeded by his brother Humphrey: Humphrey died in 1784,
succeeded by his eldest son George, whose sister Rebecca was married to the 1st
Lord Northwick. On George's death, unmarried, in 1817, his estates passed to Mr
Rushout, who assumed the name of Bowles. Mr Rushout was married to Lady
Caroline Stewart, daughter of the 7th Earl of Galloway, who died in 1818, leaving
three daughters and a son, George (see above). The Rushout property at Burford
included Dean Park (462 acres), Dean Lodge, Harpfields and Whatmore Court,
Nash.

Russell, William (born *c*. 1806)
A linen draper of Teme Street, Tenbury, living with his wife Ann; they had three
children.

Salwey, Lt-Col. Henry MP (1794–1874)
A son of Theophilus Richard Salwey, see below, and younger brother of Edward, he
was the Whig Member for Ludlow, 1837–41, and again from 1847–52.

Salwey, Theophilus Richard (1757–1837)
Samuel Davis' landlord for his Court of Hill land, he lived at The Lodge, Richards
Castle, a 'beautiful seat … delightfully situated on an elevated spot' (according to
a contemporary). A Fellow of All Souls' College, Oxford, he married the coheiress
of Court of Hill, Burford, Anna Maria Hill, who predeceased him leaving twelve
children, the eldest being Edward (born 1790), his father's successor as Samuel
Davis' landlord: another son was Henry Salwey MP, and a further son, Humphrey,
married the sister of George Johnstone (see above).

Samuel – See Davis, the Revd Samuel

Sayer family
Robert (born 1798), a retired Navy lieutenant of Boraston, had brothers Benjamin
(born 1792), a road surveyor, and George (born 1800). They also had younger
sisters, Mary and Decima.

Scarborough, Earl of (1788–1856)
John, 8th Earl, formerly a Whig MP, succeeded to the title in February 1835: he
had several illegitimate children (one, a diplomat, became Baron Savile), but died
unmarried.

Scott, Sir Walter (1771–1832)
It was estimated that the poet and historical novelist spent £25,000 in building
Abbotsford, which stood in an estate of some 1,000 acres near Galashiels.

Skey, Arthur (1806–1860)
Educated at Harrow and Exeter College, Oxford, he was a Worcestershire
magistrate and (later) High Sheriff.

Smith – Groom at Burford Rectory

Smith, Edward (born 1805)
The elder son of the late John Smith of Ribbesford and Kimbolton, and of his wife
Mary, née Mytton; see Appendix 3.

Smith, John junior
A farmer (the younger son of the late John Smith of Ribbesford and Kimbolton,
and his wife Mary, née Mytton), he married his first cousin, Elizabeth Mytton. The
newly-weds set up home at Coney Green Farm, Ribbesford. See Appendix 3.

Smith, Mary (1777–1868)
Edward Mytton's daughter Mary, she was the widow of the late John Smith of
Ribbesford and Kimbolton (see Appendix 3). She lived with her father at Boraston
House.

Stewart, the Revd Alexander (1808–1837)
A grandson of the 7th Earl of Galloway, he graduated from St Alban Hall, Oxford
in 1829, and became rector of Burford first portion in 1836. Married to Mary (née
Lawson), with two daughters, he died on 30 October 1837 in Torquay. Generally,
see Introduction.

Strafford, John (born *c.* 1796)
Farmer of Orleton Court, Worcestershire, he lived there with his wife Elizabeth and
two sons, John and William.

Stubbs, Charles (born 1807)
From Swynnerton, north of Penkridge, he farmed some 400 acres for many years at
Preston Hill: in 1862, he won the prize for four-year-old hunters at the Staffordshire
Show. Unmarried, he lived with his sister, Ann (born 1801).

Tinson, William (born 1792, in Chipping Norton)
Headmaster of a boarding school in Mill Street, Ludlow, he was married with no
children: was his possibly the school William, Samuel and Peter Davis attended?

Trumper, John
'Old Trumper' and his wife Catharine or Katharine, née Price, had five children
baptised in Orleton, on the Herefordshire/Shropshire border, namely John (born
1797), William, Matthias, Richard (born 1807), and Aaron Thomas (born 1809).

Trumper, Matthias (born 1803)
Son of John Trumper, he subsequently became Superintendant Registrar in Tenbury,
living in Park Villa, Teme Street.

Trumper, William (1801–1838)
Tenbury attorney, he was the second son of John Trumper (see above). He married
first Sarah Pitts Baker, who died in 1835; the following year, he became Peter Davis'
brother-in-law upon his marriage to Eliza Davis.

Turner, John Beresford (1775–1855)
He lived at Brockmanton Hall, Leominster with his wife Ann Ursula.

Turrall, John
Miller, of Kidderminster.

Uncle Reynolds – See Reynolds, William.

Victoria, HM Queen (1819–1901)
On passing through Tenbury in 1832 as heiress presumptive to the throne, she is said to have referred to it as 'my little town in the orchard'.

Wade, Richard (*c.* 1786–1850)
Saddler, of Market Street, Tenbury.

Watson, the Rt Revd Richard (1737–1816)
In St Martin's church, Bowness, there is a wall tablet in memory of the late Richard Watson, bishop of Landaff, whose body was buried there. Before becoming bishop, he was Regius Professor of Divinity at Cambridge, and before that a professor of Chemistry and a Fellow of the Royal Society. A contemporary *Windermere Parish History & Directory* says, 'In the midst of all his fame to which his talents raised him, Bishop Watson never forgot his humble origin; and his contempt for human distinctions is sufficiently indicated by his choice of this humble resting place, and the inscription which merely records his name, age, and death. For the services he rendered to the cause of science and of truth, and for the example he set as an independent bishop and an honest man, his memory will be ever revered.' He lived at Calgarth Park, Troutbeck Bridge; Wordsworth and Coleridge visited him there, and Wordsworth wrote his *Letter to the Bishop of Llandaff* (1793) in response to his defence of the French monarchy.

Whatmore, John (born 1805)
Baker of Broad Street, Ludlow.

Wheeler, Vincent Wood (1786–1853)
He was the owner of land at Nash, Kyrewood and Lambswick, and lived formerly at Nash Court: at the time of the diary, he resided at Newnham Court, with his wife, who was also his cousin, Cecilia Maria, née Smith, of Eardiston. After her death, he married Fanny Graham of Ludlow, by whom he had a son and a daughter. A Deputy Lieutenant for Worcestershire, he was also a Justice of the Peace. He was involved in prolonged litigation with the Revd George Hall of Tenbury over tithes.

Wheeler, William (farmer) (born 1816)
He lived with his newly-married wife Mary, née Nicholls (born also 1816), at Eardiston. A son, George, was born to them in 1839.

Wheeler, William (miller) (1785–1860)
Of Pinkham, Cleobury Mortimer, he was married to Martha, née Pheysey, with four children, one of whom took over as miller on his father's retirement: William Wheeler went bankrupt in the 1850s.

Wilkinson, the Misses
The nieces of the vicar of Tenbury, the Revd George Hall, were Agnes (born 1811), Jane (born 1816), and twins Ann and Isabella (born 1826).

William – See Davis, William

Williams, Charles (born *c.* 1792 at Bitterley)
A butcher and grazier, he lived with his wife and three children in Teme Street, Tenbury.

Winnington, Captain – See Jeffreys-Winnington, Captain Henry

Winton, Mr & Mrs
George Winton (born 1806) was a farmer and auctioneer, married to Catherine, née Smith (see Appendix 3), at The Vine, Sutton; they had a daughter, Mary (born 1835).

Wrottesley, Sir John MP (1771–1841)
The 9th Bart, later created 1st Baron Wrottesley, he lived at Wrottesley Hall, near Wolverhampton. Educated at Westminster School, he was expelled for leading a rebellion. 'He was a good practical farmer, and his lands at Wrottesley were furnished with the latest improvements in agricultural machinery. While in parliament he procured the exemption of draining tiles from duty.' [*DNB*]

Wybrow, the Revd Henry (born *c.* 1807)
Of Clifford Place, Herefordshire, he graduated in 1829 from Worcester College, Oxford, and became perpetual curate of St Paul's, Newport, Monmouthshire, 1834–55. He was subsequently vicar of Stretton-upon-Dunsmore, Warwickshire, and was married to Catherine, née Mills, by whom he had seven children.

Yapp, James (born 1779)
A shopkeeper of Market Street, Tenbury, and also a farmer (of Berrington Lane) and carrier, he travelled from Tenbury to Worcester every Friday, as well as fortnightly to Stourport. He was a widower (twice) with six children.

Bibliography

Bagshaw, *Gazetteer and Directory of Shropshire* (1851)
Burke's Commoners (1836)
Burke's Peerage
Census returns, 1841 ff
Chant, Christopher, *Locomotives* (Chancellor Press, 2000)
Childe, Frances C. Baldwyn, *The Register of Burford* (1913)
Davis, the Revd Ralph Leigh's family tree
Dictionary of National Biography
Encyclopaedia Britannica, 11th Edition 1910–1911
Evans, Tunstall, *The History of Tenbury* (1840)
Foster's Peerage & Baronetage, 1882
Green, Jen, *Changing Scenes: Celebrating 150 years of the Tenbury Agricultural
    Society 1858–2008*
Greene, Miranda, *The Leominster and Stourport Canal* (2003)
Harper, Charles G. *The Great North Road, Histories of the roads* (1922)
International Genealogical Index
Jenkins, Simon, *England's Thousand Best Churches* (Penguin, 1999)
Journal of the Royal Agricultural Society of England
Joyce, F. Wayland, *Tenbury, Some Record of its History* (OUP, 1931)
King James' Bible (1611)
London Gazette
Maddocks, Robert, *Penkridge, Lord Hatherton and the Railways* (2006)
Maund, Benjamin, *The Botanic Garden* (1825)
McLaughlin, Dr G. Harry, *The Barons Northwick*
Milne, Graeme J., *Trade and Traders in Mid-Victorian Liverpool: Mercantile
    Business and the Making of a World Port* (Liverpool University Press, 2000)
National Burial Index
New Jerusalem Bible (1985)
Noake, John, *Guide To Worcestershire* (Longman, 1868)
Oxford Dictionary of National Biography
Peile's Biographical Register of Cambridge
Pevsner, *Buildings of England – Shropshire* (1958)
Pigot, *Directory for Cumberland, Lancashire & Westmorland* (1828–9)
Pigot, *Directory of Shropshire* (1835)
Pigot, *Directory of Worcestershire* (1830)
Pigot, *National Commercial Directory 1835 for Worcestershire*
Slater's Royal National Directory, 1850
Trouteaud, Chris & Peter Bevis, *The Tenbury Workhouse*

Venn's Cambridge Alumni
Victoria County Histories: *Staffordshire* and *Worcestershire*
White, Francis & Co., *History, gazetteer, and directory of Warwickshire* (1850)
Wikipedia
Williams, Richard, *Mytton of Bayton, Worcestershire*

Compiling any significant biographical index for the diary would never have been possible without the resources of the internet, many of which are of course provided anonymously.

Acknowledgements

First, I wish to thank my second cousin once removed, Trevor Webster of Sydney, New South Wales: many years ago now, he sent me a photocopy of Edith Freer's manuscript transcription of Peter Davis's 1835 travel diary. Subsequently, he has made helpful suggestions for improving its presentation. As significant, however, is the contribution made by Peter's great-great-great-niece Susannah Davis, a descendant of his brother William Davis: she took on the onerous task of transcribing this manuscript version onto disk, and further inserted a number of pithy footnotes – to which additions have now been made.

The incentive I required to move towards publication came in the autumn of 2009, with an excited telephone call from another cousin, Bruce Coates of New Brunswick, Canada. Bruce had first contacted me having discovered my website (www.freerangephotography.co.uk/MDg3-0/index.htm) in March 2004. His call now was to inform me of the unexpected discovery of the original travel diary, together with the subsequent 1836/7 diary, more particularly described in Appendix 4. Bruce and his wife Genie, besides providing the all-important source material, photocopied the originals for me, transcribed the 1836/7 diary, and have given generously in terms of both advice and support.

I have many others to thank for their help; I only fear that this list is nowhere near comprehensive. The order of names is of no significance.

John Broad of the British Agricultural History Society has been particularly generous with his explanations and suggestions. In addition, I have been helped by the following and their organisations in one way or another: Jennifer Glanville (The Museum of English Rural Life, Reading); Roger Crofts (former CEO of Scottish Natural Heritage); Laura Deacon of Christian Ecology Link; Dr Sam Riches of Lancaster University; Hugh Fenton (chair, East Midlands RCE); Don Thompson, Merseyside Cycling Campaign; Andrew Meredith (Manchester Archives and Local Studies); Morag Fyfe (The National Archives of Scotland); David Tilsley (Lancashire Record Office); Jackie Fay (Kendal Local Studies Library); Liz Bregazzi (the Durham County Archivist); Claire Fowkes (Northumberland Collections Service); Helen Foster (Shropshire Archives); Lorna Standen (Herefordshire Record Office); Robin Whittaker (Worcestershire Record Office); Kate Holliday (Cumbria Record Office); and a most helpful man at Liverpool Central Library, whose name I noted in my own travel diary (now alas lost).

Thanks are also due to many individuals, including my sister Sarah Davis, my daughter-in-law Katsumi Davis, Polly Rubery, Alex Campbell, Freddie Freer, Julia Brown, Phil Heeks of Weston-super-Mare, Alan Brown of the Bodleian Library, Dominic Rose Price, Richard Lockett, Fee Berry, Sue Colquhoun, Charles Tweedie, Thomas Bohm of User Design for re-drawing maps, and especially to Alan Sutton for sharing with me his experience in devising the biographical index for the magisterial Witts Diary, for the use of his view of Bridgnorth on page 92 and generally guiding me through the unfamiliar process of book publishing.

Finally, I wish to thank my dear wife Caroline for putting up with my absence for many hours at the computer; for her constructive ideas for the Introduction; for delivering me to Dean Park at the outset of my 'footsteps' tour – and for fetching me home from Banbury Hospital when it came to an abrupt end.

Needless to say, any responsibility for errors is mine alone.

Biographical index

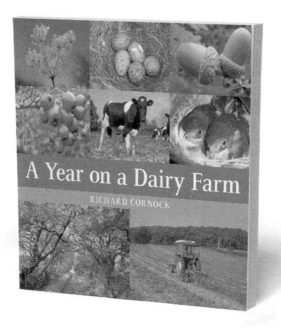

ALSO AVAILABLE FROM AMBERLEY PUBLISHING

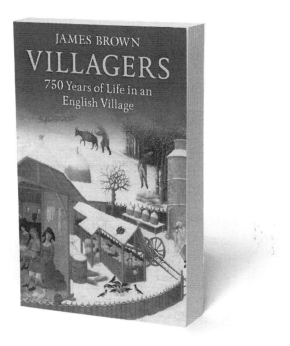

Villagers — 750 Years of Life in an English Village
James Brown

English history explored through one ordinary village.

Most of us now live in towns and cities, but until relatively recently the majority of English people were villagers. What was life like for our ancestors? Were the people of the past really like us?

By telling the story of the ordinary Cambridgeshire village of Gamlingay through 750 years of history from the middle ages to the present day, *Villagers* brings the past to life in an extraordinary way.

Villagers introduces us to a myriad of fascinating people, such as the medieval widow who took a lover and lost her home, the son of an alewife who became Mayor of London, and the strutting Tudor gentleman at war with the rest of the village. We meet the husband who sold his wife, another who was too drunk to notice his wife fornicating in public, and the man who built a mansion for himself and his mistress and almost accidentally founded a Cambridge college.

Paperback
235 x 156 mm
256 pages
ISBN: 978-1-4456-0347-6
£16.99

www.amberleybooks.com

ALSO AVAILABLE FROM AMBERLEY PUBLISHING

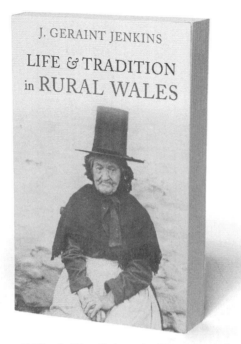

Life & Tradition in Rural Wales
J. Geraint Jenkins

A comprehensive and evocative description of life and tradition in
Wales up to the mid twentieth century.

The key to the study of rural Wales is the living past, for many features of
the culture and social life of Welsh country people are of great antiquity. The
pattern of settlement brought into being by the medieval system of inheritance
is still recognizable in the scattered farms typical of many districts today, and
its impress on the customs and character of the remoter uplands persists, not
least in the hospitality and kindness offered to strangers.

Domestic crafts using local materials and rural industries such as woollen
manufacture and leather working dependent on farm produce have many
features distinctively Welsh; so too have the cottages and farmhouses and
their furnishings, and the way of life reflected in the customs and beliefs that
have not entirely vanished from the countryside.

Paperback
235 x 156 mm
240 pages
156 black and white illustrations
ISBN: 978-1-84868-037-1
£14.99

www.amberleybooks.com